This exquisite memoir chronicles an exceptional life of challenge and joyful fulfillment. It is the author's gift to her readers who share her vision of a world without boundaries.

—Jeanne Wadleigh, lifelong friend

Janne Irvine's *Making Friends with Other Trees and Flowers* is a unique and moving autobiography in which she intimately shares the details of her unusual life. Using the talents she developed as she became a superb lecturer and teacher, Janne relates her experiences when her visual world gradually disappeared and she developed her musical talents. It becomes evident that she has led a very fruitful and satisfying life.

In *Making Friends with Other Trees and Flowers* Janne aptly describes the discovery and use of her musical talents to protect and nourish herself as her world darkens. With courage, ingenuity, and perseverance she meets the challenges of gradually becoming blind. The impressions of the natural world which she develops without her vision are unique and beautiful.

—Shirley Andrews, musician, author

As an optometrist, I've always been interested in low vision, spending one of my externships to study this field at Baylor. Knowing Janne, her story, her accomplishments, and full of life personality has shown me in an intimate manner, how profound an early education such as hers can help with low-vision patients. She has really shown me a different aspect of patient care and understanding

Making Friends with Other Trees and Flowers will be helpful to those in my profession, people with low vision and blindness, their families, musicians and music students, as well as the general public. It's plainly an excellent story.

—Dr. Carolyn Finnell, optometrist

Janne Irvine and I have been friends for over forty years, sharing similar experiences, both as musicians and as people who face the challenges of low vision. In this brilliantly written book, Dr. Irvine chronicles her early years and life lessons in a most colorful and sensitive way.

—Nancy Protzman, BME Westminster Choir College,
MFA (Music) Sarah Lawrence College

It is seldom that we are privileged to meet a figure who, when faced with adversity, grasps it and reshapes it into a positive, becoming more extraordinary and awe-inspiring in the process. Janne Irvine remains such a person.

—Robert M. Dryden, MD

So often we rush through life to get to where we are going. And we miss just about everything along the way. Isn't it a delicious irony that it takes a person with severely limited vision to give sight to one who sees everything yet nothing? I see much more now than I ever did before, thanks to you, Janne.

—Catherine Liddell, college classmate
and professional lutenist

Making Friends

with Other Trees and Flowers

A Story of Low Vision and High Expectations

Janne E. Irvine

Published by Wheatmark®
1760 E. River Rd, Suite 145,
Tucson, Arizona 85718 USA
www.wheatmark.com

ISBN: 978-1-60494-653-6 (paperback)
ISBN: 978-1-60494-702-1 (Kindle)
LCCN: 2011931406

Cover photo by Janne E. Irvine
Author photo by Christine Gallandt
Cover design by Richard McBain of Centric Photo

Portrait: Janne E. Irvine
by M. William Boyhan, 1955, Boston, Massachusetts

Dedication

In Memory of My Parents

John Withers Irvine, Jr.

who knew from the beginning

that I would survive

and

Fredna Tweedt Irvine

whose years of reading

out loud to me made my subsequent

accomplishments possible

With love and appreciation

for your countless ways

of bringing the world

into my sphere of understanding

Janne

Table of Contents

Author's Note...xi

Prelude.. xv

1 The Letter 1

2 The Battered Green Songbook 26

3 The Portrait...40

4 Brook, Lake, and Ocean 54

5 Listen, My Children, and You Shall Hear 70

6 We Sail the Ocean Blue...89

7 Matterhorn by Moonlight 110

8 Epiphany 125

9 The Discovery...144

10 The Decision..157

11 Song of the Crickets 172

12 No Time to Spare...190

TABLE OF CONTENTS

13 The Thunderstorm...202

14 Making Friends with Other Trees and Flowers 214

Postlude 239

Postscript: Messages through Time 243

Author's Note

What makes my life of interest to other people? I asked myself this as I began to chronicle the first eighteen years of my story. The answer is threefold.

It's like a triple-strand braid, in which a golden cord represents music and years of listening, performing, and teaching. A silver strand stands for words written in poetry and literature, spilling over to represent education in general. The third strand, a ribbon of midnight velvet that intertwines with the gold and silver fibers, symbolizes the medical condition that brought about my gradual loss of sight.

I could liken these strands to three melodies dancing in and out of my consciousness and making up the complex contrapuntal texture of a Bach fugue. Music has been a part of my existence since my earliest memories. The rhythm and pattern of words, so closely related to the flow of music, were also a part of my awareness from an early age, as I was encouraged to memorize and, later, to write poetry. With this constant flow of sounds—of music and of language—I grew up in the 1950s and 1960s as a person who could see beauty in the bold but blurred colors of an autumn wood, who could feel beauty by stroking a milkweed pod, and who could hear beauty in a cascading waterfall. The challenge for me was to piece together what I could see and what I could not see into a fulfilling reality that was the world around me. I was a person with low vision and high expectations, and figuring out how to appreciate my environment took years of cultivating my memory and my imagination.

As I remembered incidences, many of which took place during my family's trip through Europe when I was nine years old, I began to realize that over the intervening decades I had fused verbal descriptions with my abstract visual references in order to give me a memory that, in retrospect, was far more detailed than anything I actually saw. This fusion became so natural a procedure that only rarely was I reminded that I really could not see what other people could see, such as the stars at night, people's facial expressions, or their body language.

Defining what I could and could not see was important in describing those early years of elementary school education, especially since I was learning in the company of my fully sighted peers. Gradually, as I entered my teens and reading printed material became a visual impossibility, my senses shifted so totally to the world of music that becoming absorbed in its complexity took precedence over any other awareness and kept me from regretting this sudden decline in my already limited vision. From that time on, there was no longer much of a need to describe what I could or could not see, for I had entered a world in which I could compete and excel through ear, intellect, and intuition alone.

Imagination became an important tool as I studied my way through years of strenuous education. For imagination, the same imagination that had allowed me to fuse detailed verbal description with the actuality of blurred visual images, enabled me to dip into my memories and to make vivid whatever I was studying. If I was reading about castles, I could picture them as massive blurred forms. Better yet, I could remember walking down stairs worn smooth by centuries of footsteps, including those made by my then nine-year-old feet. These descriptions of nonvisual observations, which aided me in understanding my studies, now translate into tools that are vital to my work as a teacher.

This account of my early years closes at the end of chapter fourteen with my eager anticipation of college and the new life away from home awaiting me there. My story does continue within the collection of poems in the Postscript, for I have intimated much of what I have experienced in the intervening four decades since my graduation from college. I have also included, in their entirety, three poems that are referred to within the text.

So take my hand and run with me along the sand, or wander in an autumn wood, or taste a snowflake on your tongue. Listen as I unlock the keys of the piano and realize that, to me, the key of C sharp minor is a rich, deep purple and that A major is a silvery gray. Meet me through my poems. Some are old, and others are new, and in them you will find the world of my own reality waiting there for you.

Janne E. Irvine
Tucson, Arizona
May 8, 2011

I wish to express profound thanks to Andrew T. Greeley, who encouraged me to write about my unusual childhood experiences. His belief in my story and what I have to offer has made this project possible.

I wish to alert my readers that my name, Janne Irvine, is pronounced as though it were spelled Jan Irvin.

J.E.I.

Prelude

March 15, 2010, 10:00 AM

Today's class was different. Twenty people sat in my living room in Tucson, Arizona, where they had come for the past eight weeks for my annual series of Music History and Appreciation lectures. Instead of playing a Mozart piano sonata and discussing its structure, I was going to tell about a little girl who played with lilac bushes and maple trees. Rather than introducing the class to the magnitude of Beethoven's *Ninth Symphony*, I was going to talk about a child who loved to wade in the stream that ran in front of her house in Belmont, Massachusetts. Furthermore, I was going to inform my students that their teacher, when she was a second grade student, liked nothing better than to play, summer after summer, with foot-long plastic canoes that were bright red, yellow, or blue. Today, I wouldn't be revealing details about Tchaikovsky's *Violin Concerto* or his *Sixth Symphony*, since I was about to reveal that I, their teacher, had begun the serious study of piano at the advanced age of thirteen. I would be speaking for the next two hours about my life—music and poetry, recorder playing and travel—and about the tremendous impact that memories of brilliant colors had, and still have, on my imagination.

I had not spoken about this subject before. In fact, I had rarely spoken at length about what I considered to be a private matter. In time I had come to realize that the people who came to my classes, week after week and year after year, had a right to know something about my personal history. My students, being doctors, lawyers, teachers, an engineer, a chef, some museum docents, and all eager concertgoers, knew that I approached my teaching in an unusual and different way. My lectures were memorized, so I didn't use lecture notes. I recited historical dates, opus numbers, and facts about the lives of the great composers without using any reference books. I timed my classes by a clock that chimed and spoke the hour at ten o'clock when each class started, at eleven o'clock when it was time to take a break for homemade refreshments, and at noon when the class ended punctually, as it always was timed to do. Furthermore, it took someone saying, "Janne, can you tell me ..." to attract my attention so I could answer questions, since a hand being waved in the air could not break into the field of my awareness.

Of course, most people knew I was dealing with some kind of serious eye problem. After all, I had known many of my students for over ten years. I was friendly with all of them, and I had become close to several couples that, out of respect for my privacy, hadn't asked me many personal questions. That morning, everyone would learn the medical cause of my eye condition, and they would hear about many of the subsequent challenges that I would face. Most importantly, they would find out that I had come from a family who accepted my gradual loss of vision, and who researched and found the education best suited to my needs and abilities. Over the years, many of my students had met my parents and so were interested in how they had given me the confidence and skills I needed to survive and to thrive.

"I grew up on an acre and a third of woods bordered on one side by a brook and on the other side by a massive stone wall cut into the hillside that bordered an abandoned king's highway," I began, not knowing how this talk was going to unfold. I projected my imagination and thoughts back more than fifty years and more than two thousand miles away, to a time and place that has remained vibrantly real to me although I have spent the past thirty-five years enjoying the Arizona desert. My hibiscus bushes were beginning to flaunt bold red and golden flowers outside my front door; but as I spoke, I was not thinking of their beauty, as I was summoning maple trees, branches of wild sumac, and hedges of yellow forsythia to my imagination. I was thinking of myself as a young child scrambling down a short slope into the woods of maple and ash trees, or climbing up the stone wall to higher land to find the patch of sharply scented pine trees.

My class members appreciated my descriptions of the terrain, since many were from the Midwest, and more than a few were not just from New England or Massachusetts but also from towns that bordered my hometown of Belmont. But my friends had not gathered to hear fond reminiscences. To my surprise, I found myself speaking comfortably about what it was like to grow up with low vision, which in my case meant no sight at all in the right eye and 20/200 in the left, the latter figure being the definition of legal blindness. Since the figure 20/20 sets the standard for normal vision, the figure 20/200 indicates that what a normal person could see at two hundred feet, I could see at twenty feet. Though in time my sight was to decline and eventually was to be relegated to a memory, I never thought of myself as blind, since I could see that the sky was blue and that the leaves of summer were green, and I could read a book if the print was large enough.

Gradually, during my childhood years, more subtle problems arose that made me more aware of my visual limitations. While playing with a group of children, I realized that I couldn't understand the answers to questions asked in the course of playing games. I waited for the answer yes or no, but it never came. I think my playmates must have grown impatient with me, and that added to my frustration of not understanding what was happening. Someone explained that a nod of the head meant yes and a shake of the head meant no. The nod and shake of the head were such small movements that they were completely beyond my range of vision. Someone explained the gestures to me, and when I tried them for the first time, it felt odd to wobble my head up and down or to shake it sideways. My neck muscles felt strange, since they had not been used that way before. At least I had learned the code, and though I could not see others using it, I could use it myself and be understood in this silent language of the fully sighted.

Most importantly, I wanted to convey to my class the positive aspects of my growing-up years. In reality, there is great beauty to be seen even with defective and deteriorating eyesight, especially in the autumnal woods that surrounded my home. Year after year, I appreciated the magnificent colors that were all that mattered, since small details did not figure, or rather could not figure, in the views and vistas that defined my world. Those who know me, and this includes my students, are aware that I am unquenchably optimistic, and I believe my ability to recognize and appreciate beauty wherever I can find it is one of the reasons my outlook is so positive.

When I was nine years old, I could see distant things if they were big enough. I remember a very black nighttime sky and a very large moonlit mountain called the Matterhorn. I could see the enormity of Gothic cathedrals during the year I lived in England and traveled in Europe, though the great rose windows described to me were only blurs of light, and size was gauged by echoes rather than by visual loftiness. Thus, memories of what I could see, though flawed in actuality, still served to illuminate my years of studying history and literature.

These memories encouraged my imagination to reconstruct the things I had seen and to convert them into the realities I knew them to be. No one taught me to use my imagination as a tool to create this enhanced visualization of memories, but it has proven to be vitally important to me as a teacher, for without it, my ability to describe buildings and landscapes would have been seriously curtailed.

The visual aspect of my life was only one part of the total sensory pattern of my existence. I was, after all, addressing a music class. So I told my friends that though I was in touch with music from before the time of conscious memory, I did not know until that gray November of my eighth grade year, when I could no longer see well enough to read print, that music would overwhelm my thoughts and capture my imagination. Those early weeks of studying piano and composition would bring so much energy, excitement, and pleasure into my life that my loss of visual acuity would recede from the fore-front of my thoughts into a place from where it would never haunt me with melancholy.

So I began music lessons with the choral director of my junior high preparatory school and realized, from the first days of study, that the world of piano keys and chords, that the Mozart and Beethoven sonatas and symphonies I had heard over my family's stereo system at home, would spark my imagination, please my ear, and develop powerful analytical skills in the realm of music theory. The challenge was immense. Studying piano performance and music composition, and learning everything else I could about music, would have to be done in a concentrated and accelerated manner if I had any hope of making music my vocation. After all, I had begun my serious study of music at the age of thirteen rather than at the age of four or five or eight, which is the usual scenario for those who enter this profession.

It had been suggested more than once that the story of my child-hood years and unusual educational background would be of interest to people outside my personal range of acquaintance. I was beginning to realize that what I took for granted, as far as compensating for my poor vision in the fulfillment of daily tasks, was intriguing and fascinating to others. How do you learn piano pieces, how do you bake chocolate chip cookies, and how do you give your lectures without referring to notes? These are just some of the questions I have been asked. I began collecting my thoughts and encouraging memories from the distant past to emerge, since, for years, express-ing my thoughts in writing as well as in musical composition had been an outlet for creative expression. Over the past five decades, I had written over a hundred poems ranging from the light-hearted to the profound. I had written a handful of essays ranging from "Brit-ain's Crown Jewels" to "My Green Typewriter," and those, along with others, were already in my computer, awaiting refinement and a reason to be linked together in the recounting of my story. Once I decided to chronicle my early years, I wrote to my elementary and preparatory schools for my grades. My perusal of report cards and teachers' comments gave me a precise account of my development as a person with low vision operating and competing in a sighted world in which I was being critiqued and graded on an equal level with my sighted peers. I am telling this story from the standpoint of how music, poetry, the concept of color, my education, and encroaching blindness affected my life. Though this chronicle ends as I prepare to begin college, throughout the telling, I have referred to many past experiences that have stayed with me and that have influenced aspects of my present and future interests.

Who would have thought the five-year-old child listening to

Johann Sebastian Bach: His Story and His Music would become known for presenting seminars in advanced music history and appreciation? How could I have forecast that the thirteen-year-old fledgling pianist playing the simplest of Mozart minuets while longing for the skills to play Mozart's pianistic masterpieces would, less than twenty years later, present and defend her doctoral dissertation, "The Completion of Fragmentary Keyboard Works of W. A. Mozart"? I certainly didn't know that the nine-year-old girl visiting Jane Austen's grave in Winchester Cathedral would, half a century later, lecture on "Music in the Novels of Jane Austen" and represent Austen's heroine Emma Woodhouse in an original concert and play, performing piano pieces pertinent to the Austen era. For those hard-won skills had yet to be developed, and they might not have been developed if it weren't for my family, who nurtured my ability and encouraged me to rise above my disability.

I knew that bright colors, music, and memorizing and reciting poetry had been a part of my earliest memories. I knew too that there must be a reason why my appreciation of flowers, and my love of the acre of woods in which I wandered for a dozen years, were so strong and vital to me still. Unexpectedly, I found out why these things were so. Just a few days before I was to begin writing about my earliest memories, I discovered a copy of a remarkable letter that my mother had written when I was five and a half years old. At the request of a neighbor who knew of another family whose son had the same eye condition as I did, my mother wrote in detail about what and how she had taught me using her training as a preschool educator. The neighbor was a scientist researching retrolental fibroplasia (RLF), now known as retinopathy of prematura (ROP), the eye condition that affected me, along with hundreds, if not thousands, of premature infants. So many infants and young children were from the Boston area, since it was in Boston where the finest incubators had been developed and were in use.

The best way to begin my story is with this letter. Surprisingly, I found I had firsthand recollections of at least 80 percent of what my mother mentioned. Therefore, throughout my mother's descriptions of incidents ranging from my learning to read, to experiencing a family vacation on Cape Cod, I will add my own comments and recollections to augment her document.

1

✤

The Letter

My mother wrote this letter in 1954, to help another young mother raise her child who had retrolental fibroplasia, my eye condition. To me, this letter shows the trained teacher at work. How fortunate it would be if every low-vision preschool child had experienced this kind of environmental enrichment throughout those all-important first few years of life.

> It sounds as though your son, Larry, has an excellent start, good health, normal development, and three other children in the family to give him a satisfying social environment. His amount of sight seems similar to our daughter, Janne's, so perhaps I may be able to answer some of your questions by telling you how we've managed.
>
> Janne was five last August 6. She was a 6½-month premature baby and weighed 2 pounds 6 ounces and, as you said, had a precarious start. To complicate matters, she, when a few weeks old, with four others in the premature nursery, developed infectious diarrhea, and I was told that she alone survived.
>
> Contracting infectious diarrhea was the indirect cause of saving what little sight I had, since the infected babies were removed not only

from the oxygen-laden incubators, but also from the birthing hospital to a different hospital altogether. From as early as I can remember, my mother told me that I was a survivor, and I knew that was something of which to be proud. Though physically fragile at that time, there was an indefinable inner strength that kept me alive, not only then, but later in life as well.

Pure oxygen is still used in incubators to keep premature infants alive, and now, sixty years after I was born, the levels of oxygen are so carefully monitored that although babies continue to be born with retrolental fibroplasia, in no way is the condition as prevalent as it was in the past. The damage occurs when the delicate tissues of the retina (and, in some cases, of the brain) are exposed to air after being in an enriched atmosphere of pure oxygen for three months or more. Since air is made of 21 percent oxygen, the delicate tissues shrivel, thus causing loss of sight or brain function in varying degrees. My sojourn in the incubator was two months rather than three, so I left that environment in time to avoid brain damage and to begin life with some sight.

At five months I noticed that one eye appeared smaller, and upon examination I was told that she had retrolental fibroplasia. Her right eye has no vision; her left eye has partial vision.

I am fortunate to have had that little bit of vision. I have points of reference for so many things, such as colors, shapes, and distant vistas, if they are large, such as mountain ranges.

She is quite fragile looking; she was relatively slow to walk and talk, but development has been accelerating, or so it seems.

She has an older sister, and we are grateful that she has this companionship.

Apparently, I didn't walk or talk until I was three years old, and when I began to talk, bypassing baby talk, I spoke in complete sentences. Walking happened all of a sudden too. For several summers, we had the loan of a friend's small cottage on Cape Cod, and when I was three, we took the hundred-mile hot drive to the cottage. Mother set me down carefully on the floor so I could crawl. Since the floor was cement and covered with gritty sand, I stood up, brushed the sand from the knees of my little pink overalls, and started to run. By the end of the day, I was running down the long, rutted sand path to the beach and the ocean. Yes, my sister Kit, less than three years older than I, was a good companion, and probably she was set the task of making sure I didn't escape to the beach.

I have taught school, so I suppose I started very early to talk about and explain everything to her. Very soon she showed great appreciation for color, and she can see color at a distance, so we were looking for yellow or orange buses and bulldozers, and red fire engines. I still try to give her color to enrich her environment, and I have found color valuable in teaching her objects, sizes, shapes, etc.

I remember being shown those yellow buses and red fire engines, but my favorite memories by far are of being shown the great piles of orange pumpkins that appeared on street corners and vegetable stands as soon as the October air was scented with the smell of burning leaves. I would get close to a pile of pumpkins, enjoy their orangeness, and just to make sure that orange color was really there, I would stick my nose within touching distance of the cool, smooth surface of a large pumpkin so all I could see was orange. Then I would sniff that unforgettable pumpkin smell. Now I realize that my nose was doing a good job of learning its trade, since eventually it would take over as an important pleasure-giving sense. Somehow I must have known the time would come when I would no longer distinguish the color orange from other colors. Somehow I knew I had to cultivate and preserve these memories so I would continue to think, imagine, and speak in the vocabulary of colors.

> Very early we used phonograph records; she loved to sing even before she could talk, and for several years we had the recording machine going at any time of the day! Do you know the record-of-the-month clubs called Young People's Records, Inc., and the Children's Record Guild? I believe I found the former to be superior, but both had some very excellent records. Some have suggested rhythms that she loved, and it was excellent for her coordination.

My father had built and wired that record player just as he had the pancake grill, and both appliances were well used by the time I remember benefiting from them. I must clarify my mother's use of the term "recording machine." It did not record as did the early reel-to-reel tape recorders, which I learned to use ten years later. This was a turntable and speaker built into a simple box. In the early to mid-1950s, we were decades beyond the crank-up Victrola with its morning glory horn. I remember sitting cross-legged on the blue flagstone floor of our large downstairs living room and listening to records, and though the titles mentioned by my mother are too far back in the past for me to recall, I do remember singing along with a host of nursery rhymes such as "Jack and Jill," "Hickory Dickory Dock," and "Up in a Swing."

There were also records with lively versions of "Rudolph the Red-Nosed Reindeer" and "The Donkey Serenade," but my favorites were a pair of ten-inch records, *Wolfgang Amadeus Mozart: His Story and His Music* and *Johann Sebastian Bach: His Story and His Music*, which were both produced by Vox. These particular discs were lost decades ago, as were so many of my memories of the Mozart recording. Those memories that remain are of a performance of the minuet in F major that young Wolfgang wrote at the age of six; an excerpt from *Symphony Number 40*, splendid in its rich minor tonality; and above all, the fun-loving aria from *The Magic Flute* in which Papageno explains his work as a bird-catcher. Looking back on this introduction to the music of the man who was to become my favorite composer, I can say that I have taught many six-year-old children as well as adult beginners to play that minuet in F major. I have taught classes on the *Symphony in G Minor*, so I am familiar with every theme of all four movements, and I have shared the beauties of its orchestration with others.

As for the recording of the life of Bach, twenty years ago I found a secondhand copy in the local classical music record store, and I have just finished listening to it. I was to know the somber music of the *St. Matthew Passion* and the upbeat music of the *Brandenburg Concerto Number 5* in years to come, and my immediate thought on hearing these works was that I knew those pieces from the Bach record! From the age of five I knew about the *Goldberg Variations* and Count Keiserling, who commissioned Bach to compose some music to entertain him at night when he couldn't fall asleep. Later while at Yale, I took classes on this work from the eminent harpsichordist Ralph Kirkpatrick, who, coincidently was losing his sight from glaucoma, as was I.

From this record about Bach, I learned about the *Flute Sonata in E Flat Major*, which I heard in later years when my sister Kit played the flute while our mother accompanied her at the piano with a little brown Chihuahua dog perched on her lap! Though the Vox recording did not quote any music from the *Coffee Cantata*, I heard about it within the body of the narration. Years later, I was to hear that work in concert along with two prize-winning modern compositions for recorders. The winner of the first prize was a physics graduate from MIT, and the second-prize winner was a fledgling seventeen-year-old composer named Janne.

> Either my husband or I read daily to our girls, often several times daily, and Janne soon became a good listener. She loved rhymes and songs and soon responded to them. She has developed the ability to listen to the stories that delight our eight-year-old, so while we read some for Janne, alone she also enjoys our family Sunday evenings before the fire. *Swiss Family Robinson* is the story read to her after lunch. Usually we have a continued story going. Just now it is Thornton Burgess's *Danny Meadow Mouse*.

I don't remember the book about the mouse, and I have only faint memories of the *Swiss Family Robinson*, but the warmth and cozy security of our family time, together with a book being read out loud, is a powerful manifestation of the bonding and solidarity that made my childhood so happy and secure. When in time reading out loud became a necessity rather than just a pastime, my family, already used to this practice, accepted the challenge of reading textbooks along with pleasure books to me.

Janne also likes to have me sit at the piano with her for five or ten minutes every day. Kathryn, her sister, takes piano lessons, so Janne and I are learning things at the piano. From middle C, we have her fingers counting up with the right hand five notes and down with the left hand five notes. Then she plays her little songs by number. She picks out tunes independently on the piano. I believe that she must play at the piano three or four times daily by herself.

Now I understand why I have always known the names of the notes at the piano and understood that C was to the left of the two black keys and D was in the middle of the two black keys. I remember tinkering at the piano, picking out tunes and even making them up. One tune was all on black keys, and I called it "Little Birds Coming Home to Their Nest at Night." I'm sure it took far longer to say that title then it did to play the piece. I did say to Mother that when I grew up, I wanted to be a musician, and I probably stumbled over the last word, since I wasn't used to saying it. Was this prophetic or coincidence? We'll never know; but I do know that my mother kept me away from piano lessons. I believe she made the right decision at that time, since she knew, as I did not, that soon I would be dealing with more than my share of frustrations. I would be entering the school system as a child with very limited vision and would be studying and learning with fully sighted kids.

Physically she is timid, and only by being hard-hearted have we been able to force her outdoors to meet and enjoy her environment. I must admit the terrain is a difficult one—rocks, ravines, a brook, and almost no level land—but she does very well with it, even though her perspective is poor. She has to take more time learning about the out-of-doors. She loves her sandbox (a large one, 6' x 8') and can pump herself up in her swing. Her wagon has been fun on our sloping driveway, but I feel we made a mistake with her tricycle. It is a fragile one, and she has gone over on it several times, and now she's afraid of it. Her sister's old one is larger and has a large, squat wheelbase, and I believe, in time, she'll manage it.

It is hard to realize that I had been fearful of venturing out of doors and afraid of exploring the land around my home. There is one memory that may hark back to that time. Spring was on its way, though it must have been cool, since I was bundled up. The morning sunlight was bright, and I was met by the blur of blue sky, green leaves, and a green lawn made all the brighter since it was dotted with blobs of yellow, which were golden dandelions. I was holding very tightly to Mother's hand as we went out to explore the backyard. The lawn was soft, and the dandelions were even softer, so as I made friends with these growing things around me, my fears slipped away. I remember that feeling of starting to lose those fears, and it was a good feeling!

There were other things about which I was fearful, and some of these fears may have been generated by the distorted and confusing images that were unavoidable, given the state of my vision. I was afraid to wander around one part of the woods and for years stayed away from it, since it was there that my sister and I had found a dead rat frozen stiff to the branch of a tree. Later I realized that fear was no more than being colossally squeamish, which, alas, I still am. There were other fears that came later.

A little schoolmate had told her classmates that her furnace had "exploded," so for years I was nervous whenever I heard the furnace turn on. Daddy took me down to the furnace room to show me how things worked, to assure me that there were safety features, and to remind me that the furnace was cleaned and serviced every fall. Our talk helped me a little but not much. A few years later, our furnace did "explode," but as was true in the case of my schoolmate, this event was an inconvenience needing immediate attention rather than a serious life-threatening experience.

The most colorful fear of my childhood was being afraid of pink clouds. I could see the blue of the sky and the colors of white and gray clouds, and those didn't bother me. It was the bright pink clouds of late afternoon and evening that would send me scuttling for shelter. In 1953, a tornado made its way into Massachusetts and touched down in the town of Worcester, about forty miles west of Belmont. The following day, we drove there to see the damage, and I remember being shown great, gnarled trees that had been torn up by the roots. Certainly we could have seen pink clouds that evening, which, in error, I thought were the harbingers of tornadoes. My father, who was from Missouri, explained to me that green-black skies were associated with tornadoes, but a streak of childhood stubbornness kept me from responding to reason. Instead, if I saw a harmless pink cloud, I would run inside and hide under the couch. Finally, when I was almost too big to fit into that particular refuge, one evening my fear vanished as quickly as the color pink vanished from clouds at the onset of twilight. A child's mind, regardless of any visual impairment, can take scraps of information and twist them into a source of seemingly insurmountable terror. After years of careful thought and quiet contemplation, I overcame these fears. Yet having experienced them, I am ever vigilant in my adult life, to keep such shades at bay.

My mother mentioned my enjoyment of the sandbox. That gave me many hours of delight through a number of hot summers. I remember sitting on one of the seats, which were planks set across each corner of the box. A shiny tin bucket and a bright red shovel kept me happy and entertained. To this day, when I think of the word "evening," I see myself in that sandbox. I see, not pink clouds, but an apricot-orange sky. The trees in full summer foliage are so dark green that they look almost black. From a block and a half away, the church bells, just a little out of tune, ring the eight o'clock chime. I pick up my bucket and shovel, dust off the sand, and walk the short distance back to the house, where there may be a cookie and a glass of milk waiting and a story to be read before I am tucked into bed.

Sometimes the sandbox called, and at other times, it was the sturdy swing set built by my father; this swing set gave Kit and me pleasure for many years. That feeling of swinging, with its steady rhythm and sensation of flying, is one of so many wonderful memories revived by my reading of Mother's letter. I know I was far less adventurous on the swing, ladder, rubber tire on a rope, and "acting bar" that looked like a large letter *A*, than were Kit and our friends who came to play in the backyard. So be it. I still enjoyed what I could do, for the wind still blew in my face, even if I didn't fly as high. Later, when childhood had been left behind, that swing set was taken down. There were two bare spots where the balls of our feet, clad in sandals, sneakers, loafers, oxfords, or boots had worn away the grass, leaving patches of hard, bare ground. They were visible for years to come, and they were reminders of times when afternoons were for playing and evenings were not yet needed for studying, reading, or practicing music.

That little red wagon made many trips up and down the steepest part of our driveway, since the paved driveway was the only place where it could be used. I remember the contrast in color between the red of the wagon and the black of the blacktop. Kit and I took turns pulling each other up the driveway, and sheer momentum and the steepness of the grade took us down. Sometimes the little wagon would overturn, but that was not enough to keep us from playing with it.

When I think of the word "day," I see an oblong block of light, since I am looking out the open front door. I see tall trees with a bright green blur of leaves, a blue sky, white clouds, and a newly paved black driveway going up the hill into ... well, disappearing into the mists of limited vision. With this view, I have the feeling that new and wonderful things are going to happen. Just as my image of the word "evening" conjures the security and nurturing that a good home gives, so that of "day" to me as a child meant anticipating a fresh day filled with good things in it.

What childhood is complete without a little red wagon? Today whenever I shop for red- or yellow-flowered hibiscus plants, or refreshing English mint for flavoring iced tea, or fresh basil plants for making pesto, I use such a little red wagon to haul plants from within the nursery to the checkout station. I wonder if Harlow's Gardens in Tucson, Arizona, knew that a fleet of little red wagons would more likely than not supply me, as well as countless other customers, with a flock of charming memories as well as a sensible way to haul flowers.

I graduated from the red wagon to the red tricycle. Sometimes on

Sundays, when most of the stores were closed (there were blue laws then), Kit would ride her blue bicycle while I took to my red tricycle. I remember only pleasant, though not numerous, times with it, and at least it gave me the experience of driving something. Such experiences were never plentiful.

> Our first major problem was school. She went to nursery school and enjoyed it thoroughly, particularly any creative play. She showed her handicap only in holding her own with more aggressive children. This last fall we decided to send her to a small, progressive private school, hoping for teacher supervision and small classes. We put her into a four-year-old group, thinking that she'd have the advantage of the extra year. It was not long before she came home tearful, saying that the children didn't like her; they pinched her and pushed her. This seemed unnecessary, because there were twenty-seven children with three teachers; also Janne is by nature a very outgoing child who loves people. I talked with her teachers and they were completely pessimistic and had no helpful suggestions. This was a turning point. While my husband and I were aware that she was bright enough, we realized that she should be tested to help us determine her proper place. We then took her to the public school psychologist, who tested her and told us that we had an unusual and bright child. But, said she, we had not met her needs in a school situation. We had put her in with four-year-olds who were not her peers mentally; we had put her into a permissive school when she needed a more formal handling to ensure physical security; she needed the atmosphere of a public

schoolroom. We immediately transferred her to a public kindergarten, with thirty-one children in the room and one very capable teacher, and Janne, who has been there since October, is completely happy. The teacher recognized her need for friends, and Janne has developed friendships with little girls whom I've had over for the afternoon; although when I ask her with whom she's played at school, she'll say, "Everyone, Mommy." When the other children asked the teacher if Janne could see, she told them that Janne could see but not as well as they could, so if Janne needed help, it would be nice if they helped her. Then, of course, she had to keep the children from helping her too much. I really felt the great day had arrived when I peeked in and saw Janne helping another child get off her snowsuit!

I do remember going to three different nursery schools, but I do not recall any negative incidents. I remember wearing a green corduroy jumper with red smocking and a white ruffled blouse, for little girls were expected to wear dresses to school. I have always enjoyed clothing with texture and fabrics that felt good, and the love of romantic ruffles is with me still. At the more permissive school, I remember playing with brilliant pink Play-Doh, and for that, I'm sure, blue jeans were in order. The teacher was our neighbor, and I believe the gray stone walls of her house, which was also her school, made that dough look all the pinker by contrast. The third nursery school was associated with the church we attended, which was a block and a half down the hill from our house. The children had to have blankets for rest periods. Mine was brown, probably an old army blanket, and on it was an enormous red-and-white-striped candy cane, or so I thought, until Mother told me it was a great big letter *J* for Janne, which she had sewn on the blanket to label it as mine.

> Janne is so nearsighted that she does not recognize people, which is, of course, a disadvantage. I'm hoping that she will learn to circumvent this by listening to the voice, learning to recognize posture, gait, shape, size, clothes, etc. She is at her best with a few "known" friends and plays beautifully in her dollhouse.

Being able to recognize people is still difficult unless I know the people as well as their voices. As I think about the problems I had, it is likely that having partial sight hindered my development of the skill necessary for voice identification. In the confusion of trying to focus on looking at people as far as shape, size, and clothes were concerned, since seeing posture, identifying ages, and of course seeing faces were all beyond my ken, identifying voices alone was not properly cultivated. How well I remember those Sunday mornings when the church service ended and an ocean of well-meaning adults would swarm around me with friendly greetings in voices that all sounded the same. A few years later, even after Kit and I had sung the duet "Guardian Angel" by César Franck, all I could do was smile, shake hands, and say, "Thank you" for the many compliments we received. I still could not call these well-meaning churchgoers by name.

As far as identifying people by simple, bold, and large enough attributes I could comprehend, in school, it was somewhat easier to recognize my classmates than it was to identify the congregation of adults seen just once a week. Linda had dark hair and wore a blue dress, and Mary was blonde and wore red. As for the boys, they all had short hair, since this was before the 1960s. They wore slacks and shirts of uniformly medium or dark colors, and so boys were difficult to distinguish from one another. Only a few did I get to know by name as I heard them speak in class when addressed by the teacher.

Friends would spend an afternoon playing with my dollhouse. It was a little two-story metal dollhouse with miniature furniture, including a pink toilet. I would kneel in front of it to arrange and rearrange the furniture. I think Mother in her letter may have been referring to the larger dollhouse, which was big enough for children to enter. Her father, whose professional skills included carpentry and house painting, made a triptych-style dollhouse facade that, since it folded out, could turn any space along the side wall or especially the corner of our large living room into a cozy space for playing. The front board, into which a window and a Dutch door had been cut, rose to a point to give the impression of a pointed roof. The door was just tall enough for a five-year-old me to step inside without bending my head down, and the split aspect of the door, making it possible to close the bottom half while keeping the top half open, was a practicality as well as a novelty, since more light could be let in that way. The boards were painted a clean bright white, and as an artistic touch, there was trimming in dark green and yellow along the roof line. Since my grandfather loved pretty flowers, he made sure I had my own year-round garden: brightly colored blossoms were painted on either side of the front door, just as though lilies and tulips were growing there.

My grandfather made the house for me when I was five, and by my following birthday, I was given a set of miniature kitchen tools. These must have helped me to make friends with their grown-up counterparts, since I remember tiny slotted spatulas and what for me were large cooking spoons with silver-colored bowls and black handles that looked just like the ones in Mother's kitchen.

The psychologist suggested that I start reading readiness with Janne. The doctor could not predict whether she would be able to read or not; we had to wait and see, and we still have to wait to find out how well she can use her eyes. However, this last November I started to give her comparisons, likenesses and differences—color was most valuable to her here. The nicest book I know is *The Golden Stamp Book*. The stamps are colorful and of readily recognizable objects, such as a house, a bird, a tricycle, a dog, a ball, etc. She loved the manipulation of tearing out the stamps and pasting them in the correct frames. This was with close supervision when we were alone. Then I helped her by holding her hand (she is left-handed) while we wrote the words, just to get the feel of the words, and I helped her "read" the sentences. They are not perfectly worked out—only fair in composition. Soon she recognized such phrases as "See the baby" and "See the ball." Then I wrote these phrases using large manuscript with a big black Dixon Beginners 308 pencil, and before long she had a reading vocabulary of thirty words.

See the baby

The blackboard was an excellent tool for presenting me with large, bold letters. It was a real blackboard: a rectangular piece of slate mounted in a metal frame, with a curved tray to hold the chalk and eraser at its bottom edge. The darkness of the slate and the white of the chalk made a good contrast, so it became a fine way for me to gain ease with writing letters and for making that transition between print and cursive writing.

The blackboard was mounted on the dark pink wall of my bedroom, and I remember my mother writing such sentences as "Billy is coming to play." I would hold her hand while she created the letters, and then I would make them on my own.

There also was an easel that supported a piece of paper almost as large as the blackboard. Mother encouraged me to play with paints of pure bright colors that were easy for me to see. Later there would be crayons, but using those would necessitate finer motor skills than my fingers had when I learned to use the blackboard. New crayons have a fragrance that can't be resisted, and I have been known to buy crayon boxes, to sniff them when opened, and to enjoy that particular aroma-induced memory. That recollection brings to mind the hours of pleasure that coloring with crayons gave me when I was old enough to hold them comfortably and could see to color within the black lines of the largest and simplest drawings in the most basic of coloring books.

Now we have started a primer. We bought her a magnifying glass, which she may find helpful later; some children have, I understand, but I don't think she's ready for it yet.

That magnifying glass was never easy to use, nor did it meet my visual needs. It was that rectangular style with the handle set at a slant, and in my hands as a first-grader, and a left-handed one at that, it was heavy and tiring to my wrist. Furthermore, finding the proper distance from the page to the glass, and from the glass to my eye, was never achieved to the point of effective or comfortable use. My head had to be farther away from the print, and though the letters were magnified to a certain extent, my field of vision was so small that the distance from the text defeated the purpose of the glass. Would that I could have verbalized my discontent at that time, but that was beyond my comprehension at the age of six.

I do not work on anything of this sort for more than fifteen minutes a day, as I don't wish to tire her, and I don't work on it every day.

That was wise. Because of this, the learning experience was a pleasure rather than a chore, and to me it constituted just another mother-daughter activity, as interesting as the many others we had together. I remember sitting on that little modern couch, the same one under which I used to hide when pink clouds sent me running inside. I would sit next to Mother with my feet dangling down and not touching the floor. I would hold the book in both hands and squint at it, with my nose touching the page. I remember the sharp, clean smell of good, firm paper, ink, and glue, and whatever else was used in the manufacture of a book. I learned to see and read "See Spot run," and since red was an easy color to see, I remember the red balls and balloons pictured in that primer.

Now we know that she can read, but whether she is physically able to manage the amount necessary in school is the next problem to face. With understanding teachers, she may be able to work it out.

In a year or two, starting as a summer project, I hope that

Kathryn (my eight-year-old), Janne, and I will study Braille as insurance against Janne's not being able to read the regular-size type. As a family project it should be interesting. Kit, Janne, and I are going to take lessons in pottery. This is for Janne. I want her to use her hands and learn to "think" with her hands.

That summer playing with clay was wonderful. I think the clay was oil-based, and just as the smell of a freshly opened crayon box brings back delicious memories, so the less pleasant smell of the clay brings back memories of when I was five. Though there were three or four other children in the class, Mother told me years later that the only reason she instigated the class was to teach me how to use my hands. It is well known that the blind or partially sighted child in infancy is not programmed to reach for brightly colored objects, since the ball or balloon may be a dim red blur or maybe not visible at all. That lack of the natural impulse to reach and grab so often results in hands that are listless or weak due to lack of stimulus. Since hands need to "see," they need to work, and so manipulating clay was, to my mother, a good way to exercise the fingers as well as a way to initiate an enjoyable, controlled group activity.

When we go to a program of any kind (I took the girls to see *Oklahoma* a few weeks ago), I try to buy front seats. It is expensive but worth it. Then I whisper explanations in her ear as the play progresses. She has a remarkable vocabulary and a fine imagination, and I feel that the more experiences she has, the better she can judge life. When we saw *Oklahoma*, we sat in front and had a good view of the orchestra (in the pit) as well, and we talked about the different instruments.

Throughout my growing-up years and not just during the formative years of early childhood, Mother took me to plays and musicals. One of our neighbors was involved with a theater company in the neighboring town of Arlington, so I know we went to many of her productions, which in later years included *Iolanthe.* By then, I was an avid music student who had more than a casual interest in Gilbert and Sullivan operettas. It was around the time of that particular performance, which I think I saw at the age of thirteen, when I was told that *Iolanthe* was the first Gilbert and Sullivan operetta to be presented with electric lights illuminating the theater.

> We try to take the girls to movies of merit. *The Living Desert* was such a movie. Janne and I sat down front; the picture is large and colorful, and with my whispered explanations, she enjoyed it thoroughly. She enjoyed *Peter Pan* also, which is most colorful.

What I remember about the film *Peter Pan* was that so many things were green. That was true of Peter Pan's costume, which I wanted to have to wear for Halloween. Mother actually found a Peter Pan costume. It had green satin knee pants with a yellow-gold-colored satin tunic. A wide black belt trimmed in red added dash, but not as much as did the green pointed hat, which sported a red feather. It was cute, and I loved trying it on. When Daddy saw me, he said, "You are not my Love Bug Imp now. You're my little Peter Pan." I knew I was my Daddy's Love Bug Imp. He didn't realize he had said the wrong thing! I took that cute little costume off and would *not* put it on again. I wasn't going to change my status as Love Bug Imp, a nickname he called me for as long as he lived, though later it was shortened to Bug. That stubborn streak, which is part of my personality, rarely made itself known, but when it did, there was no forgetting the incident in question.

We watch for things that she can excel in. The girls started to learn to count up to ten in foreign languages. My husband is a college professor, so we know many foreign students. They have about ten "languages" under control, including such as Turkish, Persian, and Japanese!

Mealtimes, especially dinners, were not just for eating. They were time devoted to family interests. As children, we were encouraged to talk about whatever interesting things had happened during the day at school. The grown-ups in turn would tell of things that would interest young children, and in our household, they ranged over many subjects, but those did not include politics or sports. The foreign language game consisted of learning to count from one to ten. I remember the warm gloss and smooth shine of our dining room table, designed and assembled by my father, though built by Clore, as I focused on a string of odd sounding words. *"Eins, zwei, drei,"* Daddy taught us, as he resurrected the German he had studied many years before. That was followed by *"Un, deux, trois."* Foreign languages were not his forte, and the way he sailed through the doctoral language requirement in French was to read Marie Curie's work on chemistry and radioactivity, which he already knew by heart in English.

Mother added *"Uno, dos, tres,"* as we learned to count from one to ten in Spanish. She had been involved with that language since her days as a teacher in the 1930s, when she had taught the children of the migratory fruit workers in Redlands, California, and had encouraged them to speak and sing in Spanish. She studied Spanish all her life, and, though never fluent, she was always interested in learning about different ways of saying things. Years later, I was to study French, German, and Spanish at the high school and college levels, and later I studied some Italian so I could follow the libretti of some of Mozart's most important operas. I'm sure that basic interest in foreign languages, which has been vital to my work as a musicologist, began around our dining table.

> Janne has an excellent memory, and I'm teaching her poems; she and Kit just learned "Jabberwocky." I shall do more of this as we go along. I want her to have a lot to call upon when she must sit idle.

It was thoughtful of Mother to prepare me for a time when I "must sit idle." At that time, she didn't realize that the fine level of education she had been giving me, from the cradle onward, would banish most chances to be idle. Memorizing poems began with the simplest of children's poems, many of which were also in song form. Since some of the A. A. Milne poems were known to me as songs as well as poems, I could recite "Halfway down the stairs is a stair where I sit" as well as sing it. By teaching me to memorize poems, Mother was strengthening my memory and helping me to develop it into the inestimable tool it is today. From nursery rhymes, I graduated to learning poems for children, and thence to poetry to sustain me for a lifetime.

> We have a television set. Kit watches some programs, and Janne sits nearby, playing and listening. The best program

22

for her has been on FM radio: a program sponsored by the universities in this vicinity and the Boston Nursery Training School. The program, which is excellent, is carried on WGBH (Boston). One may obtain the songs, poems, and stories used by writing this station.

That old black-and-white TV entered the far corner of our living room in 1954. Kit would watch *The Lone Ranger* and *Rin Tin Tin*, while I would sit on the floor and play with the set of wooden blocks Daddy had made for us. I still remember the theme song from *The Mickey Mouse Club*, and I was interested enough in *The Howdy Doody Show* to have a Howdy Doody washcloth. Our house did not have a color TV until fifteen years later, when Mother wanted to watch the launchings of the space missions; today they are taken for granted, but then they were something very exciting. She also wanted to see the excellent costumes in the British series *Upstairs, Downstairs* unfold in color, but I wasn't around to take advantage of what would have been her fine descriptions, for by that time I was away at college.

We have found an excellent game, which you can all enjoy with your boy when he is five. It is A.A. Milne's Winnie-the-Pooh (produced by Parker Brothers.) Like Parcheesi, only simpler, it is based on color rather than number, and Janne can play as well as anyone and wins as often. Also we have found a slightly larger dominoes game that is very black with larger white spots.

That Winnie-the-Pooh game could have been made just for me. What could be a better combination than bright colors, the beloved

Pooh characters, and a chance to have playtime with the entire family? The goal was to bring the characters safely to the North Pole without, if possible, falling into the Heffalump Trap, and the means of travel was to draw colored-paper discs out of a bag and move the characters to matching colored squares on the board. Those colors—red, blue, green, yellow, light orange, lavender, and black—were a delight to me, who could match the colors and who loved anything to do with Pooh and his friends. The traditional pen-and-ink drawings of the Pooh characters were printed on cardboard pieces looking rather like half of a Popsicle stick stuck into a small marshmallow. Christopher Robin was red; Rabbit was blue. Piglet was yellow, and Pooh was green. Pooh made his appearance in other places too. For years, an enormous white teddy bear sat on my bed all day. He was probably the biggest available at F.A.O. Schwartz. Tiny bears, some no more than two inches high, were displayed on my whatnot shelves and are there to this day.

Janne is a very friendly little girl. We have friends in quite often, and Janne is not only on hand to greet them; she will entertain them until we take over. She is particularly at ease with adults, though she loves children also. She is very much her daddy's girl, and they are constantly kidding each other.

Janne is also very affectionate. While she is stubborn, she can be reasoned with, so that we have no real behavior problems so far.

I hope that you will all have as much fun with your boy as we do with Janne.

Reading this letter affected me profoundly. As a teacher myself with over four decades of experience, I can understand all the more how creative my mother was as she worked with me through those formative years. In reviewing my report cards from kindergarten on through the early grades, I realized for the first time, from the standpoint of the teachers, that meeting my needs was far from easy; and that it was due entirely to my mother's years of patience, for what was virtually preschool education around the clock, that I was prepared to enter school and survive among sighted children.

I think it is fair to say that if I had not had this degree of individual attention before entering public school, made possible by my mother's professional expertise and loving devotion, my education would have had to have been undertaken at a school for the blind, where I would have learned different skills and other alphabets, which undeniably would have been helpful. How well would I have fit in there? I was neither totally blind nor totally sighted.

I can express this moment of choice best in the words of Robert Frost:

Two roads diverged in a wood and I

I took the one less traveled by

And that has made all the difference.

The world is filled with sighted people, so while I still had some sight, I entered kindergarten in the Belmont Public School system. I now know that my parents' true legacy to me was the constant attention given me during those preschool years that, in retrospect, shaped my positive outlook on life and developed my innate understanding of the importance of learning.

2

The Battered Green Songbook

I wore a little dress of red and green plaid with a crisp white collar for my first day of kindergarten. I remember a large room with lots of children and a teacher whom I liked right away. I heard the word "cloakroom" used for the first time, without realizing that the time would come when I would know the difference between a cloak and a cape, not to mention a coat. I heard the term "cubby" in reference to the small half-cube shelf on which I was to store my belongings. I learned to ask for help, and that was not easy when we had arts and crafts. Using right-handed scissors with my left hand was hard at best, and when that was coupled with not seeing in detail what I was to cut, things were made even more difficult.

I remember the smell and texture as well as the color of construction paper. I responded to the bold red, pumpkin orange, and kelly green, and I folded, cut, drew, and scribbled on all of them. Those fat, stubby crayons were just the right size for uncoordinated little hands to hold while attempting to create alphabet letters. I didn't realize until I studied my report cards that I began that year working below grade level in penmanship and art, which was to be expected, given my visual limitations. By the end of that year, although those grades were still C's and D's, they were at grade level. That not only represented an improvement, but by grading me on a level with everyone else, my teacher was awarding me a vote of confidence regarding my abilities and acknowledging my potential rather than catering to my disability.

I was fortunate to have a kindergarten teacher who gave us a great deal of music. We learned a song about selling lollipops, and to turn it into a group activity, enormous lollipops cut out of construction paper were handed to us as the song was being sung. Another song, which many people know as "Lightly Row" was a catchy little tune that, as I later learned, has only five notes in it. I enjoy knowing a piece I learned in kindergarten that, over the years, I have taught to numerous students, beginning their music studies on the piano or on the recorder.

Our teacher played the piano for us during midday rest periods. I don't recall any specific piece, but I do remember gentle, flowing music that was comforting and soothing. By the end of that first year in public school, the teacher had written. "Janne has improved a great deal. Her handwork is still below average, but it is much better. She is becoming a good group worker. She is a joy!"

This thoughtful and generous teacher gave me a beautiful gift at the end of the year. The rag doll was clean and bright and fresh, with long blonde yarn hair, big blue eyes, a pink face, and a dress of crisp blue-and-white-flowered cotton. My fondest memories are of that teacher, and thanks are due her for her thoughtful present as well as for her comforting and gentle piano playing.

Besides hearing the piano being played at school, I also heard it played at home when my mother found time to play a prelude by Chopin or a sonata by Mozart on our square grand piano. Now, as a piano teacher who favors working with adult students, I have taught many people who studied during their childhood and college years and who returned to music lessons after a hiatus of ten or twenty years. My mother, Fredna Tweedt, was such a student who took pleasure in her music and who gave pleasure to me especially during my formative years.

Mother, born in 1910, began piano lessons at the age of five and a half, and she was taught by the teenage daughter of a family friend. When my grandparents and mother moved from Washington State to San Fernando, California, Mother, at age eight, had various teachers until she met Marcia, another family friend, who showed her the splendor of true concert repertoire coupled with the artistry and technique of an acknowledged concert performer. Marcia, a child prodigy, played the piano with delicacy and strength that my mother admired but never could emulate. Mother worked hard on works by Beethoven, Brahms, Chopin, and Mendelssohn, and in time, she shared her enjoyment of these pieces with me. Music was always a part of Mother's life. In her early nineties, she could still pick out a hymn tune to help during group singing at her retirement home, and her ability to lead group singing, especially from that beloved battered green book, *The Fireside Book of Folk Songs*, is a skill I remember from my earliest memories of her at the piano.

Sometimes Mother would play a Mozart sonata, especially the one in A major that begins with a haunting set of variations and ends with the flamboyant "Turkish Rondo." She was studying Mozart sonatas while pregnant with me. Is my affinity for Mozart due to prenatal influence? We'll never know, but it is not beyond the realm of possibility. At other times, she would play waltzes by Chopin. On special occasions, at Kit's and my insistence, she would play the rich, dark chords and somber melody of Chopin's "Funeral March" as background music while we paraded into Daddy's workshop. There, deftly and quickly, a couple of times a year, he would pull out our loose baby teeth with his pliers.

In 1954, our family, like many others, began to play the recorder. Kit, by then in the fourth grade, had played the Flutophone, a stubby, simpler version of a recorder that for years was taught to generations of third-graders. Kit wanted to play the genuine instrument from which the plastic Flutophone was derived, so a woman came regularly to our house to teach Kit, Mother, and me to play the recorder.

A picture of the three of us shows Kit at the left of a small, round coffee table with her alto recorder, for she preferred the mellower, lower-pitched instrument. Mother is seated on the right, and I am sitting next to her. My soprano recorder was appropriate for a beginner and fine for me at that time. Kit's and Mother's instruments were quite fine and purchased from the Boston Music Company, probably in 1955. Manufactured by Koch Recorders, they had a sweet tone, and they were made of exotic cocobolo wood.

Fifty-five years later, I attended a banquet honoring a long-time friend who was an Italian three-star general. The occasion was his ninetieth birthday, and since many guests were military, I found myself seated next to an American four-star general who had found out that I played the recorder. The American general asked if I was familiar with the name Koch. I thought for an instant and then remembered that long-ago trip to the Boston Music Company. "Yes. I do recognize it," I told him. "My sister now plays the alto and soprano bought many years ago when she was learning to play." The American general told me that he was a close relative William F. Koch, who started Koch Recorders in 1934, and that his childhood memories included spending time in their New England workshop, watching the building of these excellent recorders.

Though by the age of six I had learned the rudiments of playing the soprano recorder, it was probably two years later when I could play several little pieces. Since many of the recorder books we used were collections of German folk songs, I learned several charming tunes that used only five notes. I also learned to play some melodies by well-known classical composers. There was a pleasant little gavotte, which I knew to be an early kind of dance. I never saw the name of the composer on the music; in fact, I didn't see the music at all, since I was learning these pieces by ear. This was easy, for unlike piano music, I was learning a single melody line, which meant playing just one note at a time. Decades passed, and just a couple of months ago, a recorder student played a piece for me. I recognized every note of that gavotte, and when I asked her the identity of the composer, he turned out to be Handel.

I did learn Papageno's aria "A Bird-Catcher Am I," which I already knew from the Vox recording of the life of Mozart. It was my soprano recorder line that played the ascending five-note scale in imitation of Papageno's panpipes, a touch of charm that Mozart wrote into this particular opera aria. A couple of years later, I attended a performance of *The Magic Flute*, and when I heard that aria, I felt a proprietary feeling about it, since I considered it to be my song.

Just as I associate the music of Mozart with my mother's playing at the piano, so I have a similar association with the music of Bach and the music of Bob. Mary Jane, my oldest sister, was in college during my early growing-up years, and during that time, she was dating a brilliant young doctor who was a research scientist with a lifelong affinity for music and a love of playing the organ. They married, and

Bob Haynes filled her life and those of their children with his music. When Bob would visit, we always had the piano tuned in readiness for him. We even had the right book set out on the music rack, for in it were my two favorite pieces, which I would beg him to play, not once but many times. He had never seen a child weep over hearing Bach, and there were other signs, he later told my parents, by which he recognized some sort of affinity I had for music.

When Bob turned eighty in 2005, I wrote him a letter reminding him of the close musical ties we have had for so long, and though part of this letter goes beyond the chronology of my story at this time, I will quote it in its entirety:

My Dear Bob,

Once upon a time there was a brilliant and soft-spoken young man who went to the Redwood Modern House in the Big Woods of Belmont to court a Beautiful Redhead. He would always take time to pay attention to his Intended's little sister, who liked nothing better than to sit beside him at the piano while he played for her. He would play out of that green-and-black book that had BACH, BEETHOVEN, and BRAHMS written in bold letters on the cover, and the pieces he would play most often were those of BACH.

I don't remember sitting in my high chair at the age of eighteen months while singing a Bach fugue, but I understand you were the one who alerted the family to what I was doing. It could it have been the C minor fugue from "The Well-Tempered Clavier," which goes *da-da-DAH-dum-dum*, since that piece is in the green-and-black book.

I do remember that when I was three or four years old, I

31

would sit beside you while you played my two favorite pieces. One was "My Heart Ever Faithful," and the other was "Bourée." It was some twenty years later before I heard that piece played on the instrument for which Bach wrote it, but to my ears it never sounded quite right on the violin, since my earliest memories of it were your playing that piece on the piano.

We have shared so much music throughout the years. When I spent time with you in Chesterland, Ohio, in the summer of 1959, I heard you sing, in your gentle voice, so many beautiful songs that would lull your children to sleep. I remember "My Old Kentucky Home" and "Too-Ra-Loo-Ra-Loo-Ral." On a more cheerful note, you would play from the Gilbert and Sullivan songbook, and as Mary Jane would fix dinner, we'd sing "Poor Wandering One" or "Behold the Lord High Executioner."

I also remember going down the steep stairs into your basement and seeing the organ you had built. It wasn't quite finished at that time, but it still could be played. It must have been then when you started to introduce me to the organ pieces of Bach. I also heard you lead a choir rehearsal at your church in Chesterland.

In Shaker Heights, your organ had the place of honor in the library. By now you were playing pieces of a later era and were introducing me to the organ works of Mendelssohn, but at the end of an evening, I'd always ask for "My Heart Ever Faithful" and "Bourée."

Time passed, and you moved to the Modern House in the Big Woods of Charlottesville, Virginia. By now you had a more powerful organ, and you were playing works by some of the early twentieth-century composers. When I visited you in 1996, you played for me Bach's mighty "Passacaglia and Fugue in C Minor." Whenever I teach classes on the music of Bach, I often teach this piece, and I always think of you.

I think of you, dear Bob, as you celebrate your eightieth birthday. May it be happy and filled with love and family. And remember this. When I was little, I thought the names "Bob" and "Bach" sounded so much alike that they had to be connected in some way. When I'd think of one, I'd think of the other. Now, fifty years later, those two names are still closely entwined, and I will always be grateful for the way you and your music have enriched my life.

All my love,
Janne
August 17, 2005

There were piano lessons being given on our square grand piano, but they were not my piano lessons. Kit was studying from the same teacher from whom Mother had learned, but sometimes a teacher works better with adult students than with children; and so it proved to be in this case. Nevertheless, Kit worked during her first year on a waltz and a march by Dmitri Shostakovich. I would sit on the floor during her lessons and entertain myself by playing with blocks while listening to the music being taught and played. I was to find that Shostakovich wrote the waltz and march for his eight-year-old daughter to play. This was my first exposure to the music of Shostakovich, that brilliant and tormented genius who helped to define twentieth-century Soviet music.

As Kit grew more advanced, she learned "Invention Number One" by Johann Sebastian Bach along with "Solfeggietto," a flamboyant study by Bach's most famous composer-son, Carl Philip Emmanuel Bach. I never studied those pieces, but I did learn them without realizing it until twenty years later, when I began to teach them. The Bach "Invention" shows that composer's skill in creating a piece for two virtually independent voices, one being played in each hand. Carl Philip Emmanuel's piece is a glittering array of sixteenth notes; its precision of composition shows its composer to be indeed the son of the great Johann Sebastian. Nobody knew that I had these two pieces memorized in my head and all ready to play. I did not know that myself. I didn't have the keyboard knowledge or finger skill at that time to pick them out at the piano; nor did I have any idea that both the roles, first of piano student and then of piano teacher, were, at a later date, to be mine.

The record player continued to entertain as well as to instruct me. By now, the "Donkey Serenade" had given way to Gilbert and Sullivan's *The Pirates of Penzance*, and the biographical recordings had been put aside for a recording of *Beethoven's Seventh Symphony*. Besides the record player, there were many music-making devices in the large, stone-flagged living room that occupied the entire lower floor of our house. There was the piano. There was the record player. There were a handful of smaller instruments, mainly percussion, including a tambourine, some finger cymbals that I still have, a triangle, and some castanets. Mother told me years later that these all came into our house to give me some way to make musical sounds. Interestingly enough, of these smaller instruments, the one that influenced me most profoundly was the xylophone.

It was just a simple, one-octave toy xylophone with eight metal keys going from low C to high C. A couple of mallets came with it, and I know I enjoyed the clear metallic tone, which sounded something like bells when I struck the oblong metal keys. Ping. Ping. Ping. I would play up and down the little scale of glittering notes, listening to the different tones and associating them with the colors painted onto the metal keys. Most children's toy xylophones today have keys painted all of one color. My xylophone had silver-colored keys with an oval of color in the middle of each one.

I cherish those colors, for they have left the realm of paint-box reality and have morphed into something combining sound and color; in retrospect, this laid the foundation for my extensive knowledge of music theory. As I thought about the eight pitches that sounded whenever I played the eight notes on the xylophone, I would hear the pure tone and associate it with the color of the key on the instrument. C was a rich, dark purple. High C was lavender, indicating that the two notes were related in one way and different in another. The basic pitch was the same, though the quality of pitch was different. The dark purple colored my understanding of the lower C, just as the lavender or lighter purple colored my impression of the C that had a higher and lighter sound. D was a silvery royal blue. E was a green like maple leaves in springtime, and F was a sunshine yellow. G was a russet red, A was a silvery gray, and B was the warm brown of brown sugar.

As my musical awareness grew, these colors stayed with me and became integral, defining aspects of the sounds of the notes themselves. C is purple. When I think of that pitch, or when I play the first movement of the Mozart *Sonata in C Major*, K. 545, I think of purple. When the tonality shifts to another center of tonality (which is that of G major, in this case), my internal color monitor tells me to think of russet red. In retrospect, I was grasping aspects of analytical music theory, called "key relationships," that I would not study for years to come. When I did study them, I had the feeling that I already knew about them and was just being reminded of what they were called.

Furthermore, my imagination, helped with the xylophone colors, gave me a concrete image by which I figured out the theoretical background for understanding the pairing of major and minor keys known as relative majors and minors. D major is a silvery royal blue. In my musical imagination, D minor is a lighter silvery blue shot through with yellow in a marbleized manner, so that the two colors do not mix to form green. My xylophone's yellow key, F major, is strongly associated with the blue D minor and so is called its relative major. By the same reckoning, the green of E minor, rather like a fire agate, is flecked through with the russet red from its companion key of G major. Somehow I had worked out the intricate aspect of quite a bit of music theory long before I had begun to take lessons in that subject.

Many people who have perfect pitch, as do I, who have the ability to identify the name of a note by aural recognition alone, do associate pitch and color, thus exemplifying and defining an example of synesthesia. I have my xylophone to thank for these musical colors that now exist only in my head and explode into my being as I listen to and analyze music.

I had not met the majesty of Beethoven's *Ninth Symphony* at the time the little xylophone lived downstairs. Now, thanks to that xylophone, that symphony speaks to me in a somber blue for D minor and in brilliant blue for D major, thus making it a jewel-box of lapis lazuli, turquoise, and sapphire. Of course, I did not start with the pinnacle of the symphonic repertoire to evolve and define my unusual blending of internalized colors, sounds, and the intellectual pursuit of music theory. I had to start on simpler pieces to test my colorful musical imagination, and that chance came every Thanksgiving and every Christmas as we gathered around the piano while Mother played our favorite songs from *The Fireside Book of Folk Songs*.

"Angels We Have Heard on High" radiated the warm color of yellow, since it was in F major, just as "Joy to the World" was brilliant in the silvery blue of D major. Folk songs, especially from England and Scotland, as well as those sung by the pioneers who settled the American West, such as "Clementine" and "Sweet Betsy from Pike," rounded out our evening of singing. Each song had its own key and, for me, its own color.

By the time I was ten, Kit would play the flute, and I would play the recorder, while Mother kept the group together from the piano, reading from what I came to think of as the battered green songbook, that green *Fireside Book of Folk Songs*. She began that tradition of singing together for pleasure as a family, and it has now linked us through four generations.

Four decades later, in 1998, my family had gathered in Newport, Rhode Island, for my niece's wedding. The ceremony took place on the grounds of the Villa Marina, a house of historical significance, since it was designed by a cousin of Ralph Waldo Emerson, and it had been a refuge for Boston's infamous Lizzie Borden. No one of that ilk was spending the night; the house was filled throughout with family members. After dinner, I wandered into the living room, where I had a choice of not one, but two grand pianos that, if not quite as old as the house, certainly fit into its nineteenth-century atmosphere. I sat down at one and began to play something introspective and soft.

First I played a prelude by Bach and then a Schubert impromptu that filled the space around me with musical images of rushing streams and sighing trees. Then, one by one, family members came in to sit quietly and to listen.

When my niece's new father-in-law came in, I switched from Schubert to a Scottish love song; being a Scotsman, he began to sing it. One song ran into another without taking time to figure out which should come next. We kept the music going without breaking that golden chain of melody, as Tom sang first one and then another song by Robert Burns. Gradually more family members joined us. My sister Kit, our eighty-eight-year-old mother, and our cousins from Connecticut sat down quietly while Tom sang through "Ye Banks and Braes" and "My Love Is Like a Red, Red Rose." I switched from the Scottish songs to those from that battered green book of folk songs that all of us knew. We sang the Irish "Cockles and Mussels," the English martial song "The British Grenadiers," and songs of our American forefathers who had traveled from Missouri to California by covered wagon a century and a half before this family gathering.

My sister, Mary Jane, her husband, Bob, and their three grown children and their spouses were filling the room, and they stayed there as I played from memory for four hours. My mother had played these songs for her children. My brother-in-law, Bob, had played them for his family, and now I was playing them for the next generation, for Mary Jane's grandchildren were there, completing that family gathering. We were being linked by strands of melody and bonds of memory, for these songs joined us through decades as well as through distance and time. From Scotland and England to New England, to Virginia and California, and back to New England, these songs brought comfort and a tangible feeling of togetherness.

The old house, which probably had heard a dozen decades of family musical gatherings, heard ours to the end, at which "Auld Lang Syne" became a benediction as well as a hymn to the remembrance of times gone by. "Should auld acquaintance be forgot?" It was the final memory of an evening to be treasured.

3

The Portrait

A Harvard professor who lived across the street had a daughter who was Kit's age and who had learned to count to ten in Russian. The two girls must have decided on a competition to see how many languages they could learn, and I tagged along for the experience.

Our parents taught us to count from one to ten in French, German, and Spanish, but we didn't know Russian, so there was the danger that the competition would end before it had begun. Then my parents hosted a party, and a grand party it was. A number of my father's foreign students, who were studying chemistry from him at MIT, were invited.

The large living room was filled with tall grown-up people who seemed, to the six-year-old I was then, a veritable forest of tall forms somewhat like trees. But these "trees" spoke and had different and distinct voices, for English was to them a foreign language, and their speech was colored by the richness of their intonations and accents. There was Kaya from Turkey and Dr. Bazergan from Persia. With pencil and paper in hand, Kit wrote down how to say the numbers from one to ten in several languages, including Turkish, which begins *bir, eeki, oosh,* and Persian, which begins *yek, doh, say.* I followed her and listened to how the numbers were pronounced. Fifty-five years later, I can still recite these series of numbers. When I've had the occasion to mention this particular experience to an acquaintance, a student, or a salesperson who is native to one of the countries in question, I am delighted to find that these abstract syllables that I learned by rote are comprehensible as numbers! After that party for the foreign students, it was pretty clear that the language competition with our neighbor was over.

Now it was time to learn what to do with numbers and letters in my own language. It was back to basics for first grade! Students' desks were lined up in rows facing the blackboard, actually a green board, and from the first grade on, there was always a "Janne's Row": I had a front seat, so that if there was any chance of my seeing the blackboard, I could do so. Actually, I never could see the blackboard well, so whenever necessary, I would walk up to it and stare at it or write on it when called upon to do so. My desk was always to the left of center and, as I realize now, it was placed in front of the teacher's desk, so that if I needed assistance, I could receive it.

On one side of the room there was a large chart that was kept rolled up most of the time, but when it was let down during reading periods, I could tell that it displayed large, bold versions of the letters of the alphabet in both lower and upper case. I would move to a chair on that side of the room whenever that alphabet chart was in use, and I remember being so close to it that I could smell the paper.

It may have been on the first day of class when we were presented with a piece of good white paper on which we had to draw a line of the letter A across the top of the page. To everyone's surprise, the papers were removed after writing that one line. We were told that we would see those papers again at the end of the year, when we would be asked to draw another line of the letter A. Then we could see how we had improved, as could the teacher. My penmanship remained a

C for that year. I had an A in reading readiness and a B in reading and arithmetic, and by the end of the year, I had A's in both music and art, and the overall report was good.

The teacher wrote, "Janne has become very much a part of the group situation! Only on a rare occasion does she need more than the average amount of individual help and attention. (She's a love!) Janne has done remarkably well throughout the year. (I think you know how much I have enjoyed her.)"

I was ready for the second grade, but a different kind of learning experience, otherwise known as a summer vacation, was about to happen. Daddy remained at home to work at MIT, while Mother, Kit, and I were to take a train trip across the country and visit our grandparents along the way.

Mother had made Kit and me cotton dresses of red and blue plaid with white collars and trim. In those days, that was appropriate attire for train travel. I remember being intimidated by the large, echoing train stations; and the noise, the hiss of steam, and the sharp smells of dirt and fuel, confused and bothered me. Once inside the train, the muted sound of the clickity-clack told me of the speed of our passing, since I couldn't gauge that from the views out the long, large windows. Those, to me, were blocks of color. The blue block was sky, and the green block appeared whenever the train tracks took us through wooded areas. I could see a different kind of green outside the window as we traveled west and passed by fields of wheat and corn. The train seats were, to me, very large and high-backed, and as I was small for a six-year-old, my feet would touch the floor only if I sat on the edge of the seat.

We would walk up and down the narrow aisle to get to the bathroom or to the dining car. Crossing from one car to another was a trial for me, since in the couplings, the floor was uneven, the train swayed terribly, and the clickity-clack of the wheels, now amplified into something ferocious, was terrifying. Fortunately the dining car was comfortable, and like a restaurant: there were real tablecloths and cloth napkins; if not linen, then something white and crisp. It is easy to please a six-year-old with good food, and I have no negative memories from my dining experience on the train.

Mother, always the teacher, brought along projects to keep me interested. In 1955, Magic Slates were popular. When I drew on a plastic sheet with a pointed wooden stylus, lines or words or whatever I created would appear, and when the double layer of plastic sheets was lifted, the artwork would vanish. This was perfect for playing tic-tac-toe or hangman, so the hours of cross-country travel passed comfortably. I also had a map of the United States that was a piece of white paper with the states outlined in black. I had brightly colored crayons with which to color the states through which we would pass by train and which we would visit. Though the idea was good, that project was never finished, since the states on the east side of the country were far too small for me to color comfortably.

Our first stop was Marshall, Missouri, a small town in the middle of the state and practically in the middle of the country. The town was filled with large, leafy trees and quiet, old houses made of red brick or of wood painted white. Such was the house of my father's parents on Eastwood Street. My Grandfather Irvine worked in the local bank; he knew the entire town, and everyone greeted him with affection. He loved sitting on the wide couch swing on the front porch of his house in the green twilight, where he would tell family stories, and he found in me a ready listener. After dinner, he would go to his secret stash of candy, usually Russell Stover's, and share a treasured sweet with his visiting granddaughters. What I remember most about my grand-mother was the way she said, "Hi, there!" in her sweet, soft Southern accent. She was dignified and quiet. I am said to resemble her, since I inherited the shape of her hands, and as an adult, I wear my hair up, as did she. I am touched and honored when cousins remark on the likeness between us.

I turned seven while at my grandparents' house. An unusually severe drought was affecting the farmland, and the magnificent Midwestern corn was shriveling in the fields. There were just a few pink and orange zinnias in the garden to decorate my birthday cake frosted in a white buttercream icing. My grandmother was a wonder-ful cook, and my guess is that we had fried chicken for that dinner. I still remember the rich flavor of grain-fed chicken and the smooth chicken gravy that accompanied it.

When bedtime came, everyone was restless, for both the tempera-ture and the humidity were high. The electric fans gave little relief, so Mother tried to keep us children cool by putting damp towels on us. Air conditioning, which now we take for granted, was not in general use, so these memories of more than fifty years ago of unbearable heat, damp sheets, and restlessness are a reminder of the yearly dis-comforts of the Midwest summer heat. Soon after, we saw the end of that drought, as fierce and intense thunderstorms came through town with their saving rains, frighteningly loud thunder, and the soothing coolness of rain-washed air.

We boarded the train en route to New Mexico, and when we disembarked, I noticed that everything was different. Something was different about the air, and the pale blue sky seemed to go on forever. I was not used to seeing nothing but sky overhead; in my little woods in Massachusetts, I had to look at a mosaic of pieces of green and blue, since most of the sky I knew was overlaid with a fretwork of leaves or a tracery of bare branches. If I stood in the backyard in that area, which in colonial times had been a king's highway, I could see a wide strip of sky between two walls of green trees. But here in the West, the vastness of the sky and the fragrance of the air, a combination of sagebrush and sun-baked clay and soil, was a new experience.

On arriving in Santa Fe, we stayed at the Hotel La Fonda, a grand old hacienda style of hotel. During the sun-filled days, we would wander into various shops, and when it was time for lunch, we found a place that served us tall glasses of iced tea, and it was there that I had cherry tomatoes for the first time. It is these vignettes of eating cherry tomatoes that are my memories of Santa Fe; though I could see, to some extent, that the buildings of sun-baked clay were different from those I had known, the visual images did not take pride of place in my memory. Yet I am glad to have seen these Spanish-style buildings in the limited way available to me, since such images were always augmented by colorful conversations and comments made by Mother. Now that I live in Tucson, Arizona, I recall my introduction to descriptions of the desert rose and sand-colored stucco buildings of the Southwest, for my own townhouse is of sand-colored stucco with a hint of rose.

We visited Packard's Trading Company, one of the oldest and most reputable stores for buying Native American arts and crafts, especially jewelry. Mother bought me a little bracelet made with Zuni inlay, and I still remember squinting at those clear, bright turquoise stones and seeing the sun spark bright light off of the silver of that bracelet. Later we found jewelry suitable for children, made of shell and wood, that was somewhat in the style of the turquoise and silver or pure silver massive squash blossom necklaces.

Instead of the floral-inspired squash blossoms radiating out from a basic chain of silver beads, the white shell-bead necklaces had five modified rounded triangular shapes radiating out from each side. These were decorated with patterns in black, white, red, and turquoise. The central pendant was not the horseshoe-shaped *naja* of the squash-blossom necklace, but instead it was a thunderbird in the same bold collection of Southwestern colors.

Mother had just read a book called *Maria: the Potter of San Ildefonso*, and though this world-famous ceramicist was in her nineties at that time, we took the trip to her pueblo and met her. I remember seeing rows of pots drying in the sun; adobe dwellings, sun-baked to a warm, pinkish tan; and rounded adobe structures that were "beehive" ovens. Mother, always the teacher, showed me the ovens and told me what they were. After our day trips, we would return in the evening to the hotel. One night we experienced the intense rhythms of drums and stamping, moccasin-clad feet as a group of dancers, including some children my age, performed Native American dances.

I was enthralled by the bright costumes and jewelry that I saw in Santa Fe, and of course I wanted to dress in the flamboyant manner of the classic Navajo dolls that, along with Mother's "Maria" bowl, were souvenirs of that trip. The doll of the Indian woman wore her black yarn hair up; her blouse was of dark blue velvet with "silver" buttons; and her long, full skirt was of patterned cotton. Her jewelry was plentiful, and she wore little moccasins. Now, by the door of my study in my Tucson home is a picture of a little New England girl with brown braids dressed in full Southwestern splendor. The shirt that Mother made for me of royal purple corduroy had "silver" buttons like tiny pinecones all down the front, and the long sleeves were cuffed so I could display my turquoise bracelets. The rich purple, which I could

46

see when Mother sewed it, complemented my thunderbird necklace and went perfectly with the skirt that Grandmother Irvine had made. This was of bright turquoise cotton, trimmed with rows and rows of rickrack and braid in white, gold, red, and blue. Turquoise moccasins from Santa Fe completed the outfit that I wore proudly to school or to a party, or whenever I had the chance to dress up. I have always enjoyed costumes. I could touch as well as see them on dolls. As far as wearing them is concerned, especially if they are in velvet or corduroy, I enjoy doing that now as much as I did fifty years ago. I am lucky that I have the chance to dress in period costumes for some of my musical presentations.

My mother always lit up when she spoke of California. I could hear brightness in her voice as she shared her sun-drenched memories of redwood and pepper trees, eucalyptus trees, and flowers, which were all a part of her childhood. Her parents' home, a modest bungalow in San Fernando, had, as she said, a fruit tree of every kind, and countless kinds of flowers. Certainly fragrances as well as colors bright enough for me to enjoy were plentiful. There were lemon trees and peach trees offering fresh fruit to be picked, to make eleven-inch pies. Both of my grandmothers were excellent cooks, and fried chicken was also a favorite at my California grandmother's house. Fresh fruit salads and lettuce from the garden were truly delicious and colorful. All of these foods, along with baked ham, baked beans, and maybe some enchiladas made by my great-aunt, made a most plentiful and colorful spread for family picnics, which were novel experiences for us girls who had grown up so far away from grandparents, uncles, aunts, and cousins.

My grandfather took pride in his garden, especially in the redwood tree he had planted as a tiny seedling in the front yard at the corner of his property. The tree grew rapidly, and Grandfather Tweedt lived to see it grow taller than the telephone poles. He loved the enormous California walnut tree whose wide-spreading branches made a tree much larger than those to which I was accustomed. My grandfather had planted the pepper trees that lined his driveway and had provided my mother, when she was a little girl, with a sweet-smelling and shady playhouse during the hot summer days. He also enjoyed a couch swing, and this one was in front of a persimmon tree and shaded by a eucalyptus tree whose dry and spicy leaves color my memories of that summer visit.

Another memory is filled with white, lavender, yellow, and black. There was a white pergola over the front porch of that little house in San Fernando, and when we were there in the summer, the wisteria was at its height. Darting through the pale lavender blossoms, especially on the side of the house that was in the sun, were so many yellow tiger swallowtail butterflies that I could see them as occasional flecks of gold. Kit would catch them for me so I could touch their wings and have an understanding of their beauty. That was a special gift, and ever since then, I have had a fondness for butterflies.

Both of my grandmothers were from an era in which women excelled at sewing. My California Grandmother Tweedt took her ability in this area to the level of a cultivated hobby, for she made clothing for dolls. Some of the dolls were perhaps five inches tall and had dresses and bonnets crocheted in thread. I enjoyed the textures as I touched the ruffles on these tiny dresses. Like the dolls of an earlier era, most of these represented adults rather than little girls or babies. The doll my grandmother gave me, which I had for years, had black porcelain hair and a white porcelain face, arms, hands, legs, and feet. Her dress was a rich fuchsia taffeta trimmed in bands of black ribbon, which was the style of an earlier era. I realize in retrospect that I was becoming attuned to appreciating different textures. Though I could see the vivid deep pink of the taffeta and the black of the contrasting trim as well as the black of the doll's porcelain hair, I was equally aware that the trim gave texture as well as a contrast in color, and that the porcelain was both smooth and cool to the touch. Later I found that dolls like this are mentioned by Laura Ingalls Wilder in her "Little House" books, and these dolls of ladies with their porcelain heads and tiny hands and feet were the epitome of luxurious toys for little pioneer girls of eighty years before.

After saying good-bye to the tall and fragrant eucalyptus and redwood trees, we boarded the train and returned to the trees I knew best. The large shagbark hickory that grew outside my bedroom window, and the cluster of pine trees above the stone wall, welcomed me home. The host of maple trees, including the Little Lone Maple Tree and its cousin, the moose maple or striped maple, received special greetings, for they were saplings just as tall as me. Their leaves were still green, but by the end of August, their brilliant change to autumn foliage was not far off and, as always, I would explore the woods almost every day to discover the first signs of fall.

At the end of summer, it was time for school, so I began the second grade at Winn Brook School, where Kit was in the fifth grade. The year was uneventful. I earned A's in music and oral expression. Art was now a B, as were arithmetic and penmanship, and reading was a C. As I think about it in retrospect, the grades had slipped because my vision was slipping. The print was just small enough to make reading a little more difficult for me. This sign of eyestrain was so slight that I did not make the correlation until I examined my school grades and related them to the memories about which I have been writing. Even if it was a little more difficult, I could still accomplish any given task, so that at this time there was no question about altering my method of education.

Though I could enjoy the pictures in books if they were clear and the colors were bright, there was another way in which I could appreciate images, especially those that were popular during the holidays. Fortunately for me, they were three-dimensional, for I collected wax candle figures. Though they all had wicks, I never burned them, since I enjoyed these candles as little statues. The tallest candles, probably six inches high, were a pair of Christmas trees, one green and one red, which were both encrusted with silver sprinkles. I would look at them, touch the shapes, feel the rough texture of the sprinkles, and smell the wax, which gave off its own special scent. There was an orange jack-o-lantern candle and a Halloween witch with a black pointed hat. My favorites were a pair of Plymouth pilgrims wearing period costumes. The man had a tall hat and a white collar, and he carried a gun over his shoulder; and the woman had a gray dress with a white collar and white trim on her gray bonnet. The waxen folds of her long dress seemed to flow as my fingers stroked them.

In order to house this collection of candles, Daddy built me a beautiful whatnot out of a pine so light in color that it was almost white. It is eighteen inches from top to bottom and ten inches wide, and it held that candle collection for many years. The whatnot, which has now mellowed to a warm deep tan, is still in my bedroom and reminds me of the bright and eager way I greeted those days when I was seven or eight years old. I would reach for a red Christmas tree or an orange pumpkin, smile as I saw the colors, and smile all the more as I picked up a figurine, sniffed the aroma of wax, and stroked its familiar, well-loved shape. Now I realize I was learning new things all the time, as all of my senses joined forces to enlarge my knowledge of my world.

Kit was playing kickball in school. I was not playing sports, since I was never scheduled into any activity. I spent the recess periods standing outside, talking with this or that classmate who couldn't play games for one reason or another. One day, Kit said she was going to teach me how to play kickball. We marked out four bases on the flat surface at the top of the driveway, and we used a large reddish-orange ball that showed up well against the blacktop. Kit taught me about kicking the ball and running from base to base. I remember the bright sun shining through the green leaves and the gurgle of the brook, which flowed and chuckled its way as an accompaniment through so much of my childhood, as Kit called out the numbers of the bases. I remember laughing and running, and running was something I rarely did alone. No wonder this episode has stayed with me as one of those growing-up experiences for which the reward was getting tired and dirty, and feeling like any other kid who has just won a game.

During the warm weather, and that extended into fall, the stream was our favorite place to play. This little brook cascaded thirty feet across the front of our property, so there were at times small waterfalls at one end, and a calmer flowing where the brook went under the walking bridge. Daddy had built that rustic-looking wooden bridge so we could cross the brook without walking clear up to the driveway, but the bridge was also built on top of the utility conduit to hide the large ceramic pipe. We played all around the bridge. We went under it and over it. Kit was adventurous in engineering the water to flow into this or that channel. I was satisfied with wading or just letting my hands trail in the smooth current and listening to the unforgettable musical sound of flowing water. I would sail my red, foot-long plastic canoe in a part of the stream where it would not escape from me, and Kit would take her yellow and blue canoes through her channels. One day after a storm, she saw what she thought was a red canoe that had been left in the stream. It turned out to be a large carp or giant goldfish that had been washed down from a pond farther up on Belmont Hill. The excitement for that day was taking the fish in a bucket and returning it to the pond.

When it was too cold to play outside, Kit and I had to find entertainment in the downstairs part of the house. Hidden in the back room was the acting chest. I especially liked to dress up in anything of interest that I could find that might be a long skirt and a fancy blouse. Mother's Scottish outfit consisting of a kilt skirt and a velvet jacket and hat, which had been made for her as a little girl by a Scotswoman, was always a favorite. This costume was stored in a chest along with a royal blue taffeta evening skirt and a deep green taffeta gown that Mary Jane had enjoyed. Strings of poppet pearls and other pieces of costume jewelry added glitter to the costumes I created. Though the two of us did play at dressing up and sometimes neighborhood children joined us in this entertainment, this was a pastime I could and did enjoy on my own.

In my second-grade school picture, though the picture is in black and white, I am wearing a dark green cardigan sweater buttoned at the top and showing a frilly white blouse underneath. My braids are hanging down my back, as they always did throughout my early school years. When my parents decided to have a portrait taken of me, this was the outfit I wore. My mother had seen the work of a Boston artist, and I remember the sittings at which Mr. William Boyhan sketched me while keeping up a pleasant conversation so that

I would be focused yet entertained at the same time. I must have told him all about catching butterflies in California the previous summer, for when the portrait was finished, there I was in my sweater and frilly blouse, and on my outstretched hand, a butterfly was alighting on my finger.

The portrait is in sepia and was drawn on paper that at the time was one hundred and fifty years old. Now that paper is two hundred years old, and so it dates to about 1806. It means a great deal to the adult and music historian I am now that the paper must have existed at the time of Beethoven, Haydn, Schubert, and Jane Austen. How I wanted to share that information with the artist and to tell him that my portrait, along with shadowboxes of mounted butterflies, hangs on the wall near my piano, and that it has been enjoyed for decades. It has been admired by students, family, and friends, who comment on the sensitivity of the work. I knew I wanted this likeness of me to be featured in this book, since it captures me at that special age at which my personality and interests were developing. So much of the early part of the book takes place when I was seven, eight, and nine, when I was wearing my braids down my back, and when I was reaching out for new experiences that were floating around me like so many butterflies.

I was too late. I was deeply saddened to find that the artist had died fifteen years before, in 1996. His specialty was drawing animals. No wonder the sepia-tinted butterflies alighting on my hand were exquisite.

4

❦

Brook, Lake, and Ocean

By the age of seven, I was completely comfortable roaming over the entire property on Hickory Lane. The brook flowed and bubbled over and around glacial New England rocks and boulders, and since trees lined both banks, it was a shady place to play. There were swamp maples at one end of the stream, with leaves that would fit into the palm of my hand; and at the other end of the brook were the larger Norway maples, whose leaves, as big as my face, would turn a buttery yellow when, at autumn's end, most of the rest of the trees were bare. The wood had ash trees, maples, locusts, a large oak, and a grand old hickory tree in front of the house that may have given its name to the small street. Yes, it was an official street, though it could best be described as a long driveway that split to serve our neighbor's house as well as ours.

As I return in my imagination to this acre and a third of New England woods, stone walls, and stream, I divide it into the lower and upper woods, the lower being below the old roadway, and the upper being above the stone wall. There were trees I knew by name. The Leaning Ash had been partly knocked down by a hurricane, and though its roots were still well buried in that rocky New England soil, the trunk, with its smooth bark, leaned so close to the ground that I could play at climbing without being in danger of falling off. There was a tree-house platform in a wild cherry tree, but the sharp twigs that stuck out from the branches did not make it finger-friendly to me, so I rarely played there. There was a Little Lone Maple, which I found as a sapling when it was just about my height, so I watched it over the years as it grew far taller than I could reach, and in time it grew into a full-sized tree that in the fall turned the most beautiful, rich gold. A clearing in this part of the woods had become the Sumac Patch, enjoyed in the spring, since that shrub, with its graceful branches, was early to come into leaf, and adored in the fall. These same long branches turned a brilliant red about a month before autumn was at its height.

From the Sumac Patch, I would climb the short, shallow slope onto the flat, grassy area: the abandoned king's highway. To reach what I called the upper woods, I had to walk back to the house to climb the embankment fronted by the stone wall that was just outside the kitchen window. Placing my sneakered feet in just the right places for balance, I could step onto the next level of uneven, grassy ground covered with trees and shrubs. In these upper woods there was the Linden Tree, which at one point supported a green hammock. We had planted several pine trees that, even during the fifteen years of my childhood spent on Hickory Lane, grew to be big enough to produce a pine-scented shade and a carpet of pine needles that was always a little slippery underfoot. Pine pitch on sticky fingers was always a memento of visiting that portion of the woods. Wherever I wandered in the woods, the house was near enough so that I never had the feeling of being lost, though I was on my own for much of my woodland wandering and musing. The house was a warm red, as the facing was of stained redwood, so it was not too difficult to see where it was. I could catch glimpses of the red that contrasted with the green leaves of the trees surrounding it. When I wandered outside in the late fall and winter, the red of the house was clear to see through the thin gray trunks of the bare trees, since that strong color stood out against the white of the snow.

I've mentioned the large living room on the lower floor that was perfect for playing with dolls or listening to records. At one end was a door leading into a small greenhouse, for my father raised orchids. I loved going into that greenhouse every so often, where I'd be met by that exotic smell of growing things: ferns and moss, and occasionally the sweet smell of a spray of lavender cattleya blossoms. When a particularly beautiful flower was in bloom, it would be brought upstairs so that it could be enjoyed as a centerpiece on our dining table. Sometimes there would be a plant with a long spray of thumb-nail-sized yellow flowers called "dancing ladies," called such because the lip of each flower flared out like a skirt.

It is very hard to grow orchids outside of a greenhouse, but here in Arizona I am attempting that with half a dozen plants that live on my kitchen counters and table. I have encouraged a couple of them to bloom, but even though blossoms may be scarce, I enjoy touching those wide, thick, flat orchid leaves, or thin leaves a good two feet long that drape themselves over the counter or over the breakfast table. It is most satisfying to have plants that speak to me of other places and of earlier times when the assuming of adult responsibilities was still in the future.

The Hickory Lane kitchen, dining room, and three bedrooms were on the main level. The wood floor still echoes in my imagination with the rapid, authoritative click of Mother's high heels, the softer, slower tread of Daddy's shoes, and the scurrying of tiny-footed chihuahua dogs as they scampered throughout the house. The patter of chihuahua feet is not relegated to childhood memories, since for years these little desert dogs have kept me company in my Tucson home. The Hickory Lane kitchen, long and narrow, had a window over the sink that looked out onto that part of the stone wall where it was easy to climb up to the next level of land. Sometimes the view out that window was of gray tree trunks and fawn-colored leaves on the ground; other times, a blanket of snow made the boulders of the wall look almost black. Best of all was in the spring, when the shaggy hedge of forsythia burst into a tangled mass of golden-yellow flowers. I would pick branches from that forsythia hedge as early as February and bring them inside, where warm water and sunshine would force the flowers to bloom a good six weeks early. That yellow bouquet in the heavy square-shaped glass vase, when placed on the smooth surface of the walnut dining table, would gather the sunshine from the west-facing windows and make the room itself glow with a golden anticipation of spring.

Beyond the dining room was a short hallway, off which were Kit's and my bedrooms, and at the end of the hall was the master bedroom. During those early years, my bedroom had a twin bed, a dresser, a desk, and that blackboard on one wall that was used for drawing, tic-tac-toe, and hangman, as well as for educational purposes. The Old Hickory Tree was just feet outside my bedroom window, and every so often a gray squirrel, with fur as gray as the tree itself, would entertain us by sitting on a branch and nibbling on a nut before disappearing into the hole in the hollow part of the tree trunk wherein was his nest. Mother, Daddy, Kit, and I would stand for minutes at a time to watch the squirrel, whose branch was probably eight or ten feet away from us. Mother would try to point out the little gray animal, but I could not focus on the direction in which her finger was pointing, so she would turn my head in the right direction. Sometimes I would catch the slightest movement as the squirrel disappeared into his hole, and I do remember at times seeing a blur of gray that moved. By the time I was seven or eight, the excitement of seeing this little wild animal was lost for me.

"He's there. He's over there on the branch. Can't you see him? There he is. Look where I am pointing." My mother's voice rang with eagerness as she attempted to help me see this little woodland creature. How frustrating, at the age of seven or eight, not to be believed. I could not see the squirrel. I know now that my mother was more frustrated than I, since as always, she was heartbreakingly eager to bring the world she saw into my reach. All that Mother wanted was for me to enjoy what she was seeing at that moment. It wasn't that she was denying the existence of my eye condition, since my gradual loss of vision leading eventually to blindness had always been for her, the defining aspect of my being. As an adult, I was to realize that my mother was living constantly with the self-imposed burden of guilt for having given birth to a blind child. Over the years I tried to assure her there was no need for her feelings of guilt, for my innate optimism, inherited from my father, and my total lack of resentment, a tribute to my own creed of positive thinking, had kept me from being emotionally handicapped by any such physical limitations. Nevertheless, my mother's insistence of defining me by my limitations ended only after Alzheimer's dementia had wiped her memory clean at the age of ninety-nine, and that happened more than fifty years after she tried to show me the squirrel outside my window. Mother's attempts to show me what I could not see were inspired equally by frustration and by love, but when I couldn't stand the tension of the constant questioning, which was her attempt to will me to see what was beyond my range of vision, I would mutter that I could see the squirrel even though the reality was that I could not.

Incidents like this happened infrequently, but when they did occur, the feelings of frustration and a sense of failure left me emotionally drained. How could I describe what I could or couldn't see, especially since I did not realize that even then, my left eye was slowly deteriorating and that what I could see one season, I might not be able to see twelve months later?

In retrospect, I may have unwittingly brought about my mother's conception that I could see more than was actually possible, since from my earliest years my vocabulary was that of a person who could see. In the spring I would raid the garden and bring Mother red roses, white mock-orange blossoms, and deep purple-blue violets. In the summer my hands would be filled with crayon-box red, orange, and yellow nasturtiums; and in the fall, I would bring her the prettiest peach-colored maple leaves that I could find. As we spoke of these colors, my appreciation of them was intense, and certainly it was proof that I was receiving great pleasure from what sight I had. For me, sight brought the beauty of intense colors coupled with the fragrances and textures of my harvest of flowers. For Mother, who enjoyed my floral offerings as much as I, my responsiveness to the visual world—that is, my own personal version of the visual world—led her to believe that if I could see the flowers, then I should be able to see the squirrel.

Over the next few years, as my vision continued slowly to decrease and Mother came to the realization that the woodland creatures were beyond what I could see, she developed the skills of describing things that she knew would interest me. Through her concise and artistic descriptions, I could appreciate birds, woodchucks, people, and vistas seen through the car windows. It was then left up to me to file away what I could see and to graft onto my memory what I could not see, for by this time I was definitely learning to see with words.

I didn't need to see with words to know when summer had come to Hickory Lane. With so many places to play, Hickory Lane was a grand setting for enjoying summer, though before the days of air conditioning, the high humidity did make us long for a place to swim. The brook, being too rocky and too shallow for swimming, was for wading only, so when we wanted to swim, we'd take the half hour drive out to White's Pond. This private lake was approached from the parking lot by a long, steep stairway of concrete steps that always seemed too large for small legs to negotiate in comfort; but at the bottom was a picnic ground among the pines, and beyond that lay a sandy beach and the lake itself. The sand was coarser than beach sand, but it was sand, and I was content as soon as my feet found it. The lake was shallow for quite a ways out, so I could swim, never very far out, with the security of putting a foot down if necessary. Mother would sit on the sand and wave her arms in a wide arc so I could catch the motion of that movement and know where to come ashore. The water was too cold for comfort; after all, I really had learned to swim the previous summer in Marshall, Missouri, where the municipal pool was as warm as a bathtub. But the White's Pond swim was refreshing, and even though we would be hot again as we took that half-hour drive home in the family Plymouth, those afternoons of swimming were always happy outings.

Sometimes we would take a picnic lunch to White's Pond, where we'd eat watermelon under the pine trees and search for Coke bottle caps in the sand. At other times, we'd have picnics at home in the backyard on the dark green picnic table that my California grand-father had built for us. Fresh sweet corn, boiled for six minutes, was served dripping with butter. Ground-steak patties and tall glasses of iced tea flavored with leaves of pungent mint, which I always made it my job to pick, were the flavors of those Hickory Lane summers. No such picnic would be complete without calorie pie. My mother was known for making delicious pies, as indeed were both of my grand-mothers. Pecan pies and apple pies made their way onto the picnic table, but the one I liked best was my mother's French strawberry pie.

Certainly, by the age of seven, I was finding things to do in the kitchen. Mother would have me sort the strawberries and save the biggest ones to chill in the refrigerator before placing them in the piecrust. She was very good about finding things that I could do easily, so that I would feel comfortable working in a kitchen. Of course, a few of the strawberries were eaten along the way, and the cooked strawberry pie filling had to be sampled several times as it was being stirred over the stove. Lined with cream cheese and topped with whipped cream, this calorific strawberry pie was a favorite for many years.

Daddy worked at MIT throughout the summer, except for a two-week vacation; that time became our vacation trip to Cape Cod, where we had the use of a friend's summer cottage. Sand, sun, and family togetherness were what made those vacations so special. The vacation of 1954 was cut short by Hurricane Carol. A small cottage near the ocean, with no radio and no newspaper and a telephone that might or might not work, is not a good place to be during a strong hurricane. I remember the gray sky, the heavy rain, the sound of the ocean waves pounding the shore, and the feeling of urgency to return home. What at first we thought was a little rainstorm was the famous

Hurricane Carol that, in August of 1954, left a path of destruction throughout the greater Boston area and toppled the steeple of the historic Old North Church of Paul Revere fame. Daddy was concerned about our house in the woods. Depending on the path of the hurricane, tree limbs could fall, the stream could rise, and in spite of the superlative skill of the Scandinavian craftsmen who had built the house five years before, wind-driven rain could seep into the basement. Fortunately, our house was unharmed, though there were many tree limbs down throughout our woods. The brook did wash out part of its bed, which the city engineers had to reinforce with a rock embankment. The oak tree, one of the largest and tallest in the woods, was split, and though half of it had to be taken down, the remainder of that tree has lived for decades since that storm.

The last summer we spent in Cape Cod was 1956, and it is that visit I remember best. The first sight of the ocean and the first whiff of salt air were the signs that our family summer vacation had begun. After crossing the Cape Cod Canal on the Sagamore Bridge, but before reaching Dennis, we would stop at a fish-and-chips restaurant for lunch and be greeted by that smell of deep fat frying, sweetened by the scent of salty sea air. Stands of beach grass and cattails grew in the sand outside the restaurant, and these strange and different plants, dried by the salt air and sun, would remind me that I was no longer in the thick, summer-green woods at Hickory Lane. After a lunch of hot, crispy fish, we would return to the car for the remainder of our trip. Soon Kit and I would become hot and tired from being cooped up in the car, and we would try to entertain each other. She might suggest the game of counting how many red or blue cars we could see out the window. I would play that for a couple of minutes until my eyes grew tired from squinting at blurs of cars that went by so quickly that it was hard to tell if they were red or blue. I knew that when she saw a red car, she could read the license plate and count the people inside the vehicle. If I looked out the same window, I might see a red blur, but it could be a truck as easily as a car. I always tried to play the game, since somehow, even at the age of seven, I knew that being considered "normal" was far more important than being successful at playing the game. I would stop playing only when my eyes became too tired to focus.

My entertainment of choice was to sing songs, which we did in two-part harmony. "I've Been Working on the Railroad" and "Down in the Valley" were favorite songs for which the harmony, higher than the melody, was called a descant. Of course we sang "Frère Jacques" and "Scotland's Burning" and other rounds in which the two voice parts are identical but are not sung beginning at the same time. Finally when our old blue Plymouth turned off the paved road onto a sand track, when we were hot and thirsty and tired of being in the car, we knew we had arrived at the Harrisons' cottage.

This cottage, loaned to us for two weeks every summer by one of Daddy's MIT colleagues, gave us a chance to experience a true vacation with sights and sounds, smells and experiences perfect to entertain a lively seven-year-old. The first thing to remember was to wear sneakers while crossing the sand trap, a platform of thin, weathered wooden boards spaced about an inch apart, which spanned the entire front of the cottage, for it was painful to walk over those boards with bare feet. Since the cottage was a converted garage meant to serve a house that was never built, most of our living was in one room, which gave us good family time together. From breakfast time till long after dinner, we were laughing, enjoying breathing the ocean-scented air, eating our simple meals, doing dishes, playing board games or cat's cradle, reading, and, of course, walking along the sand dunes and playing on the beach.

But before we could do that, we had to set up house. On entering the cottage for the first time, the air smelled old and musty. Throwing open the garage-style front door let in the sunshine and sweet air, and it helped banish the stale air as we put our few belongings away. I remember the odd assortment of colors, of furniture, and indeed of everything in the cottage. The floor was a dark red concrete, and in spite of the sand trap, it was always gritty. There were bunk beds with faded blue bedspreads, and it was on those that Kit and I would sleep. There was a massive old upright piano in one corner, and though the sea air had knocked it out of tune, I do remember picking out a tune or two on it. After all, what is a home without a piano? To the left of the instrument was a step that led up to the master bedroom, the only addition to the original structure of the cottage. That floor was of wide wooden boards painted a gray blue, so the room was always quite dark. The small bathroom was on the left wall of the bedroom, and it was always dark and damp and so had that unpleasant old bathroom smell.

In the main room, the round table with straight-back wooden chairs, all different sizes and styles, was near the garage-style front door that, when opened, gave us a panorama of sunshine and pine trees; we had the feeling of eating outside with the comfort of being inside. Each morning would begin with a cheerful breakfast that for us girls would be cereal and orange juice. The next activity was helping to clean up; ten-year-old Kit would wash the dishes, and I, at seven, would dry them and put them away. It was never a chore, because we laughed a good deal. The dishes and silverware were all mismatched; there were dark blue milk glasses and those tall, brightly colored aluminum glasses that were wonderfully cool to the touch when we drank chilled milk in the morning or iced Coke in the afternoon.

But morning was morning, and there was nothing quite like those mornings on Cape Cod. Of course we wanted to finish doing the dishes as soon as possible, so we could go down to the beach, which was the best entertainment of all. The long, sandy road, two tire tracks with a grassy mound separating them, cut through fields of bayberries, and the sweet, spicy scent of warm bayberry wax rose from the sun-warmed ground and accompanied us as we scuffed through the loose sand underfoot. A sharp right took us to the paved road, and very soon we were at the edge of the world, for there were the sand dunes and the beach. The tall, dry grasses sang in the wind as we raced up the dunes and tumbled down them on the other side. There in front of me were the blue sky and the blue ocean, which were so close in tone that it was hard to tell them apart. But that didn't matter. They were both that light, slightly grayed summer blue, which seemed all the more blue when contrasted with the expanse of clean white sand all around us.

First, there was a wide swath of dry sand, followed by a band of sand that was still a little wet, though like the dry, it had been blown into ripples and ridges. We were nearing the ocean, and finally at our feet was that smooth, even band of moist sand that proved to be better than my blackboard and magic slate, for it was one magnificent, enormous writing surface. I had to kneel down on that sand right away, feel it on my skin, and get my hands into it. What a place to print J A N N E in letters a foot tall. I would erase my name and write it again, this time in cursive script, connecting the letters with care, using my finger as a pencil and guiding it with my entire arm. Mother had taught me the rudiments of the cursive writing that I would be learning in school as soon as I entered the third grade. She knew that writing was a challenge for me, and in retrospect, I know she must have been pleased to see me enjoying writing as I played in the sand. I was using large arm muscles rather than the small finger muscles, and that made everything easier. I would write numbers, lots of numbers, and maybe write and solve a few arithmetic problems. I would draw circles, triangles, squares, and boxes, and I thought the sand was the most wonderful stuff in the world. Ahead of us was the ocean, and the lapping of the waves was calling Kit and me to come in and play in the water in our red-and-white Hawaiian-print cotton swimming suits. The water was cold, so I pranced and danced, got wet, swam and splashed a bit, and then came out of the water to look for shells.

We waded in the pools and walked where the waves washed the shells up on the beach for us to discover. If the shells were big enough, I could see a blur of white and find a clamshell, or better still, a perfect sand dollar. The starfish were harder to find, being a color and texture similar to the sand, so I'd look for those while squatting on a good, shell-laden part of the beach, and then I'd brush my fingers through the sand to look for aquatic treasures. I hunted for long, white razor shells; smaller, purple-black mussel shells; and all sizes of scallop shells. Some were pristine white, others were touched with apricot, and some were a dark gray, but all had that characteristic fan shape made even more fanlike by the evenly spaced small ridges on the outside of the shell. We would dig in the wet sand and watch the water fill up the depressions and make pools. I loved building sand castles, not fancy ones, but solid lumpy ones, and I never tired of waiting for the water to flow and swirl through the moats and channels I had dug, so I could experience the flow of the wet sand under my hands as it was washed back into the ocean. No wonder I loved my little sandbox at home, but this "sandbox," or rather the beach, was bigger and better.

After a morning and an afternoon on the beach, we would shower to get the salt and sand out of our hair, and then we would rinse our suits and put them out on the clothesline that was strung up between a pair of pine trees. There would be an early dinner of split-pea soup or navy beans boiled with ham hocks, which Mother had prepared in advance in her kitchen at Hickory Lane and brought in glass mason jars to the Cape. She wanted to keep the cooking simple, since she too was on vacation. Occasionally, we would have minute steaks or fried chicken, and after shopping for such fresh foods (we didn't need many), we would go to the local Dairy Queen, which I believe was a new franchise at that time.

One hot August day, after a dinner that may have been fried chicken, we did have a special dessert, which was a half of a pink watermelon with candles stuck in it, surrounding a pink plastic number eight. That was my surprise birthday cake. I remember being given a beautiful big tea set, not a delicate china one that could be easily broken, but a teapot with a lid, a cream pitcher, a sugar bowl, and four large cups and saucers made of a soft, flexible, pale blue, translucent plastic patterned with sparkly bits of color throughout. I remember unwrapping and opening that large box while sitting on the hammock in the pine trees just outside the cottage's front door, and I knew that I would enjoy serving tea in my dollhouse at home.

That was the summer for bubble stuff and bubble gum. That was the only summer I ever chewed gum, and it had to be bright pink bubble gum. That unforgettable flavor, tinged with sand and salt air and maybe a bit of pine sap, initiated my eighth year. Blowing bubbles with bubble stuff, sniffing that slightly soapy-scented solution, and waiting for the bubbles to pop on my face, is one of so many memory pictures from that summer. Kit and I also enjoyed eating M&Ms. I could see those M&M colors, for we ate them outside and picked them out, one by one, from plastic bowls of crayon-box red or yellow. Of course I went for the red ones; that is, we both did, since there were fewer of them, and they stood out brightly against the boring browns, tans, and yellows.

Since the summer twilights were long and Kit and I were still filled with energy, we would play with beach balls. Oh, those wonderful beach balls that were patterned with delicate swirls of red, pink, yellow, and blue, which made a soft ping as they were bounced on a hard surface. Yes, I remember that taut, smooth rubber, which resonated when I flicked the ball with my fingers, and always, during the course of our two-week stay, those beach balls were popped and then patched. For some reason, they never held the same Cape Cod charm after being brought home to the woods and the brook at Hickory Lane.

When the long twilight turned to night, we would go inside, close the wide garage door, and maybe have a game of Chinese checkers on the round breakfast table. Mother would read aloud, or if Daddy brought his favorite Kipling, we would hear him read *Just So Stories*. We'd go to sleep to the sound of crickets and the wind in the pines, with the knowledge that the next day and the one after that would be as wonderful as the day we had just spent together.

A two-week vacation does not last forever, and the time came when the next day was the last day. After one quick early-morning visit to the beach, picking up one more shell I couldn't do without, and one more sniff of the bayberry-laden morning air, we'd return to the cottage to pack our belongings into the car. We'd clean the kitchen for the last time, but without the laughter that had accompanied that chore since the beginning of our stay. The birthday presents, the beach balls, and shoeboxes of shells joined the suitcases, wet swimming suits, and empty soup jars in the trunk of the car. We swept the sand off of the dark red floor, stripped our sheets off of the bunk beds, and replaced the faded blue bedspreads on the mattresses. Finally we closed and locked the cottage and drove away from the pine trees and hammock, down the rutted sand path to the road; but this time we turned left, away from the ocean. That was the last time we summered at the Cape.

The following summer I was to encounter the Atlantic Ocean again under different circumstances and surroundings. I was to see the ocean as a deep, rich blue that could be distinguished from the blue of the sky overhead, and I was to learn of its vastness, for I would be crossing it on an ocean liner.

5

Listen, My Children, and You Shall Hear

Reading out loud continued to be a family pastime and pleasure. There is a picture of Mother, Kit, and me, taken at the same time as "The Recorder Trio," only instead of making music together, Mother is reading aloud from *Little House in the Big Woods*. I was captivated by the story of Laura Ingalls Wilder, who in this, the first of several books, described her life as a little girl growing up in the big woods of Wisconsin; and by the time I was in the third grade, I was starting to read that book on my own. The print was a good size for me, and the pictures were bold charcoal drawings. If the pictures were in black and white, the verbal pictures from Laura's detailed style of writing were in full color, as she described the calico prints of pink or blue that she and her sister, Mary, wore, as well as the rich, dark green of the long dress her Ma wore for the sugaring-off party at Grandma's.

My California grandmother also knew the stories about Laura and Mary Ingalls. She found two dolls, one a brunette and the other blonde, and dressed them according to the descriptions in the books. "Laura's" dress, to complement her brown hair, was of a dark, pinkish red. The fabric used was known to have come across the Great Plains by covered wagon when our ancestors had made that journey from

Missouri to California. I wondered at that fabric being so old; in fact, it could have been as old as the real Laura, who had been born in 1867! It draped in very soft folds in the full-skirted dress that little girls would have worn in the pioneer days. The "Mary" doll wore pale blue, which was considered to flatter her blue eyes and blonde tresses. The fabric for this dress was not antique, since it went back no earlier than 1953. It was made from scraps of fabric of the dotted Swiss type, out of which Mother had made Kit's and my bridesmaid dresses for Mary Jane's wedding. The fabric had patterns of lilies of the valley embroidered throughout. I enjoyed seeing that fabric in that little doll's dress. These dolls were kept in an antique box and were for admiring rather than for active play. Nevertheless, once again, thanks to my grandmother's hobby, through the dolls' clothing I had a tactile image of the costumes of Laura's era.

My imagination feasted on many other stories besides those about Laura Ingalls. Mother read the tales of the Norse gods, gods of thunder and fire, and the Greek and Roman gods, deities of the sun and moon, gods of hunting, of wisdom, and of the sea. The Greek and Roman names of Zeus and Hera, Apollo and Minerva became household words. Heroes as well as gods entered my imagination as Mother read me stories from the *Iliad* and the *Odyssey*. The tales of Paris confronted by three goddesses, an old king mourning the death of his son, Hector, and Odysseus, the wily tactician, became my bedtime stories. I had a book, *Myths and Legends of the Ages*, and could enjoy some of these stories on my own, especially since the book had simple and boldly executed illustrations of heroes in tunics and sandals and goddesses with long, flowing hair and floating gowns. Though I did read some of these stories on my own, it was always more enjoyable to hear them read aloud. Mother was carrying on the tradition established by her mother, who read aloud to her husband, nephew, and little daughter in the white bungalow on ten acres of garden and farmland in San Fernando, as well as earlier in the small house near a cherry orchard in Washington State. In fact, a golden wedding anniversary photographic portrait of my grandparents shows them each in an armchair on either side of the fireplace. My grandfather has a little chihuahua dog on his lap, and my grandmother has a copy of *War and Peace* on hers, for she had probably been reading out loud for entertainment.

From gods and goddesses, Mother and I graduated to the heroes of legend, of Camelot and Sherwood Forest. I became well versed in the concept of chivalry and looked forward to each reading session because I would learn more about bold knights, beautiful ladies, kings, and magicians, and of a sword whose jeweled hilt was an invitation to many to try to free it from the confining stone, but whose ultimate possession was destined for the one who would be king. After finishing the book of Arthurian legends, we read about Robin Hood, men in green, astounding archers, and a massive oak tree, that stalwart symbol of England's strength. Years before, when Mother taught ninth grade English, she had shared the book *Ivanhoe* with her classes, just as her own junior high teacher had shared it with her; so it was only natural that Ivanhoe, Rowena, and Rebecca soon populated my imagination. Bible stories had their place too, as did memorization of several psalms, including Psalm 23, and later St. Paul's letter to the Corinthians, that exquisite hymn to love.

Though reading was always a pleasure at bedtime, and children's stories gave way to myths and legends and later to literature to be enjoyed for a lifetime, my reading skills in school were still graded C. Music and oral expression continued to be my best subjects, each rewarded by an A, and by now, art was upgraded to a B. There were C's in arithmetic, written expression, and spelling, but penmanship, including letter formation and legibility, had sunk to a D. Writing was so much easier when I could make very large letters in the sand! Fortunately, I was in the hands of Miss Barbara Jack, an excellent teacher, esteemed by the school system, and resourceful enough to address my problems with penmanship. I remember being held after class in order to rework an assignment. I was in tears, afraid I would miss the school bus. Tears blotted the yellow paper with the widely spaced lines as I made rows of letters and numbers, especially the numbers two and eight. Finally the assignment was finished to the teacher's satisfaction; I caught the bus in time, and I finished the year with a B in penmanship. Miss Jack gave me a most unusual present; teachers at that time were not used to sharing any personal information with their students. I must have told her about playing in the brook, to which she responded that when she was a little girl, she too had played in that same section of my brook, which bore the name Winn Brook, just like the name of my school. By now, that would have been one hundred years ago. I can imagine her, the child who grew to become a skilled teacher, as a little girl in pigtails and pinafores. Was she a Belmont version of Anne of Green Gables? Did she have names for her favorite trees as did I, and were her woods sparser than mine, filled with saplings and fledgling trees rather than mature maples and ash? The king's highway must have been more clearly defined, since neither houses nor paved driveways would have interfered with its progress through the Belmont countryside.

The third grade marked my second year as a Brownie scout. I enjoyed wearing the uniform that at that time was a medium-shade brown dress and a dark-brown beanie hat. During the group meetings we learned scouting skills, and I was often selected to go to the front of the room so that if an arm needed to be bandaged or a knot needed to be tied, I could see what was happening by performing the service or by having it performed on me. The same procedure happened for the two years I was in Girl Scouts, and though I was shown how to tie knots, I never figured out the difference between a granny knot and a square knot. What I remember best is the group singing. Sometimes we sang scouting songs and sometimes camp songs, American folk songs, and patriotic songs. I was standing near the piano when one of the group mothers asked me to select a song. I may have asked for "Oh Susannah," and then I was asked if I knew on which note it started. I said it was a D and sang it. When the woman found the song in the book, she found it did start on a D and that the note I had sung was accurate as well. This episode dates my awareness that I could recognize musical pitches. Thinking back to my toy xylophone, I knew that D was D just as I knew that blue was blue. Making the correlation between musical tones and colors is the easiest way to explain the nature of this awareness, or rather gift, known as perfect pitch.

Over the years, I had classes on Saturdays in several subjects. My memories of the classes in art are not clear; I'm sure I enjoyed working with blocks of color, which meant I probably would have drawn trees and houses rather than people. I was never comfortable drawing people, and it was one of Mother's rare pointed remarks that alerted me to the reality that "people's faces don't look like that." A round ball for a head, two blue dots for eyes, and a small curved red line for a mouth may have served me while drawing in preschool, but by the time I was eight, I should have known my representations were too simplistic. I would have known that if I had been able to see faces, but since faces were expressionless blobs, it is no wonder

I couldn't represent them on paper. Though I knew the makeup of a face by touching my own features, I couldn't transfer that tactile knowledge to paper. Nevertheless, I still enjoyed drawing! Rarely was I ever reminded of my visual limitations, but gradually, whenever Kit and I would entertain ourselves with drawing, I knew that she drew far better than I. She could draw horses and people, the former being her passion at that time; whereas my attempts were clumsy and didn't look right. Somehow I never worried about the limitation, and I just kept drawing whatever I wanted. The art teachers at the De Cordova Art Museum understood this and helped and encouraged me in any way that they could.

I have a clear recollection of an afternoon class in ceramics. I wanted to make a Statue of Liberty, for I had seen her on a brief trip to New York City during the summer of 1956. We had climbed the narrow metal stairway up and up, around and around, and finally reached the lookout point at the crown, for at that time the arm and torch were inaccessible. Rather than a panoramic view seen through the windows in the crown, the view I remember was of hundreds of shiny pointed metal stairs underfoot, since that is what I stared at during the ascent and descent. I knew I had to walk carefully, so all of my attention was directed to those steep and narrow steps. Mother described the view, and my view of the statue itself was enhanced by buying a bronze figurine, from which I was able to admire the shape of the statue and the grace of her flowing robes. So the ceramics teacher had me stand up and assume the position of the statue, with one arm raised as though I were holding a torch and with an open book in my other hand. From that experience I created a very wobbly Statue of Liberty, which was glazed in an improbably bright turquoise blue.

The classes in modern dance took place in the auditorium near the front entrance. I liked wearing a black leotard and learning to move to the music. Once the teacher had shown me the basic dance positions, I could follow her verbal directions, even though I couldn't see the footwork as her feet executed position after position. I found out later that these classes in dance I had off and on during my childhood were considered important in teaching me confidence and grace in movement. I did enjoy moving to the piano music and would gravitate toward the piano, and maybe, during a break, visit with the pianist.

While Kit and I took these Saturday classes, Mother would entertain herself with a book, and between the morning and afternoon classes, the three of us would drive a short distance to where there was the most glorious copper beech tree overlooking a lake. The tree was so large and thickly foliated that it was like a great, dark tent under its branches. We would have our lunch with just enough tree shadow to protect us from the direct sun; Mother would have brought cherry tomatoes, slices of green pepper, and a piece of chicken, since I never cared for sandwiches. In good weather, Mother would read aloud from a book called *Family Sabbatical,* which was about an American family who lived in France for a year. That was my introduction to the word "sabbatical," and during that summer I did not realize how important that word was to be for me within a very short period of time.

On returning to the museum building after our lunch break, I remember always being greeted by the fresh, clean smell of air-conditioned air with a whiff of turpentine. Sometimes we would attend lectures, and one of those was on music. A man brought several instruments, which he demonstrated. He picked up a French horn, blew into it, and produced a note. "Does anyone know the name of that note?" he inquired of his audience. I raised my hand and was called upon to answer. Mother was startled and embarrassed. *What does Janne know about the names of notes?* she thought. *She'll probably make a mistake.*

But I did not make a mistake. I knew the note was an F and said as much. Once again, without realizing what a powerful tool I had, it was coming to my attention, as well as that of others, that I had an unusual ability regarding the recognition of musical pitches.

It was at this time, when I was eight years old, that Mother decided to find a piano teacher for me. I began going to the Longy School of Music in Cambridge, which was located in what was once a grand old house with a massive central oak staircase. Kit had already begun piano studies there. My teacher, a young woman, started me with a simple primer that, like all such primers, had large enough notes that I could read if I almost touched the page with my nose, but that is a very hard position to maintain while seated at the piano! At least I learned about the lines and spaces; whole notes, white on the page and without stems; the half notes, white too but with stems; and the quarter notes, which are black note heads with stems. I learned about the treble and bass clefs, each of which has a distinctive symbol that identifies the name of one of the lines within the five-line staff. Of course, I could memorize the simplest pieces after hearing them once. The teacher was frustrated. I couldn't see print music well enough to read it, and I didn't know Braille music. She did recognize that I had a good ear, and it was by ear that I learned my recital piece, "Arabesque" by Bergmüller. This is a lively little piece in which a pattern of five notes in a row goes up or down. It is a piece that I teach to this day. Every time I do so, I remember that massive front hall turned into a recital hall, where children, dressed in their best, performed on a very large, very long, black grand piano.

I participated in another recital that spring of 1956, for I was one of the few students chosen to play my Flutophone in a group concert. The Flutophone, designed in 1943, was an inexpensive way to introduce schoolchildren to music. Obviously a cousin to the soprano recorder, it is fatter and stubbier than the soprano, and most importantly for children, each finger hole is outlined with a ridge of plastic that makes it easier to find. The mouthpiece is longer and narrower than that of the soprano recorder, and again, that makes the instrument more child-friendly. The tone is not as refined as that of the recorder, and a classroom of eight-year-old kids blowing into these instruments is truly an example of cacophony. Yet those of us students who were more accurate in our performance on this instrument could and did make music on it. When I played my little solo in anticipation of being chosen, I knew that my counting and rhythm were rock solid and accurate.

Recently, I purchased a Flutophone, for I wanted to give an accurate description of it. Now that memento of the past shares shelf space with the red, green, and blue Yamaha plastic recorders I use for teaching young recorder students. These in turn inhabit my teakwood shelves, along with fine wooden sopranino, soprano, and alto recorders and a myriad of quality plastic instruments, including tenors and a bass that I've played throughout the years with great pleasure. I found that on graduating from the third grade with my Flutophone, I wanted to resume playing the recorder, which I had started learning two years before.

The recorder is so well suited to the playing of the traditional Christmas carols, and fortunately, the selections from the old, battered green book of folk songs were set in keys friendly to that instrument. Christmas really began after the traditional Thanksgiving dinner, for that was the time when family and guests adjourned from the dining table to gather around the square grand piano that, in 1956, was in the large living room downstairs. First came songs we enjoyed singing, ranging from Scottish ballads to American work songs, and finally, as though turning over the page of the year to the Christmas season, we sang "Angels We Have Heard on High," the first carol in the book. It was in the key of F major, a comfortable key for the little soprano recorder, and I could play all of those scales in the chorus. Sometimes I would sing the melody for a verse and then switch to the clear sound of the recorder. Of course, "What Child Is This" was perfect for the recorder, since that instrument had been popular when this tune, also known as "Greensleeves," had come into being sometime before the mid-1600s.

As I think back to those early holiday celebrations, I realize with a smile that what I remember most is a feeling of fulfillment and feasting for all five senses, for sight, hearing, smelling, tasting, and touching were all stimulated. The Christmas season began when Daddy brought home the Christmas tree, which, during those early years, was a tall balsa fir. He'd bring it through the downstairs door and into the far end of the living room, where he'd trim the branches and cut the trunk to fit the tree stand. Immediately, that end of the room was filled with the clean, sharp fragrance of balsa fir and that indefinable fragrance of cold winter air with a hint of ice crystals and snow. He'd set the tree upright in its dark green metal stand that held water. It took a few days for the tree's branches, freed from their rope bindings, to unfold and to take shape.

The Christmas ornaments came out of an old six board chest

that was kept in storage in the workshop. The cardboard boxes, with dividers for the balls, even then were fragile with age, and when we opened them, the ornaments seemed like treasured rubies, emeralds, sapphires, and the gold and silver of a hundred ancient myths and legends. Our only decorations were brightly colored glass globes, whose metallic surfaces shone gold and silver, red, blue, and green. The lights we had in the mid-50s were large, bulbous teardrops that echoed the same colors of the balls. First the lights were placed on the tree, and finally the delicate balls were set on the ends of all of the fragrant, prickly branches. My job was to thread delicate shepherd's hook hangers through the small rings set into the tops of the balls, and to hang them on the branches I could reach, for the tree reached the ceiling. When I would see other families' trees with tinsel hanging from all the branches, smaller lights, and fancy balls of differing sizes, some etched with patterns, I realize now that I reacted negatively because the visual effect was confusing and unclear. After seeing and identifying the component parts, I would try to fit the image together as a whole, and I found it to be a sensory overload. The plain, pure, bold colors on the familiar simple ornaments gave me much pleasure during my childhood and vivid memories for the years beyond.

On Christmas Eve, we would walk down the hill to the congregational church to be greeted by the fragrance of many wax candles, evergreens, wet woolen coats, and a myriad of perfumes. I remember great banks of red poinsettias and the organ playing well-loved melodies. At this time, I was too young to be in the choir, though I did come to the attention of the choir director when, on being asked, I volunteered to sing "Away in a Manger" in front of the entire congregation.

Kit and I always had the chance to open one gift the night before Christmas, and that gift was always a brand-new set of flannel pajamas. One year the pajamas might be red with white snowflakes, and the next year they would be blue with white reindeer. Whatever the color, the texture of that cloth was the softest thing ever, and the smell of new flannel is something I still remember. That fragrance of new cloth never survived the first washing, nor did the softness of the flannel, so we would just have to wait for the following year to enjoy that scent and softness again.

On Christmas morning, Kit and I would tiptoe downstairs to enjoy the gifts in our Christmas stockings, "hung by the chimney with care," for opening the major presents would come later, after breakfast. I still have that solitaire game Yogo, that jump-a-peg game with its yellow pegs and round blue board that, being only three inches in diameter, was a good stocking stuffer. Usually, wedged into the toe was that traditional gift of candy, which would be a small box of pure maple sugar from the Concord Country Store. Some of the candies were shaped as tiny maple leaves; some were plump ears of corn, and others were flower-inspired. All were that perfect maple sugar tan with a slight glitter of sugar crystals that added a subtle sparkle and crunch.

In time, the smell of frying bacon would lure us upstairs to the breakfast table. The dining table would be set with Mother's best dishes, the beautiful Spode Blue Colonel bone china edged in gold, and the breakfast would be our very special pancakes. The whole-wheat pancakes, oatmeal pancakes, sour milk pancakes, or cornmeal pancakes would do for Christmas. As a special treat, we would have my favorite pancakes, which were called "fluffies" because they were filled with beaten egg whites. As always, it was a teamwork breakfast. Mother would mix the batter, and Daddy would bake the cakes on that grill he had made at the same time he had wired the record player. The syrup, a family recipe, was of brown sugar seasoned with cardamom seeds. Later, Daddy created his own version that included maple sugar along with brown and white sugars and Karo corn syrup, and since the maple flavor was so delicate, the spices were left out.

There were four generations around the tree that Christmas of 1956. Mother's parents, Mother and Daddy, Mary Jane, her husband and their first two children, Kit, and I can be seen smiling, either standing or seated by the Christmas tree, in that year's family portrait. Mother had sewn three identical bright-red corduroy jumpers with gold and white trim for Kit, me, and Marilee, our niece, who was only six years younger than me. Mary Jane and Bob had been married when I was four; they had lived first in Colorado and then in Ohio, so their visits, once or twice a year, were always welcome and happy events. Sometimes it would be Bob who would play the carols for family singing, but always he would have to end the evenings with "My Heart Ever Faithful" and "Bourée," my two favorite pieces by Bach, which had charmed me ever since I was three years old.

Mary Jane brought color to my gifts around the tree, for she was skilled in knitting. There was nothing more boldly red than those bright red woolen mittens with heavy cable stitching down their backs. In later years, she made me a navy blue pair and a deep gold set, but it is those red mittens that I remember best, since they showed up so well when little hands were playing in fresh, white snow. One year Mary Jane's gift was the most magnificent collection of clothes for a beautiful doll that was big enough to dress easily. I still remember the navy blue corduroy skirt and matching bolero vest with a crisp, long-sleeved, blue and white cotton blouse. There may have been a corduroy tam to go with that ensemble. I believe another outfit was a blouse of Royal Stewart tartan with a black velvet skirt. The long-sleeved evening gown trimmed in white lace was of a deep royal blue taffeta, made from a remnant of fabric from her evening skirt, which for years resided in our costume chest.

Mother and Daddy would always select a gift with educational importance. I was given a large box, fresh from the publishing house, in which there was not one but eight books. Now I had what was, at that time, the original and complete set of the Little House series by Laura Ingalls Wilder. I could follow Laura's family life and adventures from the age of five to the age of eighteen. There they all were, waiting to be read. All eight books were redolent with the smell of fresh new paper, and as I unwrapped them, one by one, I was in such a hurry that by the time I reached *These Happy Golden Years*, the eighth book, I tore the corner off of the back cover, and on the book jackets were the only pictures that were in full color. Mother helped me protect those pictures on the dust jackets by cutting them carefully so that they could be pasted into the inside of the front cover of each book. Those Little House books given to me over fifty years ago are still on my bookshelf. The corner of the cover of *These Happy Golden Years* is still torn off as a reminder of excited, eager fingers tearing through wrapping paper a little too quickly to find the treasure inside.

Poetry was as important to our bedtime readings as was literature. Some of my earliest memories are of singing some of the lullabies I had heard from infancy; after all, songs are poems set to music. I also learned the charming poems written for children about a robin, a nest, and a secret. Soon longer poems such as "The Night Before Christmas" were memorized, along with the lovely rhythmic jumbles of words found in "Jabberwocky." "The Tale of Custard the Dragon" by Ogden Nash had a rhythmic beat that tripped off the tongue, creating a kind of verbal music, as did Kipling's "Song of the

Banderlog." Having always loved Winnie-the-Pooh by A. A. Milne, the poems about Christopher Robin and his bear, which I had first learned as songs, were added to my library of memorized poems, as was the following:

> They're changing guards at Buckingham Palace.
>
> Christopher Robin went down with Alice.
>
> Alice is marrying one of the guards
>
> A soldier's life is terribly hard
>
> Says Alice.

The British guards in their signature red coats took on a different significance when viewed through the eyes of Longfellow:

> Listen, my children, and you shall hear
>
> Of the midnight ride of Paul Revere,
>
> On the eighteenth of April in Seventy-five;
>
> Hardly a man is now alive
>
> Who remembers that famous day and year.
>
> He said to his friend, "If the British march
>
> By land or sea from the town to-night,
>
> Hang a lantern aloft in the belfry arch
>
> Of the North Church tower as a signal light—

In a quiet and compelling voice, on that day in March 2010, I recited more than half of this landmark poem to my music class, and through Longfellow's images, I brought into my Arizona living room the sights and sounds of a Boston, Lexington, and Concord two thousand miles and two hundred years away from the present. Given that so many of my students, my age or ten or twenty years older than me, had lived in New England and had also learned "The Midnight Ride of Paul Revere," it was not surprising that a murmuring chorus of voices accompanied my recitation. I had visited Paul Revere's house. The historical sites of Lexington and Concord were familiar, since we always took visiting family and friends to view the Concord Green and the "rude bridge that arched the flood where once the embattled farmer stood and fired the shot heard round the world."

My mother had wanted me to learn plenty of poetry so that, as she stated in her letter describing my early years, I would have something to think about during the times when I would have to sit idle. Those times were very few, but they did occur, especially when I had to sit in a hospital waiting room, which I did once a year for my eye examination.

During World War II, my father, an inorganic nuclear chemist, stayed in Cambridge, Massachusetts, working for both Harvard and MIT by keeping the cyclotron open for nonmilitary purposes that, more often than not, were medical. One of the Harvard doctors he met was David Cogan, an ophthalmologist who was to follow countless cases of premature infants with retrolental fibroplasia. This doctor took over my case as soon as my condition had been identified; and along with so many others, I was involved as a subject in a research program. I remember those visits as a parade of men with subdued voices and gentle hands who asked me questions but more often spoke amongst themselves. My memories also include the series of examinations utilizing lights that were glaringly bright and painful to dilated eyes. I learned to keep the pain at bay by holding my breath, clenching my teeth, and trying to think of something else, such as the sound of the brook or the taste of shortbread cookies fresh out of the oven.

My right eye was always without sight, and I was told that when I was older, I would have an operation to remove the cataract, purely for cosmetic reasons, because the retina was far too damaged for any vision to be restored. That projected surgery never took place, since fifteen years later, when I was twenty-three, the entire right eye had to be replaced with an artificial one: the only remedy to alleviate the extreme pain from acute glaucoma. That condition, not recognized as a consequence of retrolental fibroplasia when I was eight, was in later years found to affect any number of people with RLF.

The doctors were pleased that I was managing as well as I was within the public school system. The prognosis regarding the stability of my vision was still not known, since this condition was so new. My mother had mentioned in that letter written three years before, that sometime we might take summer classes in Braille so I could at least acquaint myself with the Braille alphabet, which I could then use at a later date, depending on the state of my eyesight.

Plans do have a way of changing, and during the summer in question, I was not going to be in the Boston area at all. I wasn't even going to be in the United States, for my family, like the family in the book we read during our lunch breaks at the De Cordova Museum, was going to experience its own family sabbatical. We were to cross the Atlantic Ocean on an ocean liner and live for fourteen months, not in France, but in England.

Part of our preparation was already done, since by now I was well versed in the knowledge of kings and queens, knights and castles, archers and crusaders, and crowns and gowns. I also knew several important poems of Kipling and Milne. Other types of preparation included buying proper clothes for sailing the ocean blue. This included acquiring a new pair of sneakers, the purchase of which marked the beginning of every summer.

Sneaker Summer (1997)

There was a time when canvas shoes were blue;

We called them sneakers then.

The salesman would open the box.

You'd listen to the paper crackle

And sniff that fresh sneaker smell of stiffened canvas.

Then you'd wait for grown-up fingers to thread the laces.

You'd wriggle your feet

Into bright blue shoes.

Not navy. Not royal blue, but

Sneaker blue.

Of course they had white laces

And bright white edging on their rubber soles,

Which only made the sneakers look more blue.

Summer blue. Vacation blue.

You'd hop around the shoe department,

Flexing your feet inside stiff canvas walls;

And once out in the sunshine,

You'd strut on rubbered toes

And think of how you'd walk on coarse, wet sand,

Or upon an ocean liner's deck,

Or wherever else vacation time would take

Your little blue-shod feet.

Summer is sneaker time.

6

We Sail the Ocean Blue

"We sail the ocean blue, and our saucy ship's a beauty." Kit was a sailor in *H.M.S. Pinafore* that spring of 1957, and though I was too young to participate in the annual church-choir Gilbert and Sullivan production for children, I did learn all the songs. We sang lustily as we rocked in that green hammock strung up between the linden tree and an ash tree above the old stone wall, and I imagined we were swaggering across the decks of the *H.M.S. Pinafore* and feeling the swell of the waves underneath our hammock boat.

Once we had selected our blue sneakers, our travel outfits were navy shorts and navy slacks to go with our sneakers. We made a point of not buying denim jeans, since we wanted to avoid the negative image of the stereotypical American tourists of the 1950s. We knew from the beginning that we would tread on English soil with respect, so we would wear no blue jeans, and more often than not we would wear skirts rather than slacks. But summer was summer, and jerseys with bright, bold red and white stripes; white socks; and blue Byrd cloth jackets with reversible bright red tartan plaid were appropriate travel outfits, especially for very young sailors.

A train trip to New York City began our journey. When we arrived at the dockside, there was a massive dark gray wall in front of us. It was hard to believe that it was a ship: the *M.S.T.S. Geiger*. It looked like a tall building that was far too big to float. We were taken up to the gangplank and soon were on board. I remember the narrow hallways and a small cabin with two double-decker bunk beds. Everything was gray. The hallways were gray, as were the floors, and the thin wool blankets on the four beds were charcoal gray.

There were lots of children running around on the deck, shouting and playing shuffleboard. That was not a comfortable activity for me, so I found a more peaceful pastime. I stood at the polished wooden rail and looked down into blue. It was a blueness beyond blue, a rich, dark, bright blueness that is with me still. The ocean water was a darker version of the blue that was there in the cloudless sky overhead, and that sky was an uninterrupted expanse of bright, light, intense blue. A long ways down, I could see the crisp white wake coming out in a large V as we ploughed through the water. Not all the days were blue. The water and the sky turned gray like the ship, and the decks were wet with rain, making the white lines of the shuffleboard show up like chalk lines on a blackboard.

Finally, there came that day when land appeared on the horizon. "There's England," I heard voices all around me call out. *Where's England?* I thought, for the land was too far away for me to see. Mother was describing green trees and sunshine, and then I saw a smudge on the horizon. That finally became a blurry line that gradually darkened into something that was recognizable as land. It was foreign land and yet not foreign; weren't we from New England?

The trip from Southampton to London was long, and we were hungry. Finding a dinner that first night was difficult, but eventually we had good food at the officers' club. My memory of that dinner was not about the food, for music was being played that made the surroundings special. A violinist and a pianist were playing a piece that I learned later was Vaughn Williams' version of "Greensleeves." What an appropriate welcome to England.

We spent the first couple of weeks at Judge's Guest House, in which we occupied two bedrooms on what we call the second floor, and in which we learned some interesting things about breakfast in England. We were used to eating hot toast, but when the waitress apologized for serving the toast too warm, we found that toast was cooled on purpose on a cooling rack. Our days were spent in looking for apartments, or flats, as such residences were called. I liked the neighborhood of Knightsbridge since the word "knight" was in its name, but the apartment there was very dark, so we moved on. Within a short time, we found just the right place in Mayfair, a location immortalized in the Lord Peter Wimsey stories by Dorothy L. Sayers. This central location was of particular importance, since at that time we had no car.

The apartment building at 55 Park Lane overlooked Hyde Park. What was appealing to American visitors was that it had central heating—a true commodity—and what was special to us was that family friends, Dr. and Mrs. Edward Brady, were already living there. Once we moved into Flat 52-A, the Bradys were our next-door neighbors. Ed, my father's first MIT postdoctoral student, was by this time the liaison officer for the Atomic Energy Commission, and his wife, Evelyn, was a noted hostess and a wit. They were wonderful to Kit and me, and they kept us laughing and happy all year. When I think of Evelyn, I think of the gleam of silver, for she loved silver and had imposing and impressive pieces on display on sideboards and tables. I remember tea services, decorative large bowls, and large, shiny platters. I loved polishing silver, and before long I was polishing Evelyn's silver, since I could see so much light that glinted and gleamed from its surface. The metal became warm to the touch as I rubbed it, and I could see the sparkle intensify as I rubbed away the tarnish. Evelyn took to calling me her Little Silver Polisher, and the nickname lasted all year.

In our apartment, I was polishing everything I could find, but since we had no large and lavish pieces of silver, I made do with coins. What a wonderful way to realize I was in a different country. The English coins at that time were larger than American coins, so the half crowns and florins, the little silver sixpence coins and the five-shilling pieces, almost an inch and a half in diameter, came under my polishing cloth. On the largest of the coins, I could read ELIZA-BETH, and on the face of the coin was the image of the young queen who had come to the throne just a few years before. It was in that year that I learned to spell the name Elizabeth. I had to. After all, it is my middle name. I also polished the coins that were copper in color rather than silver. These pennies and ha'pennies changed from a worn dark bronze to a golden copper color, and by looking closely at these large coins, I could make out the head of the young Queen Elizabeth II; and on the older coins I could see the blurred image of the head of Queen Victoria.

Our flat opened onto a hallway that was carpeted in a deep purplish red. To the far left was the small kitchen with yellow walls and a black-and-white checkerboard pattern on the floor. The kitchen was so crowded that two people had trouble maneuvering in it, and the sink, refrigerator, and stove were one size larger than dollhouse appliances. Though many people might have chosen to eat in the well-known restaurant on the ground floor, that wasn't the right thing for a family with young children, so we used that doll's-house kitchen, where Mother cooked meals that were as excellent as ever.

At the opposite end of the red hallway was the bathroom, which also had yellow walls and black-and-white squares on the floor. A tub, a sink, and a Royal Dalton toilet were all it could accommodate, and the bathtub was used for washing our clothes as well as for washing ourselves. The two bedrooms and the living room opened onto the hallway. In Kit's and my bedroom, there were twin beds covered with heavy copper-bronze colored bedspreads, and on the far wall was a window through which I could glimpse the blurred green forms of a few trees in Hyde Park. On the near wall, there was something we had never seen in Belmont, though we had read about it in books. We had a wardrobe. It was a tall cupboard of dark wood. Two doors opened onto the closet section, which had a clothes bar near the top and a shelf above that; underneath the closet was a drawer for shoes. It really is a practical piece of furniture, since it can be moved to any part of the room. Now I find wardrobes all through the English novels I love, from Charlotte Brontë to Mary Stewart, and since I lived with one for a year, I can always picture it in my imagination.

August came just a few weeks after we had settled into our flat, and on August 6, I celebrated my ninth birthday. We had been reading a book about the fifteenth-century English King Henry V, who in 1415, with a handful of determined knights, defeated the French army at the Battle of Agincourt. My birthday gifts that day came in small boxes that were heavy for their size, and in each one was a knight of Agincourt. Mother bought these little warriors at the toy store since she knew how important brightly colored things were to me. She realized that my interest in costumes of the past was as strong as ever because I was learning what I could about English history. This wonderful gift consisted of enough little fighters to protect King Henry for a long time. These lead knights were brilliantly colored and painted in a great deal of detail. My first knight carried a sword and had a stag's antler on his helmet, and his heraldic colors were a brilliant blue and yellow. The standard bearer, the most impressive knight, about four and a half inches tall from his horse's hooves to the tip of his lance flagpole, was clad in red and blue. To this day, they fight the Battle of Agincourt on the pine whatnot shelves that Daddy had made for me years ago.

When September came, we had a real cold snap. The central heating would not be turned on until the first of October, and even though the September temperatures were uncomfortably cold, that rule was not changed. We wore our newly acquired clothing for school—wool skirts, sweaters, blazers, and woolen underwear—as we huddled around the electric fire. This heater, which glowed red at its center, threw out quite a bit of warmth, only it was so directional that you either roasted or froze. We may have kept the oven on, and that was an excuse for me to learn to mix flour, white sugar, and butter to make shortbread cookies. We may have eaten those during an evening while sitting around the table playing hearts. Large-print cards were available even then; the pleasure of playing games kept us from minding the damp cold that was ever present.

We went grocery shopping several times a week, since the tiny refrigerator was too small to hold much food for a family of four; because we had no car, it was necessary to carry home what had been purchased. Each store we visited had its own specialty as well as its own characteristic aroma. Oliver's was the small grocery store where we bought excellent fruit. Hannel's was the grocer's where salad greens were sold. At Alan's Meat Market, we would see the carcasses hanging up in the front window; I can still remember that unpleasant smell of unrefrigerated meat. Once the meat had been cooked, we did enjoy the fresh beef roasts, lamb chops, and pork chops. At Bailey's, we bought flavorful fresh chickens and an occasional goose. Here in the States, where one buys red meats, poultry, and fish all protected by shrink-wrap and all in the same supermarket, it is worth remembering that there used to be separate stores, each with its own personality and specialized merchandise.

A store that had a wonderful fragrance was Hovis Bakery. Now when I go into a bakery, the alluring aroma of freshly baked bread is overshadowed by the heavier sweet fragrance of sugared pastries; but at that small bakery in London, the smell of fresh yeast bread was predominant and irresistible. Maybe we would pick up Scottish bap, a crusty, small, rounded loaf of white bread. Sometimes we would buy what we called knotty bread, which we later learned was the Jewish delicacy challah. We loved its bright yellow insides and the unusual braided shape of the loaf, which made it possible to pull pieces off of the bread rather than to cut slices from it. Probably the loaves we bought most often were whole wheat.

No wonder we had bread left over. By Sunday, we would take the bread to St. James's Park and Green Park to feed the ducks. Summer, fall, and winter, we'd squat down on our haunches and toss pieces of bread into the water and watch the ducks swim toward us, snap up the bread in their bills, and swim away. I could follow where the ducks were going by their persistent quacking. Daddy enjoyed feeding the ducks as much as we did, and these Sunday outings gave him as much pleasure as they gave us. Then, one day in the spring, when we went to feed the ducks, something was different. When the ducks came out on land, there were tiny, soft brown balls of fluff trailing behind some of the larger birds. Daddy saw to it that I had a chance to touch one of those amazingly soft dark brown duckling fluff balls.

One weekend, instead of going to the park to feed the ducks, we went with Evelyn and Ed Brady to the famous flea market at Portobello Road. We went by stalls filled with clothing, jewelry, shoes, and anything else we could imagine. Kit stopped by a table covered with swords. We handled some of the swords in their long scabbards decorated with silver and black. Kit was anxious to acquire a sword, but on reflection, she decided that it was too expensive. At least I had the chance to see a sword up close, to feel how heavy it was, and to see and feel the silverwork on the scabbard.

The next booth that was interesting sold old coins, and we bought some Roman coins. How fascinating it was for me to hold something in my hand that was almost two thousand years old. The coins were small and bronze and had Caesar's head on them. They were oval in shape and a little frayed around the edges. They had been well used and had probably been buried in the ground for hundreds and hundreds of years. To keep them as they were, these coins did not see my polishing cloth. Living history, touching it, memorizing it, and feeling it was at the forefront of practically everything we did during that sabbatical year.

As we went through the crowded market, we headed toward one establishment that was important enough to be in a building rather than in a temporary stall. At the outlet for Minton china, sitting on the floor, Kit and I reached our hands into boxes and barrels of china. This was white china with fluted edges, for these plates and bowls were "seconds." The trick was to find plates that looked good enough to use, and though they may have been too flawed to be sent through the rest of the painting and firing processes in the Minton china factory, it was easy enough to find pieces that did not have obvious chips or cracks. Before long we had stacked white fluted dinner plates and salad plates by mounds of fragrant wood chips. Then we found some shallow bowls that were excellent for cereal, prunes, or small salads. The smallest bowls I found that were added to the collection of what was to become our second best dinnerware were smooth rather than fluted. They were the perfect size for serving melted butter or mayonnaise to go with artichokes. The small white teapot, which holds probably no more than two cups, is still in use, and it is a charming reminder of that colorful day at the Portobello Road Market.

The Roman coins were not the first in our coin collections. We were fascinated by the so-called bun pennies, which were given their nickname in reference to Queen Victoria's severe hairstyle depicted on the coins. Because the particular coins which we had collected had been minted between the 1860s and the early 1890s, and the older coins had been in service for ninety years, they were worn so smooth that at times it was hard to distinguish the outline of Queen Victoria's head on the one side and either Athena or Britannia on the reverse side. Use, dirt, and wear had make the coins little more than warm brown discs, quite dark in color, but the fact that they were so old was an important part of their charm. At Oliver's Grocery Store on Mount Street, the saleswomen would save all the bun pennies and give them to us in change. These women were intrigued by the two little American girls who were so interested in old English coins.

For years, my bun pennies and ha'pennies stayed in a wooden cigar box with COIN COLLECTION written on it in scrawling, uneven letters in black magic marker. Then, about thirty years ago, I had an idea. English currency had changed, making the farthing, the bronze ha'penny and penny, the tiny silver threepenny bit and the twelve-sided brass threepenny bit, the silver sixpence, the shilling, the florin, and the half crown all obsolete. I took the bun pennies and ha'pennies to a friend, a clever jeweler, who assembled the coins into a collar-style necklace about eighteen inches long. Two of the ha'pennies were made into earrings, and I had a bracelet made as well. The Victorian coins are by now over one hundred years old, and the Queen Elizabeth coins sprinkled throughout the necklace, with the portrait on one side and an armada-style galleon on the reverse side, are over fifty years old. They are dated 1957 and 1958 and so are reminders of the years spanned by our sabbatical. When I wear this necklace, I am aware that this piece of art is displaying a tangible reminder of the passage of time. This necklace of memories always garners compliments whenever I wear it.

Saturday morning was the time for special lessons. While Kit took riding lessons every Saturday, I took art lessons. Mother and I would board a double-decker bus to Edgeware Road. We'd pass by copper and brass shops; Mother was good at describing the things we passed. We'd walk along a road whose blacktop made a thin layer over the superior paving of the original road, built two thousand years before by the Romans. We reached the apartment of Mr. Francis Kelley, a friendly young American artist who gave me painting lessons at his kitchen table. I was always drawing things and had enjoyed my Saturday morning art lessons at the De Cordova Museum. I loved to draw costumes: long, flowing robes worthy of Lawrence Olivier in his film role of Henry V. I used purples and reds and even knew to draw the little black tips on the ermine trim. I could draw golden crowns with round dots of purple, red, green, and blue to represent my imagination's treasury of crown jewels. Mr. Kelley and I didn't deal with faces, and he never made me feel inadequate because of my limitations. We dealt with larger things for me to draw.

I remember taking a piece of thick, white artist's paper and moistening it with water. While it was still wet, I took a quill pen, dipped it into black India ink, and drew the outline of a tree. The water on the paper made the ink spread so that the tree, with its stylized trunk and graceful branches, looked something like an Oriental tree by the time the paper had dried.

One morning, Mr. Kelley had me draw a picture not on paper but on glass. Using different shades of green in the watercolor box, I made squares, like the fields of England that we saw out the window when we took bus trips out into the country. A bit of blue paint on the glass made the sky, and part of the glass was left bare for the white clouds. At this point, a piece of heavily textured white paper was laid on the glass and pressed down upon it. When the paper was lifted, the picture, or monoprint, had been transferred to the glass. By a fluke, the Fields of England turned out well enough that Mr. Kelley said he wished he had painted it! That comment of gentle flattery is still treasured. Now this picture hangs in my computer room as a reminder of those sun-filled and paint-filled Saturday mornings. Fifty years later, with the help of the computer, I am in touch with the artist and his wife, and I am glad to have reached out to them to thank them for bringing more color and craft into my life.

Pictures would fill my world on other days of the week besides Saturday. I loved looking at royal purple robes, gowns, and crowns, diamond scepters and gold orbs, gold-leaf coronation coaches, and jewel-encrusted coronation robes, for the queen's coronation had happened just four years before we lived in London, and people had kept their printed souvenirs.

We had a woman who came in once a week to clean the apartment. Mrs. Turner was very nice to us and took a special interest in me. Knowing I would treasure the magazines and pamphlets she had saved since the coronation in 1953, Mrs. Turner brought me the souvenirs she had collected at that time. I still remember the sharp smell of the ink on the newsprint of these collector's copies of magazines and leaflets over which I pored for hours. To see them at all, I lay tummy down on the bed with my hands on the paper, chin resting on the backs of my hands. Through the blurred pictures and captions, I learned all about the crown jewels, the great diamonds known as the Stars of Africa, and the historic sapphires, spinels, and rubies.

There were other things to study besides royal crowns and gowns, for I was in the fourth grade at the American School of London. In Rosamunde Pilcher's *Coming Home*, two little English schoolgirls meet while being fitted for their new school uniforms. I could picture that scene so completely, since I too had been fitted with my gray blazer, pleated dark-green plaid wool skirt, yellow pullover sweater, and navy blue trench coat. More recently I took delight in reading about the ritual of being fitted for the proper boarding school attire as Harry Potter and his friends were fitted for their robes before beginning their journey to Hogwarts. Harry and his friends may have traveled to school on the special red train. Kit and I, however, journeyed daily to the American School of London on a red double-decker London bus, Number 74 to Camden Town. Just as I had learned my colors by seeing and identifying the bright yellow school buses of my earliest years, so I could appreciate the bright red of London's public transportation buses.

The American School of London, then quite new, was located at Porchester Terrace. The older students had the building on the left, and we younger students had the building on the right. I remember a pleasant classroom with a young teacher. Miss Oakley taught us what fourth-graders needed to know about math and science, Egyptian civilization, and how to draw maps. She kept our knowledge of America current with that of England, and the maps we drew were of our home states.

Math meant learning the times tables. I doubt that kids today are called upon to memorize the multiplication tables, since they can count on calculators, but in 1957, such electronic aids were not a part of our culture. Alas, my memories of math and school cafeteria food are linked. It must be remembered that the food in postwar London was not delicious. Protein substitutes were already in use to augment our diets, so it was always questionable as to how much real meat there really was in our meat patties. One day, the lunchroom was becoming very noisy. We had helped ourselves to sickeningly sweet baked beans and jellies and were trying to eat them. That day, the dining hall monitor was the notoriously strict fifth-grade teacher before whose scrutinizing glare we had to pass as we left the dining hall. We learned the fine art of rearranging our food on the plate to make it look as though we had eaten our lunch, when in reality we had eaten as little as possible. The monitor did not scold us for not eating our lunch; she scolded our table for being too noisy. How unfair. Neither my friend Becky nor I had been making any noise beyond normal conversation. We were caught, however, and along with our louder classmates, we were assigned the task of writing out the times table for the number nine, and we had to write them four times! Nine times one is nine. Nine times two is eighteen, I wrote laboriously and as neatly as possible. That night Daddy was taking pictures of family life in our flat, so there I was, sitting at my desk, wearing my red Royal Stewart tartan kilt skirt, my braids hanging down over my shoulders. I wouldn't need this picture to remember that I was staring at my math book, committing to memory that nine times nine is eighty-one.

I always enjoyed our music classes. We learned some old English songs such as "The Keeper," who "did a-hunting go, and under his cloak he carried a bow." Of course, we learned "Greensleeves," so from then on, the old English words "Greensleeves was all my joy, Greensleeves was my delight" were as familiar to me as were those of the Christmas carol "What Child Is This," which shares the same melody.

Kit, being in the seventh grade, studied Chaucer, and since what we were taught at school constituted our dinnertime discussion, I learned as well. I knew about *The Canterbury Tales* long before I studied them myself in high school, and the same was true of Shakespeare. Whatever speeches she learned, I also memorized. How we loved attending the play *Henry V* and later Olivier's film version, and hearing our hero proclaim, "Once more unto the breach, dear friends, once more; or close the wall up with our English dead."

Our woolen clothes from Harrod's kept us warm at school, and we grew accustomed to wearing our blazers all day. I felt very grown up in my blazer and skirt as I attended the student council meetings, for I was the representative from my class and so wore a small green bar pin on my lapel. Later, I also wore an oval pin made of the same green material, for by the end of the year I was deemed the student who had made the greatest improvement and was given the Improvement Badge. My name was also engraved on the honor roll, and it is nice to know it is there still, even though it was inscribed over fifty years ago.

In 1957, November 5 fell on a Tuesday. Many of the students

from the American School of London lined the streets to watch the procession as the queen rode to the Opening of Parliament. At school, we were encouraged to learn as much about England as we could, by participating in public occasions such as observing the procession to the Opening of Parliament and Trooping the Colour. It was ironic that November 5 also happened to be Guy Fawkes Day—the day a renegade, during the reign of James I, tried to blow up the parliament buildings. However, on this day, the only glitter came from diamonds rather than explosives, and the crowd watching the procession of historic coaches carrying the major members of the royal family to and from Parliament, were happy and supportive.

I must explain that at such processions, what I saw in actuality and what I saw in my well-trained imagination were, in many cases, two very different things. I knew the royal coaches were passing by, hearing the rhythmic clopping of the horses drawing them, as well as the increased cheering of the crowd. Although the coaches them-selves were little more than a blur, I had seen the coaches up close when visiting the Royal Mews and so I knew what they looked like. I remembered the black, crimson, and gold grandeur of the Irish State Coach, which was the conveyance used in this November procession, so I superimposed the image I remembered over the moving blur that was the reality of what I was viewing. As far as seeing the queen, with a flash of diamonds and a wave of her white-gloved hand, I saw nothing. My mother's description became so much a part of my rec-ollection of the experience; it is virtually as though I had actually seen the queen in her coach in that degree of detail.

I describe this episode in the opening of my poem "English Rose." In 1957, my friend from fourth grade, Rebecca Rolph, and I watched the young queen of England ride in a grand procession. In 1997, we were drawn together in thought, which, if one reads the poem very carefully, can cross all barriers, including those of mortality. That summer I was absorbed in following the funeral service and solemnities of a beloved princess who, forty years before, had yet to be born. I wanted to share my nostalgic thoughts of England with my friend whose doctoral work had been in English history, and with whom I had shared the experience of observing that procession to Parliament in November 1957. I was too late, for Rebecca had died of cancer just days before the death of the princess of Wales. Somehow I must have known of my friend's passing, for every time I heard the line "Good-bye, England's Rose," I thought of my classmate as well as of the passing of a princess.

As November moved into December, my family and I were caught up with the excitement of the Christmas season in the land that had given us so many of our carols and customs. We needed to have some music in the house, and since I had not brought a recorder with me, we decided to pick one up at the world-renowned store Boosey & Hawkes. That soprano recorder from London lasted for many years, and many seasons of carols were piped on it. "The Holly and the Ivy" was one such carol. When Daddy brought us a Christmas tree, it was not the tall and fragrant balsa fir of my early childhood; it was a holly bush. We were delighted that our Christmas tree was to be a holly tree, and it needed no metallic trimmings, since it was already trimmed with red balls, or rather, red holly berries.

The December days came but brought no snow; it was to be a mild winter in London. It is possible that we saw a dusting of snow in the parks two or three times, but we found we didn't need snow to celebrate the season. A mound of presents was growing under the tree. There were those wrapped in newspaper with bright red ribbons, cheerful against the newsprint, but other packages sparkled and shone as much as the traditional metallic tree decorations left in their storage boxes in New England. Some of these presents were wrapped in the new foil papers whose jewel-bright tones delighted me, especially when the winter sun shone onto the packages that glinted red, blue, and green. We could guess all we wanted to, but opening those packages would have to wait till Christmas morning.

We were spending Christmas Eve with our friends Lise and Geoffrey Wilkinson, whom I had known during my earliest years, since they had lived in the MIT community. Geoff had been one of Daddy's colleagues, and part of the pleasure of being a part of the MIT community was that we had the chance to meet so many interesting people. As we arrived at the Wilkinsons' front door, I pulled out my little recorder and played "The Holly and the Ivy," and as we were welcomed into the Wilkinsons' lovely, cheerful home, we were caught up in the celebration of three generations. Lise's parents, a gentle, soft-spoken couple from Denmark, were there, as were the Wilkinson daughters, who were just a few years younger than me.

The first thing we saw upon entering their living room was the Christmas tree, a live tree lit with live candles. Both Mother and Daddy had seen wax candles on Christmas trees in their childhoods and were glad to see the precautionary bucket of water near this tree. I still remember my mother's repeated urging that I look at this tree and try to remember the sparkle of the candles, for we probably would not see such a lovely tree again.

"It is so beautiful, and the tree seems to shimmer," she continued to explain, and she insisted that I look carefully at it. I looked as hard as I could but could see no shimmer. All of the lights looked the same. Though I knew I was being directed to look at something beautiful and rare, I have to admit that in reality, the sight meant little to me. The candle flames' points of light were too small and distant for me to see clearly, and so they made little impression when compared to the boldly colored red, green, and blue electric tree lights that were far easier for me to see and enjoy.

Since I always gravitated to bright colors, I was intrigued by the long teak table that was decorated, not with traditional red and green, but with a narrow runner of deep electric blue. Against this background of the blue runner and the warm brown of the teak table, there were oranges, bright bold orange oranges, along with the soft brown of nuts in their shells. Those served both as decoration and as a final gourmet note to that Danish dinner of roast goose and red cabbage.

We were not to know until years later that we were being entertained by a future Nobel Prize laureate and a knight, for Geoffrey Wilkinson was awarded the Nobel Prize in chemistry in 1973 and was knighted in 1976. To commemorate his knighthood, I suggested to Geoff that he needed a minstrel to tell how he had gained "honor and fame," so I "applied for the job." By then I was in graduate school and had heard and studied many ballads exemplifying the archaic tonalities and authentic modal cadences of the times when knights lived in castles. The melody for "The Ballad of Sir Geoffrey," along with my text with its refrain and simple rhyme scheme both had a robust and almost troubadour flavor, except that in order to tell his story, I had to use some modern terms for such lines as "From nuclear he changed to inorganic chemistry, my lads, to inorganic chemistry."

The winter sunshine on Christmas morning lit up the jewel tones of the foil-wrapped packages under our holly tree. The small, heavy packages were more lead soldiers, but they weren't knights of

Agincourt this time. Now I had some of the Queen's Guards, the red-coated Palace Guards, the Horse Guards with their black mounts and silver breastplates, and a solitary Highland bagpiper. There was a figurine of the queen herself sitting sidesaddle on her brown horse in the uniform she wore for Trooping the Colour. We were to see that annual ceremony later in the year. I realize now that the importance of those lead figures was that I had the chance to see an impression of the costumes up close, since when we did watch various parades, I was always too far away to see any details. Sometimes the Horse Guards paraded outside of our windows. At other times the Palace Guards were on parade when we walked through St. James Park or Green Park or when we stood outside of Buckingham Palace along with flocks of other tourists to watch the Changing of the Guard. As always, the Horse Guards were too far away for me to see more than a fleeting glimpse of color, so seeing the real people made less of a visual impression than did seeing and handling the keepsake figures. What thrilled me about attending live parades was that sometimes they were accompanied by the rousing melodies of military marches: the silvery boom of the drums and the clear call of the high flutes and fifes. The music stirred my blood, and I wanted to march in time with all of the other marching feet!

One gift under the tree was a large wooden chess set on which I learned the rudiments of that game. Then there was a tall beefeater doll standing guard under the tree. We saw his like at the Tower of London, and I could enjoy the contrast of the beefeaters' red and orange costumes against the ancient gray stone tower walls. My beefeater continues to stand guard on my bookcase, as he has done for the past five decades. Though dust has fallen on his shoulders like snow, and his velvet hat and lace cuffs are shabby, on his chest is still the golden ER with the royal crown above the herbal insignias of the British Isles: the Tudor Rose of England, the Thistle of Scotland, the Shamrock of Ireland, and the Leek of Wales.

The book-sized packages wrapped in foil paper were indeed books, for once again, as had happened the previous year, my parents gave me something to encourage my enjoyment of reading. I had become acquainted with "The Secret Seven" series of detective stories written by Enid Blyton, an expert writer of stories for children my age. I already had the first couple of books, but now I had the entire series to read. For the first time, I was actually making friends with reading. I loved reading about children my age who wore the same style of raincoat that I wore to school. I reveled in their conversations, filled with English expressions such as "Jolly good" and "Smashing!" For the first time, I knew what it was like to get lost in a book. These were little mystery stories, and I was enjoying mysteries as much as anyone. During those winter afternoons I learned what it was like to surface into reality when it was time for dinner. When the sharp smells of clean, new paper and printer's ink mingled with the aroma of good, fresh meat roasting, I knew it was time to close my adventure book and surface into the reality and into the coziness of a family living in close surroundings, who were experiencing this year abroad to its fullest and gathering memories for a lifetime.

New Year's Eve was soon upon us. How fitting it was to hear Big Ben chime out the old year and ring in the new. Kit and I were awakened just before midnight so we could perform our little New Year's ceremony. On one piece of paper we had written in large, clear numbers the year 1957, and on another we had written 1958. As the great clock began to chime, we went out onto our small balcony and threw out the paper with the old year written on it. Triumphantly, we brought in the paper with the new year on it and sang "Auld Lang Syne." We now had a book, a beautiful little book bound in the brilliant red of the Royal Stewart tartan and trimmed with gold leaf on the pages. That book, filled with the poems of Robert Burns, including "Auld Lang Syne," resides on my bookshelf, and when I handle it and touch the smooth, cool surfaces of the gold-leafed pages, the book does indeed evoke many memories of times gone by and of days of long ago.

7

❧

Matterhorn by Moonlight

As we settled into our routine of living in London, it was clear that Kit and I were not the only ones enjoying this year to the fullest degree. Mother enjoyed being a homemaker and loved her daily shopping expeditions to the many stores where she would purchase good things for dinner. She cooked simply because she was on vacation along with the rest of us, so when she wanted to surprise Daddy with an apple pie, she rolled the crust out with a glass milk bottle because she did not have a rolling pin. It was Daddy who was fond of saying that if he could live anywhere he wanted, walk to work, and be happy in his work, then he had fulfilled those wishes during that sabbatical year. He worked at the Office of Naval Research and sometimes would leave for two or three weeks at a time, for his job was visiting the chemistry laboratories from Copenhagen to Rome, many of which were run by his former students from MIT. When the chance came to visit Holland, Germany, Belgium, Switzerland, and France, he made this a family vacation. Fortunately, the American School of London was accommodating, and so armed with our school books and a month's worth of homework assignments, Mother, Kit, and I left bleak and rain-chilled London to go on a boat train bound for Holland to join Daddy, who would meet us in Germany.

It was March, and the flowers were blooming as we began our

European trip in Holland. We were to enjoy the spring flowers at both the beginning and end of that trip, so I experienced the rich fragrances of daffodils, hyacinths, and tulips, as well as the blurs of rich, bright colors as we passed by fields of red, yellow, and lavender.

From Holland, the train took us into Germany, where the train tracks paralleled the River Rhine for a while. Mother loved looking out the train windows and seeing the ruins of many robber baron castles, and for these I had to rely on her descriptions because the castles were too far away for me to see, and the train was moving too quickly for me to focus on where they were. What I did focus on was the novelty of hearing the sounds of languages other than English being spoken around me. I was to hear the voices of men, women, and children speaking German and French throughout that entire month. Years later I was to study both languages, and I was glad that I had those early memories of native accents.

We met Daddy in Munich in the evening, so my first impression of his new Mercedes-Benz, which he had picked up in Stuttgart, was not what it looked like but how it sounded, felt, and smelled. The deep throb of the engine, the authoritative sound as the doors closed, and best of all, that opulent aroma of new leather made my first experience of being in such a car a memorable one. The next day, I saw that the car was gunmetal gray and the upholstery was a rich, dark red. Neither Kit nor I had smelled a new car before, because the only family car we had known was the hard-working, sixteen-year-old Plymouth that died three months before we left for England. No longer did we have to deal with small holes in the upholstery and smaller ones in the floor through which, according to Kit, the road could be seen as we drove over it. Now, the seats were comfortable and cozy, which we enjoyed as we wended our way through Germany.

The view from our rooms in the General Patton Hotel was like the descriptions I have had of postcards. It was a thrill to be in the Alps; the mountains seemed close enough to touch, and the colors were paint-box bright. I could see the blue sky and a green pasture area, hear the clang of cowbells, and see the steep slope of the mountain in front of me as I stood on the hotel balcony. This scene often came to mind throughout the years as I read romance novels set in Germany and Austria.

Our first major place to visit was Mad King Ludwig's castle, Neuschwanstein, and unlike the robber barons' castles along the Rhine River, this castle was not a ruin; in fact, it was not very old, having been built in the 1860s and finished in the 1890s. There were only two ways up to the castle, and the approach was very steep; one could walk or take a horse-drawn carriage. We took the carriage up, and the clip-clop of the horses' hooves stayed in my memory to furnish a realistic setting to many a fairy tale and historical novel that I was to read in the future. There was a nip to the air and some snow on the ground. The day was sunny, so the green of the evergreen woods, the blue of the sky, and the white clouds presented colors for me to enjoy.

Once in the castle, I remember seeing great oaken doors adorned with elaborate metal hinges. Those massive hinges were close to face height for a nine-year-old child, and I was able to reach out and touch them. Being both bold and intricate, they made a lasting impression. One room was a bedroom, where for the first time I noted bed hangings. How glad I was to get close enough to see that, for I was to read so many stories of castles, chateaux, and palaces in which beds of this style were described. I found out those hangings would keep the heat in and keep the cold drafts (and maybe a rat or two) out, and they would give some privacy in a room that might have been a sleeping chamber for several people. The contrast in color between the medium blue of the hangings and the rich, reddish brown of the floor and wood-paneled walls left a pleasant memory that to me was of far greater import than the magnificent and dramatic views for which this castle was famous.

But before we went outside to enjoy the views from the castle's terraces, we visited the throne room. I saw the gleam of a great deal of gold leaf on the walls, and I remember an area with a number of circular white marble steps, but at the top of the steps, there was nothing—no throne at all. That was a disappointment to the imaginative child I was then. We went out on a terrace and looked out over the Alpine vistas, a lake, and ruined castles beyond. I could see the shadowed, steep sides of the mountains and a valley filled with golden light, which was beautiful in its own right, though there were no ruined castles or lakes within my range of vision. Mother described this vista beautifully to me, and though I did not see those distant castles, my imagination stored that scene away for future reference; in later years I was to read that at one time, Germany was made up of more than three hundred principalities. I must have known I was cataloguing memories for a future of reading novels and of studying history. That afternoon, I enjoyed breathing in the clean, crisp mountain air and enjoying the beauty of a day that was either late winter or early spring. Because we had taken the horse-drawn carriage up to the castle, we walked down that very steep hill—or very small mountain; I'm not sure which it was. I do know I gained a sense of the extreme steepness, which I could not have grasped by looking out the car window at the mountains. After all, we were in the Alps, and I needed a little hands-on experience.

My first memory of Austria is of eating lunch while sitting on a hillside. The grassy area where we sat was so steep that I couldn't go more than a few steps before there was a rocky slope. Once again, this memory has stayed with me to demonstrate the ragged nature of the mountains through which we traveled. There were mountains all around us, the Tyrolean Alps. Though I'm sorry we missed seeing Mozart's home in Salzburg, I'm glad we had the chance to see the lovely Austrian scenery. In Innsbruck we bought some special clothing; my choice was a perfect little dirndl. I still remember the white, puffed-sleeved blouse and the deep pink dress that had white flowers on it. A blue apron completed the outfit, which I was to wear the following year for my fifth-grade school portrait.

In Switzerland, we visited Lucerne, the city of watchmakers. In the windows of watch shops, we saw giant gears moving the insides of great, oversized clocks. Our new watches were smaller affairs, and mine, with larger-than-usual numerals, was self-winding, though it didn't tick. I did keep waving my arm around for the first couple of weeks, just to make sure it would stay wound, and because it was my first watch, I will always remember it.

Before heading out of the mountains, we took a side trip to see the Matterhorn. This meant a ride up a mountain to the little town of Zermatt, on a cog railway. When we reached this small village, winter was in the air, and snow was on the ground. After settling into the hotel, we took a moonlit walk away from the village, and there in front of us, I saw that great, gleaming silver cirque of the Matterhorn as it thrust its way up into a sky that was blacker than black. That silver mountain set against a black velvet sky is one of my most dramatic visual memories. The next day was a gray, cloudy day, and there might even have been a little snow. The mountains were completely hidden; we were fortunate to have sought out the Matterhorn the previous night, or else we would have missed seeing it altogether.

The village of Zermatt in the gray light of a snowy morning had a charm of its own. We strolled along narrow streets, enjoying the sound of sleigh bells, for at that time there were no cars allowed on the streets. It was our main chance to visit with snow, ice, and a clear, crisp breeze, since that year, the temperature in London had been too mild to give us much snow. We went into a shop, where Mother found me a black velvet cap lined with bright red flannel, and all over the cap itself were the loveliest Alpine flowers embroidered in red, gold, and blue. Of course, featured against the black velvet were the snow-white edelweiss. I still have that velvet cap. What a feast for the fingers and a source for fond recollections. Whenever I teach "Edelweiss" from *The Sound of Music,* I show my students this cap so they can see that specific Alpine flower.

The next place of interest I remember is the Castle of Chillon on Lake Geneva. As I walked through the great rooms, my footsteps echoed on stone floors as well as wooden ones, and the castle, which was devoid of much furniture, seemed lonely in its emptiness. Many of the windows looked out onto Lake Geneva, and some of those windows were glazed with the round, thick bottoms of wine bottles, fitted into frames. When the windows were open, the water looked blue. Otherwise the lake looked wine-bottle green. In one window-sill there was a hole placed strategically over the water, and I knew that if this medieval castle didn't have what we would call modern plumbing, at least it had some creature comforts!

Having well-built dungeons was probably considered a convenience more necessary for a medieval castle than primitive bathroom facilities. The dungeons, built below the level of the lake, had Gothic arches, pillars, and windows high up in the wall. The floor was uneven, and the pillars still had rusted chains used for securing prisoners. Though we couldn't explore that dungeon for safety reasons, I was so close to it that I believe I stuck out my foot and felt the beginnings of the stone-littered floor. *This is a real dungeon,* I thought, and as we wended our way out of that castle, I knew that whenever I would read about castles and their dungeons, I would have a memory to bring the written words to life. Indeed, so many memories from that month's trip in Europe, kept vivid through the decades by conversations with Mother, were to enhance and illustrate scenes from my reading of medieval history, European history, and in years to come, of music history as well.

As we drove into France, we encountered a spring snowstorm. The trees along the side of the road were covered, and each branch had a thick layer of white, just as did the trees at our home in New England after an April blizzard. We had to stop the car and step out along the side of the street to throw a few snowballs. Of course I had no mittens, so my hands grew wet and cold from making snowballs. In that way, I could really experience the snow, which was more important to me than just to be told it was there.

As we left the mountains and the snow, it was sad to say good-bye to the Alps. I had loved being in the mountains, smelling the crisp air, and visiting a castle or two. Now, our destination was Orange, a part of southern France well known for ancient Greek and Roman ruins. There was no snow here, but instead a sun-baked landscape and sun-baked stone ruins. We saw a theater and an arena, but the most spectacular structure was the Pont du Gard, a triple-tiered aqueduct that soars up and over the River Gard. We watched the sun set on the warm, gold-tinted stone, and the next day we walked across it, making our way inside the channel through which the water used to flow. I remember the confines of that trough and the feeling of smooth stone underfoot. I was told that the views of the river valley were magnificent. The view I could take with me was the rich, warm, golden color of the stone arches as the afternoon sun illuminated them. Years later, I was to read Mary Stewart's novel *Madam, Will You Talk?* which is set against the background of so many of the things we saw. In the Temple of Diana, I could get close enough to see and even to touch the statue of the goddess. We walked up a steep slope to the Tour Magne, and as I looked at and touched the stone walls, I knew they had been built by the Romans and that I was experiencing a piece of history. The cypress and sycamore trees, as well as the smell of hot, dry air, are among my recollections from our time in southern France. Without having been there and experiencing all that I could, my reading that story set in Orange would have been much less vibrantly interesting to me.

The city of Carcassonne gave us the chance to see not just one medieval fortress, but an entire walled city. It was not quite as its medieval inhabitants would have remembered it, since it had been renovated in the sixteenth century. We walked around the ramparts, where towers with pointed roofs were in abundance, and the stone paths, as was so often the case, were uneven underfoot. I enjoyed walking in the moat that had been dry for years and was filled with grasses. I could touch the massive stone walls that had once been lapped by moat waters, and it was an experience to see where and how people had lived several centuries ago.

Soon thereafter, I had the chance to see how people lived several thousand years before that. Périgord was riddled with limestone caves, and it was in some of these that the Cro-Magnon people lived many thousands of years ago. The first cave we visited had narrow passages that were clogged and cluttered with stalactites and stalagmites, and though throughout the years I have been in other caves, in this cave was the only chance I have had to see and touch those amazing stone formations. I also felt and saw the primitive etchings that were scratched into the stone walls by the cave's early inhabitants. The second cave, Font-de-Gaume, was far more spacious, but it had been opened in 1901, so the pictures had succumbed not only to the natural drying-out process but to vandalism as well.

The most memorable cave was Lascaux, since it was in pristine condition. In the early 1940s, some boys were playing with their little dog. When the dog disappeared down a rabbit hole, the boys dug through the hole to rescue their pet, only to find themselves in an enormous cave with strange and beautiful pictures of giant animals all over the walls. The young man who was our tour guide had been one of the little boys who had discovered the cave some fifteen years before. In 1958, an antechamber, moist with dripping water, had been built to keep a moist atmosphere in the cave itself so that the pictures would not dry out. The caves themselves were vast, and the pictures were illuminated with bright lights, bright enough to show me the rusts and ochres and browns and blacks used in these great prehistoric paintings. The enormous prehistoric beasts were drawn large enough on those cave walls that I carry, to this day, a memory of curved black horns and great, rotund bodies in muted rusts and golds, which then reminded me of the colors of fallen autumn leaves.

It is no wonder that great effort was taken to preserve this cave. There was some natural protection, for a thin layer of transparent calcite had grown down over the pictures. This served to date them as well as to protect those great bison, antelope, and horses, since it was estimated that it had taken more than seventeen thousand years for such a layer of calcite to grow. I have heard various figures given, and this seems to be the most current.

Not many years after our visit, we heard that the cave of Lascaux had to be closed, since the pictures were in danger, not from dryness this time, but from dampness and algae. Now, by appointment only, the caves are opened only to scholars and students, but no longer are they accessible to tourists. Therefore, few tourists have had the chance to see them. One nine-year-old tourist reveled in staring at these paintings of enormous animals that were big enough for her to see. I know just what a rare opportunity it was for us to see that particular cave, since it has been closed to the public for so many years. We visited this cave only three days after it had opened.

Within a few days, we went from looking at caves to looking at palaces. My first introduction to the great French chateaux was the spectacular Chenonceau, which spanned the River Cher. The grand hall built over the river was filled with morning sunlight that flooded in through the plentiful array of tall windows. I remember the brilliance of that sunlight and the stark contrast of the black and white checkerboard tiles that paved the long, empty room. I also recall the information, from the tour guide, that this hall had been used as a hospital wing during World War I. Since Mother loved gardens, we had the chance to visit some of the elaborately artistic gardens that might have been enjoyed by the young Mary, Queen of Scots, when she was queen of France.

There are so many vignettes I have from visiting the Palace of Palaces—Versailles. I loved the Hall of Mirrors, with its seventeen windows and seventeen mirrors, and I remember going nose to nose with myself as I found my reflection. The parquet floors were as fascinating as they were elaborate, and since I was accustomed to looking down so I wouldn't stumble, rather than looking up or out, the floors made more of an impression than did the art on the walls. The great royal bedchambers were filled with silk bed hangings, draperies, gold tassels, and silk-covered walls. Some of the chambers were in a commanding deep royal red and others were in a more delicate light blue. The fountains were not playing, though we saw the vast gardens where the fountains were. We ran through the beautifully kept expanses of green lawns to secluded glades, seeing statues of gods and goddesses. Great vertical loops of white marble, startlingly white against the background of green grass and trees, made a wonderful place to imagine court revels. Years later, when I was to take classes in French baroque music, I knew that I had wandered in the gardens and the halls where this courtly music had been composed and performed to entertain the kings of France. So many of these vignettes—the royal bedchambers, the Hall of Mirrors, the Venus and Mars salons, one with an unusual oval "bull's-eye" window that I remember—are described in detail in *To Dance with Kings* by Rosalind Laker. Every time I read that book, I experience a thrill of recognition, because I was there. Every time I hear the stylized dance music of Lully, I can imagine King Louis XIV dancing in the Hall of Mirrors, because I was there; and when I think of Queen Marie Antoinette appearing on a balcony, the setting seems familiar, because I was there. It does not matter, in retrospect, that what I actually saw was a series of blurred images that to a fully sighted person would seem a travesty of the actuality, for the blurred images were all I knew. The excitement of having spent one afternoon of my life in the Palace of Versailles is as clear to me now as it ever was, and it demonstrates just how important it is to fill a child's mind with as many novel and interesting experiences as possible.

When I think of Paris, I remember the Eiffel Tower and our visit to the Louvre. As with the Statue of Liberty, the Eiffel Tower was easier for me to grasp in concept by handling a bronze figurine than it was by trying to understand it visually and sculpturally. Nevertheless I am acquainted with its iconic form, so when I think of Paris, I have the correct image to associate with it.

Mother and Daddy were wise in choosing what would be of interest to us, especially to me. They orchestrated the trip so we would see things we would remember and could appreciate. Therefore, there were only three things we saw in the Louvre—the *Mona Lisa*, the Venus de Milo, and Winged Victory. I was to see the *Mona Lisa* better in reproductions, since the original was hung in a corner where there was very little light, and the painting itself was small in size and somber in color. As for the two statues, I did show my lack of years as well as my lack of sophistication, since I could not understand why they were so famous. The Venus de Milo had no arms, and Winged Victory had no head!

Of course, we saw the great cathedrals of Notre Dame and Chartres, but as always for me, these structures were massive and far too dark for me to see any details. After leaving Paris, we did find a cathedral I was able to see to some extent. The interior of the cathedral at Reims was not blackened by the smoke from centuries of votive candles, so the walls were a creamy white. They had been cleaned fairly recently, and since the windows on the side walls were of clear glass rather than stained glass, the sunlight came in, making the interior beautifully light and bright. The stained glass in the side windows had been destroyed by bombing during World War II, and to keep the great rose windows above the front doors of the cathedral from suffering the same fate, their glass had been removed and preserved. By the time of our visit in the spring of 1958, the original glass in those windows was once more in place. Though they were far too distant for me to see any detail, I could appreciate a blur of color. There was organ music as we looked around that cathedral where, in centuries past, the kings of France had been crowned, and to hear the tones of the organ reverberating in so vast a stone chamber enhanced the entire experience for me. A wedding was in progress, and seeing that made this historic cathedral a living church.

I loved our visit to the Taittinger champagne cellars, a vast stone chamber of a different kind. We walked along narrow passages lined with dusty green bottles in wooden racks. We were shown imposing wooden doors with heavy ironwork hinges that had come from a fifteenth-century Spanish monastery. The walls were uneven, and in places damp; I recognized that tangy smell of wet chalk and so knew that these cellars had been carved out of chalk caves. How had I known? That blackboard in my bedroom on which I had learned to write had a trough that collected the chalk dust from the erasers. Once I had dribbled water onto that powder and noticed an unusual, sharp, clean smell that I recognized in that champagne cellar. We bought a bottle of Taittinger champagne, which was opened four months later in London on my tenth birthday. That was a very special bottle of champagne.

On leaving France, we entered Belgium, where it seemed that the city of Brussels had just been cleaned up for display. The black wrought-ironwork on the old buildings such as the Guild Hall and the State House, and on many of the fences, had been tipped with gold. This could have been to please the tourists who were swarming

122

in to attend the 1958 World's Fair. It certainly pleased a nine-year-old tourist who loved looking at anything shiny and bright. Bright and shining was the symbol of that World's Fair, the Atomium, which was a large metal structure of silver-colored balls and connecting rods. We used to have a paperweight version, which I liked since I could gauge the architecture and shape of the entire structure, which I couldn't do while approaching the real thing. It was so large that people could go up into it for viewing the surrounding countryside, which we did.

The last country we visited before returning to England was Holland, which had been the starting point for our month's sojourn in Europe. Since museums were on our list of things to see, along with castles, cathedrals, and caves, we went to art museums and saw some of the works of Rembrandt, such as The Night Watchman. It was hard for me to appreciate the heavy, dark oil paintings. Either they were too dark to see any colors, or they were displayed too far away for me to see them comfortably. Sometimes, when I could get close enough to a picture, I could appreciate the colors of the velvets and satins represented on the canvases. We saw The Laughing Cavalier, who was playing his lute, an instrument of great beauty as well as of tone. Little did I know then that within a few years, I would become interested in the lute and its music.

We stayed in a quiet hotel outside of Amsterdam. Mother and Kit must have gone to the famous flower auction, so Daddy and I had one of those rare father-daughter moments. We walked together on a quiet sunlit afternoon along the canal that was just outside of our hotel. There were greenhouses along the bank, and as we walked into one, we were met with that wonderful and familiar smell of dampness, soil, and growing plants. Those fragrances reminded me sharply of our little greenhouse in New England filled with orchids, but here we saw other flowers. Daddy showed me for the first time what a gloxinia was. Some flowers had petals of royal purple, and others were of wine red, and some had white centers that made the colors seem even more sumptuous. I had just seen velvets portrayed on canvas, and here were velvets found in flowers. These were velvets I could touch, and I did so; Daddy showed me flower after flower and let me touch as many as I wanted.

Some people might describe my recollections as "Europe through a flawed lens." The fields of flowers were blurs of color, the pictures were too dark to see, and a spectacular mountain vista was jettisoned in favor of an intricately wrought iron hinge and set of silk bed hangings. The lens may have been faulty, but the memories certainly are not. What I could not see was described well enough for me to experience and appreciate to a considerable degree. What I could see then is as clear to me as it was fifty years ago, and the educational aspect of what I learned from that trip transcended my visual limitations. How much richer are my memories than those of the tourists who say, "If it's Tuesday, it must be Belgium!"

We arrived in England after our month away to find that, in our absence, the poignantly beautiful month of April had banished winter and had ushered in a tender and delicate spring. In the great parks and gardens, and in the smaller squares sprinkled throughout London, the trees had come into leaf, and that rarest of colors—soft green, new green, spring green—welcomed us home to 55 Park Lane.

8

Epiphany

That change of season from winter to spring was a stark reminder that our adventure in England was coming to a close. The rest of spring and part of summer were all we had left. It seemed as though we used every moment we had to experience something new, to take a weekend trip now that we had a car, and to create as many memories as possible.

Throughout the year, we had taken a number of short trips by bus. Sometimes the four of us would take a picnic lunch of fried chicken and apple pie, as when we visited Runnymede, where King John had signed the Magna Carta in 1215, thus curbing the absolute power of the monarchy. Our trip to Salisbury Plain took us to a much earlier part of British history, as we were allowed to run in and out and under the arches formed by the standing stones of Stonehenge. Fifty years ago, there was construction equipment in evidence, since the stones, which had fallen within the memory of living people, were in the process of being returned to their original upright positions, and some of the massive lintels were being hoisted to their positions on top of the uprights. Because we were allowed to walk amongst these stones, I had a hands-on experience of feeling their texture and gauging their size. Not long after our visit, tourists were relegated to an area for observation only, which for me would have left this monument out of range of my ability to observe and experience it.

In the nearby town of Salisbury, we happened onto a small bookstore, whose rich aroma of old paper was probably spiced with a little mildew. I found a book with large print and pictures that I could see. Daddy had read Kipling's *Just So Stories* aloud to us for as long as I could remember, and now I could read these stories to myself. In years to come, as I buried my nose in that book, I would always be reminded of that sunny day in Salisbury.

We went more than once to Hampton Court, where I remember seeing Henry VIII's enormous banquet hall and the vast kitchens needed to prepare the king's lavish dinners. It was as we descended the stairs to the kitchens that I made a discovery. Stepping carefully so I wouldn't stumble, I noticed that the stone steps were worn down in the middle, enough to make it difficult to find a solid foothold. Even at the age of nine, I knew that the steps were made of stone and that the wear was caused from centuries of feet treading upon them. How many steps, I wondered, how many steps and how many feet had it taken to reduce the middle of those steps to little more than a ramp? This observation returned to me time and time again as I visited buildings from the twelfth century and beyond.

Outside in Henry's gardens, we saw some very old greenhouses, which were still used for growing grapes. *Only the best for the king's table,* I thought, years before my extensive study of Henry VIII and his six wives informed me of the grandiose lifestyle to which the king was accustomed. In that garden, we also saw large statues of the king's, or rather the queen's, beasts. The Lion of England, the Unicorn of Scotland, and the Dragon of Wales are the best known of these wonderful creatures, which are heraldic symbols. Since these statues were taller than people, postdating Henry VIII's reign by centuries, they were big enough so that I could get close to them, touch them, and see them easily.

Oxford and Cambridge, Stratford and Shakespeare's burial place, Windsor Castle, Westminster Abbey, and St. Paul's Cathedral became part of my experience of the meaning of England. I saw what I could see and imagined what I couldn't perceive. For me, I registered the vast spaces in the great Gothic cathedrals, not by the soaring arches that for me disappeared into blackness before they had the chance to soar, but rather by the echoing of footsteps on hard stone floors.

I enjoyed visiting Bath and feeling the warm water that still gushes from natural hot springs to fill the vast Roman baths. The Royal Crescent was a glittering blur of warm, sand-colored stone with delicate white trim, and by the time I saw it, I already knew it was a featured residence in *Northanger Abbey*, Jane Austen's novel set in Bath. We saw the Pump Room mentioned in *Persuasion*, but rather than trying to focus on the grandeur of the room through which Jane Austen's socialites promenaded, all I could focus on were a few white tablecloths and furniture made of very dark wood.

The brief trip to Scotland included more castles and cathedrals. We visited places whose names such as Stirling Castle and Loch Lomond have surfaced again and again in my thoughts during the past twenty-five years that I have played Scottish vocal and dance music. The place on that trip that meant the most to me was naturally that of the town of Irvine; all of us took delight in hearing people pronounce our surname properly. We found out that Irvine's floral emblem is holly and that its motto is "Flourishes in sun and shade." Somehow, even at the age of nine, I knew exactly what the motto meant, and I knew that there could be none more appropriate for me. This has been proven true time and time again, and I take great family pride in being associated with it.

We continued to explore London, which included several trips to the British Museum. I saw the Rosetta Stone and the Elgin Marbles, and I enjoyed seeing objects that massive. When it came to the displays of ancient Grecian pottery, Mother's descriptions gave me a running commentary, describing the black background against which the terra cotta figures seemed to move. She also told me that sometimes the beauty of the black and terra cotta vessels was interrupted by necessary pieces of pottery left a blank gray or white. Those were the modern fragments necessary to support the ancient fragments. Without them, the pots would be only a pile of ceramic potsherds in a drawer. Maybe it is from these discussions that I developed awareness of and later interest in the reconstruction of unfinished works of art. Twenty years later, I was to read some of the completed fragmentary novels of Jane Austen, and influenced by that experience, I was to complete some unfinished keyboard works by Mozart. I didn't learn until years later that Mozart too, at the age of eight and nine, had lived in London, and that one of his early manuscripts is actually at the British Museum.

Stores as well as museums were points of destination on our weekend walks. Mother enjoyed Liberty's of London, renowned for its beautiful Oriental imports and sumptuous fabrics. While passing through the children's department, and in spite of it being crowded, I must have seen a flash of something. Maybe it was a glitter of red or green or the gleam of something gold.

On our next visit, we were to discover a glass case filled with the most amazing array of dolls representing the kings and queens of England, clad in the beautiful silks and velvets for which Liberty's was famous. They represented the monarchs and their wives or husbands from 1066 to modern times, though the list excluded living people. As soon as I had the chance to look at these dolls and handle them, I knew they were extraordinary. For me they were truly three-dimensional portraits that I could appreciate, since they were done not in dark oils, but instead in bright, glowing velvets.

Standing only about nine inches high, these handmade dolls had cloth faces made simply but as accurately as possible to represent the royal subjects. The hands were small pieces of leather the size of a fingernail. Everything else about them was as ornate and as accurate as could be, for the two elderly ladies who made these unusual dolls used portraits to take the likenesses; in the case of the earlier monarchs, coins were used for the portraiture. Kit gravitated toward William the Conqueror, Henry VIII, and Elizabeth I, whereas I was captivated by the costumes of Queen Victoria in her red velvet coronation robes and George V clad in royal purple. These were not dolls with which to be played, and the costumes were permanently affixed. The gold trim was costume, and the jewels were glass beads set into sequin saucers, but the silks and velvets were real, as were the details, from velvet over-gowns down to tiny satin slippers.

We had seen the palaces and castles, and collected coins, pictures, and dolls. The next thing Kit and I had to do was to create and reenact skits based on the lives of the monarchs, which we did, courtesy of the well-written, clever, and historically accurate poems in *Kings and Queens* by Eleanor and Herbert Farjeon. We created crowns of tinfoil, gowns of our mother's dresses, knee breeches from flannel pajama bottoms, and armor from the small aluminum cake tins from the cake mixes that we had baked throughout the year. "Bluff King Hal was full of beans. He married half a dozen queens," I recited, wearing Mother's jacket stuffed with a pillow fore and aft, Daddy's

French beret, pajama-bottom knickers, and knee socks. Kit, with her flowing hair, in Mother's rich blue long dress, played all six wives in an assortment of tinfoil crowns and poppet pearls. I started the concept, by parading around the apartment one evening clad in yards of our parents' heavy green brocade bedspread and reciting, in my flawless fake English accent, "King Charles was such a gentleman. He wore the finest suits." From then on, we created little poem-plays and entertained our parents as well as our neighbors, the Bradys, for many weekends during that eventful year.

Later on, as spring drew near to summer, we joined an immense crowd outside of Buckingham Palace as we waited to see the queen salute her troops in her annual birthday celebration of Trooping the Colour. We heard the brass band playing "The British Grenadiers" and thrilled to the measured tread of the soldiers as they marched along Pall Mall. When the queen, clad in military attire and riding sidesaddle on her chestnut horse, was to pass right in front of where we stood, Mother, who was standing behind me, kept saying, "Look there. Right there in front of you. She's coming now. She's there, just about six feet in front of us."

I turned my head to try to focus on her, but then Mother placed her hands on my head and turned it so I would be facing straight; that is, in the direction where she was looking. I pulled my head back to my own position, which would appear to someone else as though I were looking away and off to the side. Mother had forgotten, or just never realized, that from the beginning I had had the use of only one eye; my interpretation of "straight ahead" was not at all like hers. She was so anxious, almost to the point of desperation, that I should actually see the queen that she repeated her correction time and time again, until my neck began to hurt. I barely caught a glimpse of a blur of brown and red, but that was all. The queen was in motion, and even at six feet, I was too far away. I pictured my lead figurine of the queen on horseback and remembered the colored pictures at which I had squinted, and so in my mind's eye I did see the queen. I had taught myself to superimpose these images onto the blurred actuality of what I had seen.

My fourth-grade year was drawing to a close. The teacher's comments reflect my growing comfort with the process of learning:

Janne's development during the year has been outstanding. She has become an excellent reader, and her ability in composition and use of language are excellent. Her few minor difficulties in spelling and reading errors are, I feel, entirely due to her limited sight. She is a careful, neat writer and has developed a fine hand. Janne has an amazingly mature grasp of such subjects as science and social studies. She has thoroughly enjoyed her study of them and has contributed immeasurably to the class study. Much of her work in these subjects has been on her own initiative due to extended absence, but she has maintained excellent standards in her work. Janne finds arithmetic very difficult, but she has put forth untiring effort and has improved a great deal this year. She now has a sound background for more advanced work. Janne has gained so much satisfaction from her unusually fine artwork and has gained a reputation among her classmates as a talented person.

Janne puts forth consistent effort; with a little help, she has been able to keep with the class in games and skills [PE].

Janne has excellent study habits. She is diligent and cooperative. She is never discouraged by failure. At times she is stubborn about her assignments, but it is an element of perseverance more than anything else, which will be modified by judgment as she grows older.

Reading, composition, grammar, science, social studies, penmanship, and art all earned A. Spelling was an A minus, arithmetic and French were B, and physical education was a C. Citizenship was an A minus.

We couldn't end our sabbatical without visiting the Tower of London. We traveled to it not by land, but by river. As we approached this fortress, part of which was nine hundred years old, we passed by Traitor's Gate, and I thought of King Henry VIII's hapless second wife, Anne Boleyn, who had entered there so many centuries ago. Once inside, we saw the characteristic grillwork of that gate from the inside looking out, and that display of intricate sunlight and shadow awarded me an interesting visual impression. Prominently on display were an executioner's ax and a headsman's block. There they were, easy enough to see at very close range. There was the curved part where you would place your head and then wait for the ax to fall. Well, as my budding knowledge of English history told me, Anne Boleyn didn't have to do that, since Henry hired a swordsman to come from France to behead her. She had spent time in the courts of France and therefore appreciated the finer things of life.

What we looked forward to most was seeing the crown jewels. We lined up along a narrow path and leaned against ancient castle walls while we waited. The walls themselves seemed redolent with history and strife and with the passing of centuries, but the time for leaning against stone walls was over, and we followed a long line of fellow sightseers into the castle and entered the chamber in which the jewels were housed.

I knew what was going to be on display. There would be the St. Edward's Crown with its thousand-year-old sapphire from Edward the Confessor's ring. There would be the Imperial State Crown with its central ruby, which was really a red spinel that Henry V had worn at the Battle of Agincourt. As the story goes, that stone had saved the king's life; the sword nick in it is still there today. Along with the crowns, we knew we were going to see the Stars of Africa, the largest of which is the great pear-shaped diamond in the scepter that the queen used at her coronation. Then there were the orbs, the bracelets and rings, smaller crowns, and even the little crown Queen Victoria wore on her coil of long hair.

In advance of our visit, I had seen pictures of most of these great named jewels in blurred newspaper photographs. With my nose touching the page, I had squinted at pictures of the royal crowns and massive jeweled objects used specifically for the coronation. Finally, the time had come when I would see these world-famous jewels in person.

We entered the chamber. The glass case was beautifully lit from within, and the wooden railing was several inches away from the glass. Inside was the sparkle of one of the greatest collections of jewels in the world. What I saw was a flickering, sparkling, dancing panorama of lights. I leaned against the wooden rail and craned my neck toward the glass display case. The flash of light cast by a king's ransom in diamonds obliterated all of the shapes and forms of the jewels themselves, for that wooden railing, built to keep the tourists at bay, kept me from getting close enough to see any of the details. I knew I couldn't touch the glass case, for that would set off alarm bells. I leaned forward as far as I could and stared into the brightness. I couldn't find Edward the

Confessor's sapphire or Henry V's "ruby." I couldn't find the largest cut diamond in the world that topped the great scepter. I was within inches of the jewels, but I couldn't see them.

I felt an overwhelming and crushing disappointment. To this day, I remember that feeling of hurt and emptiness. The delight of anticipation was thwarted and destroyed by the reality of my severe visual limitations, or was it? In less time than it took to catch my breath, the images of the blurred newspaper photographs of the royal regalia, which I had looked at for months, were superimposed over the real thing. There was the purple velvet and black-and-white ermine on the St. Edward's Crown, and there was the scepter supporting the largest cut diamond in the world.

Somehow, even at the age of nine, I knew that I had discovered something special. I had knowledge. I had beautiful, clear, illuminating knowledge. I knew the history of these jewels. I knew how old some of them were and which kings and queens had worn them. I knew some of them by name. They were my friends! I was sure that the people standing five or ten feet away from me, gazing at the jewels, even grownups, probably did not know as much about them as I did. Nobody had to lecture me. Silently, I told myself that it was enough just to be in the presence of all of those jewels and to be in that ancient tower where so much history had taken place. I had been in rooms where kings and queens had walked. I had touched stone walls that had guarded London for centuries, and unlike Anne Boleyn, my ticket through the Traitor's Gate had been a round trip ticket. That inner satisfaction has stayed with me from then till now, and the lesson I learned that afternoon in the Tower of London was that knowledge is a precious thing that is worth far more than a king's ransom in diamonds. I had experienced great anticipation, and even greater disappointment within the space of a few minutes. That had been followed by a realization so profound that it was almost a revelation. At the age of nine, I understood the importance of education and that without it, the world around me would close in upon me so that I would become increasingly confined in my own world by my diminishing eyesight. Now I knew that never need happen.

Finally, it was time to say goodbye to places we had visited for the past fourteen months. The last walk in Hyde Park, with the Serpentine pond and the statue of Peter Pan; the last visit to Oliver's Grocery Store; and the last ride on a red double-decker bus were all poignant. It was time to pack. My beautiful dolls from Liberty's, my English woolens, and my Secret Seven books were stored away in large trunks to make the transatlantic crossing in the hold of whatever transport ship was chosen. Finally we left 55 Park Lane and our Flat 52–A and found a taxi that would take us to the bus back to Southampton, where we had landed so many months before. That was where this year in England, so important to all of us, had begun, and that was where we would say farewell. As the London taxi took us past the iconic edifice of the queen's residence, I could see a smudge of red as they were changing guards at Buckingham Palace. Raindrops ran down the taxi's window, confusing the images for me, which were already blurred by my tears.

On arriving at the docks, we found we had been upgraded from a utilitarian navy transport ship to a true ocean liner, the *S.S. America*, which did cheer us somewhat. The voyage was uneventful, and my main memories are of eating amazingly large dinners to satisfy my newly developed appetite. Arrival in New York was a letdown, since we had left the magic of England behind us. Rather than spending a night there, we boarded a train to Boston and arrived at our home in Belmont in the late afternoon of a late summer day. Our house and woods and brook greeted us, but they seemed different, smaller, and almost ordinary. I also had the feeling these familiar sights were pulling us back into life as it had been fourteen months before, almost as though our adventure abroad had never taken place.

I began the fifth grade a few days late, since we had been on the ocean at the official beginning of the school year. I wore my Austrian dirndl that first day of classes, and many people came up to say hi. I found it frustrating as well as difficult to recognize people after so long an absence, but as the days passed, gradually I found my circle of friends.

September, which is that bridge between summer and autumn, served as the bridge back to the pattern of life as it had been before our year abroad. The forest welcomed me with its early signs of the coming autumn. The old horse chestnut tree across the footbridge that spanned the brook dropped its fruit for children to collect. About the size of a ball with which you might play the game of jacks, the horse chestnuts looked and felt as though they were made of highly polished wood. Sometimes the tree would drop them in their protective bright yellow-green shells, and then it was for us, the collectors, to open the shells and extract the fruit. They weren't edible, though in London we had sampled the smaller true chestnuts. "A crop is a crop, and who's to say where the harvest shall stop" was the poet Robert Frost's wisdom to gatherers of leaves, so it seemed just as suitable to gatherers of horse chestnuts.

Autumn made its way into the kitchen as Mother baked apple pies and batches of the pinkest of pink applesauce from Jonathan apples. Sometimes Daddy would fix fried apples, for which Mother would prepare fresh cornbread. Sometimes a guest would come for dinner, as in the case of Ivan: neighbor, friend, scientist, and Anglophile with a PhD from Oxford University.

"Tell me about the kings and queens of England," he asked me.

"Certainly," I said, standing before him. "First there was William I, William II, Henry I, Stephen, Henry II, Richard I, and John—he's the one who signed the Magna Carta." I continued the order of succession, rattling off lists of Edwards, Richards, and Henries until I came to the most famous of all. "Henry VIII," I said, and then I named all six of his wives. The list continued, finishing the Tudor monarchs and going through the Stewarts and Hanoverians, until I came to Queen Victoria and ended with the Edwards and Georges. Out of breath, I finished by reciting Queen Elizabeth II.

"You didn't mention Oliver Cromwell," my interrogator interjected.

"He was not a king," I said, dismissing the Puritan "Lord Protector" who, in the mid-1600s, had governed England as a commonwealth rather than as a monarchy. Then I was asked another question.

"Who was Thomas Jefferson?"

"I don't know," I answered quietly.

Later, many years later, I was to visit Monticello and learn about the statesman, writer, and inventor who had been one of the founding fathers of this country as well as its president, along with being the founder of the University of Virginia. I had the chance to touch the ivory keys of Mr. Jefferson's beautiful little pianoforte, and I knew that making music was one of his favorite entertainments, for gradually, through trips as well as reading, I was to learn the history of my own country.

One of the reasons why Ivan questioned me so thoroughly and carefully, not only then but in years to come, was that my parents, along with the help and guidance of some of their friends, were hoping to place me in one of the fine preparatory schools for my junior high years; but that transition was still two years away. Kit was already at one of the best-respected schools, where, in the eighth grade, she was learning about the American Civil War, while I, in the fifth grade, was continuing in the usual elementary school subjects.

When the weather grew too inclement for roaming around the woods as the leaves turned to gold and later to a soft brown once they were on the ground, I spent more time inside at my desk. Homework was not yet plentiful, so I played with the bright, bold colors of construction paper, imitating art projects I had done in school, such as making calendars or orange pumpkins. I embarked on another project that reminded me of sitting in our living room in London and reading the Secret Seven detective stories for children. Only this time, instead of reading about English children as youthful detectives, I was writing about such children. My short story was seven pages long, and like my models, it was filled with little English children exclaiming "Jolly good!" and "Smashing!" My setting was Stonehenge, where my four little detectives saw some men burying something amongst the great gray stones. Of course the men turned out to be bank robbers burying their loot. The children's father called the police, the money was found, and all ended happily.

By this time, I was earning A's and B's in most of my subjects, including reading. A good way to cultivate fluency was to continue to read aloud as I had started to do the year before. As Mother would wash the dinner dishes and clean up the kitchen, I sat at the aluminum-topped counter, well lit by fluorescent lights, and read of Laura Ingalls and her family, with their dog, Jack; Ma, who had been a teacher; and Pa, who throughout the stories played his fiddle to keep the family both entertained and inspired. Every so often there would be a new word over which I would stumble, but Mother would look over my shoulder and correct it. The ability to read from a book, and the pleasure of reading, actually reading, was still mine.

For the third and final time, my parents gave me as a Christmas present not just one book, but an entire series of books, for I had fallen in love with the stories of the lively and impulsive red-headed Canadian orphan, Anne of Green Gables. Mother had read the first book aloud to me, and I was most eager to continue Anne's saga. After all, this little heroine loved trees and flowers, loved her woods, stream, and pond, and had special names for her favorite places, as did I. The Sumac Patch and the Little Lone Maple were my woodland landmarks, just as Anne of Green Gables had her Violet Vale.

For me, Christmas now included singing in the children's choir at our church, which had a most talented and dedicated choir director. We learned to sing the standard Christmas carols; we sang old ones and carols so new that they hadn't been heard before, since our director, Mr. Davies, had composed them himself. I always sat next to a strong singer so that I could pick up the melody by ear by listening to her. For a while, I did try squinting at the music. I could follow the notes and could see whether they went up or down, though I never could distinguish the specific lines and spaces that indicated the pitch of those notes. I enjoyed participating in the Christmas pageants. One year I played recorder duets with Kit, and the following year I had a chance to sing "And He Shall Feed His Flock" from Handel's *Messiah*. Even now, that hauntingly beautiful aria evokes memories of wearing colorful choir robes, singing well-known and well-loved songs, and walking to rehearsals and performances in snowstorms.

When falling snow gave way to falling rain, and drifts of snow were superseded by drifts of daffodils, the first violets of spring made their presence known to me. I would touch the heart-shaped leaves as soon as they broke through the ground, and soon thereafter, I would pick that first violet and a leaf and take it to Mother, who would put my spring offering into a tiny glass vase that she would set on the windowsill. Soon the violets would burst into profusion, and I would pick large bouquets of long-stemmed purple flowers. Those were my favorites, though I also picked the pure white violets, the white violets shaded with blue, which were called shaded violets, and the little wild yellow woodland violets. One never can have too many violets.

As fifth grade drew to a close, my teacher, Miss Tracey, asked all of us students what we wanted to be when we grew up. When my turn to respond came, I said without hesitation that I wanted to become a teacher. My teacher responded immediately, saying that I would be a good one. I wasn't even sure what I would teach. Would I teach English, since now I could enjoy reading?

Over the years I have helped my high school piano students with their homework and therefore have taught *Romeo and Juliet* and *Jane Eyre* to any number of people. In the spring of 2011, I developed and presented a series of lectures on the novels of Jane Austen, in which I discuss the settings and comment on the development of the characters. At the age of ten, however, I was years away from making the decision of what I would teach. Music as a profession was as distant from my concept of what I would do for a living as were the responsibilities imposed by the approaching end of childhood to my awareness of the passing of time.

My mother was in touch with the preparatory school that I hoped to attend in a little more than a year. She was asked to send my short story about Stonehenge to the headmaster. In her letter of May 12, 1959, she wrote the following:

Janne worked on her story after school when the weather was poor and she couldn't stay outdoors, and other than encouraging her to finish, which a ten-year-old needs, this is her own. She was visiting Stonehenge and was very thrilled with all the implications, so this is the background for her first story.

Miss Tracey, Janne's teacher at Winn Brook, says that her use of words is most advanced, and I suspect that this may be due partly to compensate for her handicap. At any rate, we, along with Miss Hayes (Belmont School psychologist), wish very much for her to go to a school where she can be thus encouraged.

You asked Janne to send you a poem that she had written, so I'll include one she wrote to me on Mother's Day. She loves violets and picks bouquets daily.

Violet Queen

Little violet in the green,

Will you some day be a queen?

Will you wear a gown of gold,

Or white or blue? I'm often told

On your little emerald stem

You'll be plucked

When I come.

Miss Tracey corrected this and guided her, I'm sure, since she has been most sensitive in her guidance this year.

I remember when Miss Tracey saw my poem, for she spoke to me in a voice that was intense and serious. "Did you write that?" she asked me. I answered yes. "Did you read that anywhere?" she continued in a tense, strict voice that I had never heard her use before. I answered no. She then complimented me in her usual pleasant voice, and the subject was dropped. I knew by her response that she believed me, and from that incident, I can contradict the statement in this letter that my teacher corrected this and guided me in reference to that poem. I knew, as did she, that the work was entirely mine.

As the school year drew to a close, I began rehearsals with my choir, not of sacred music, but of some of the best operetta music that has ever been written. Every year the children's choir put on a half-hour performance of a Gilbert and Sullivan operetta. Kit had been in *H.M.S. Pinafore* two years before, and it was from her that I had learned all of the songs, both the choruses and the solos. This year's production was to be *The Mikado*, and I was to have the role of Katisha.

The original solos for this particular character were far too sophisticated and melancholy for a ten-year-old performer, so our clever director took a duet and turned it into a solo. Mother coached me on the song and accompanied me whenever I wanted to sing it. As performance time grew near, she gathered some of the other children at our house so we could rehearse together. Katisha is in love with Nanki-Poo, the son of the Mikado, but Nanki-Poo wants nothing to do with her, for he is in love with Yum-Yum. I had to sing about being the Mikado's daughter-in-law-elect, and to underscore that future relationship, I was to sing "Bow. Bow" to his daughter–in-law-elect! I was to take my fan and, with wide arm gestures, swish it at the chorus.

We had to solve the question of a costume, for everyone had to wear kimonos. Mother found some bright red polished cotton for the kimono itself, as well as some chartreuse-and-gold fabric for the obi, or ornamental sash. With suggestions and guidance from Satoshi, our Japanese friend from MIT who now, fifty years later, is an award-winning physicist for work done in both Japan and the United States, Mother made me the most wonderful red kimono. When performance day arrived, I became Katisha. My red kimono and gold-and-green obi fitted perfectly. My hair was piled on top of my head in a great bun with ornamental butterflies stuck in it, and I wore lipstick and some old-age wrinkle lines. For the final touch, I had long, red artificial fingernails. When the time came for my solo, I swished my fan, and in a big chest voice, I commanded everyone, soloists and chorus members alike, to "Bow. Bow" to his daughter-in-law-elect!

I received many compliments that evening. One lady said, "Janne, when are you going to Hollywood?" I was confused. I told her that some summers, we visit my grandparents who live in San Fernando, California, but I didn't think we were going to go this year.

I did not know what was meant by "going to Hollywood"! That compliment, though remembered now with appreciation and amusement, had at that time gone completely over my head.

9

The Discovery

After school was out for the summer, classes continued, for Kit and I were taking typing lessons. Those typewriters! If you typed too quickly, the keys would stick together. That nagging bell would talk to you at the end of every line of text, and at times my fingers would go in between the keys instead of on them. I was the youngest in the class, and the teacher was patient with me, knowing that looking at a book and copying any given exercise was not an easy task. Typing had become a necessity for me. I was not yet ready for lengthy term papers, but I did need typing skills for writing thank-you notes and letters, as well as for writing whatever original poems and stories came to mind.

I left those classes early, for my sister Mary Jane had invited me to spend a month with her family at their home in Chesterland, Ohio. That was a summer of bright flowers and fresh vegetables, for Bob, my brother-in-law, had an extensive vegetable garden. I savored the taste of sweet corn only minutes out of the garden, and I loved fresh lima beans, for the only ones I had ever known were frozen. I saw flowers unfamiliar to me and learned to recognize the true blue of bachelor's buttons, or cornflowers. When she wasn't cooking or canning or freezing the summer harvest, Mary Jane would be knitting something colorful or seeing that her three children were content. My nieces were four and two at that time, and my nephew was just a few months old. Now, all in their fifties at the time of this writing, one niece is an artist and medical illustrator, and the other, for years a dedicated teacher, now manages a flourishing yarn shop. My nephew is a geologist and college professor, and all three have children of their own.

During that summer of 1959, though I had left those typing classes, I still had to practice typing every day, for Mary Jane was an excellent typist. When I had finished my time for practice, I would pick out tunes on the piano or continue the practice of reading out loud, for Mary Jane had given me a book of Grimm's fairy tales for my eleventh birthday. That was celebrated in the backyard with a picnic and a strawberry calorie pie with green whipped cream decorated with dark green mint leaves.

Evenings were peaceful. Sometimes Bob would play for me pieces on the electronic organ that he was building in the basement, so I had the chance to hear some of the great fugues of Bach on an instrument other than the piano. Sometimes, in his soft gentle voice, Bob would sing his children to sleep, and later the crickets would sing me to sleep.

On returning home to Belmont Massachusetts, I found that our redwood modern house, which had played such an important role in my growing up years, was in the process of being remodeled. The large, stone-flagged living room had been divided to make two good-sized bedrooms for Kit and me, and our smaller bedrooms on the upper floor had been combined to make one cheerful, sun-filled living room. The square grand piano had been moved to the new living room and so was easily accessible to anyone who wanted to play it.

For the second time, Mother suggested that I take piano lessons. The teacher lived just a few houses away from us. Once again, the piano teacher did not know what to do with me. She knew I could play by ear, and at that time I was picking out such tunes as "Santa Lucia," to which I would add my harmonization. She went to the great effort of drawing notes that would be large enough for me to see. I remember those filing cards with huge staff lines on them and notes colored in with a blue ballpoint pen, and I realize in retrospect how much effort she put into creating written music for me. What no one realized, and what I was not able to explain until much later, was that though I could see the large notes and tell if they were whole notes, halves, or quarters, their size meant I could never see more than one note at a time. I couldn't see the five lines of the staff at the same time, so I would have to count up line by line to identify the pitch of the note by where it was located. Reading any music with hands together was an impossibility for the same reason.

Then Mother thought of an instrument for which one note at a time made perfect sense, so at her invitation, Mr. Davies, the choir director and mastermind of the Gilbert and Sullivan productions, came to our house and gave me voice lessons. I enjoyed those voice lessons, and I remember singing "Cherry Ripe" and the beautiful Elizabethan song "The Silver Swan." I didn't read the music, for my ear was developing to the extent that on hearing a melody, I could and did imitate it. For the first time, I learned about songs whose piano accompaniments were as important as the songs themselves, as Mr. Davies introduced me to the art songs, or lieder, of Franz Schubert. While the piano part portrayed a fish leaping through the water, I sang about a poor little trout that got caught by the evil fisherman. When I sang about a young miller who went a-wandering, I listened to the piano part as it described, in melody and texture, the images of a running brook, the splashing of water off of the mill wheels, and the grinding of the great millstones.

Christmas that year was filled with music. Mother played the piano while we sang from that beloved green book of folk songs, carols, spirituals, and songs of work and valor, and I took an active part in every song. Sometimes I would sing melody, and at others I'd make up a harmony. Sometimes I'd play my soprano recorder and Kit would play her alto recorder or the flute. A friend brought his portable harpsichord, which gave a silver lace quality to the music.

There had been music played earlier during that Christmas day, and unbeknownst to any of us at the time, it had brought about a life-altering experience for me. Now, in the closet in the living room, we had a new stereo system, turntable, speakers, and the beginnings of a collection of long-playing records. Music had entered our home through a stack of vinyl discs, and I was ready for it.

Unlike Mother, who had played the piano from early childhood, Daddy had never studied a musical instrument. His time had been spent with the chemistry set his parents had given him when he was twelve years old, and in later years, he was proud to say that he hadn't blown up their house. Nine years later, in 1934, while a doctoral student at MIT and later as a faculty member in the chemistry department, he, along with some friends, attended concerts at Boston's Symphony Hall. How I envied him when he told me that he had heard Prokofiev and Rachmaninoff, Russia's brilliant pianist-composers, perform their own piano concerti under the baton of the equally legendary Serge Koussevitsky. In years to come, I would hear recordings of those same works over our stereo system, but for that first Christmas, I heard recordings of works I already knew. Kit and

I were given our choices of what records we wanted. Kit chose the six Brandenburg Concerti of J. S. Bach, and I picked *The Mikado*. From the flute solo in the Brandenburg Fifth Concerto to Katisha's solo in *The Mikado*, we alternated discs as we went from the music of Bach to Sullivan and back to Bach. Those first stereo speakers filled the room with brilliant sound, making this quite a different experience from the little portable record player of my earlier years, yet the attraction was there. In both cases, when I was five, and now that I was eleven, the experience of listening to music spoke to me in a most direct and powerful way.

As soon as I began to listen to the recordings that made up what was to become a large collection, I made the discovery that I was doing more than just listening. For me, it would never be just background music, for as I was hearing it, I was absorbing the music into my understanding and into my very being. I was catching the melodies from this Beethoven symphony or that Vivaldi violin concerto and entrapping them in my ear and memory, where they remain to this day. My ear learned about chords and harmonic patterns years before I was to encounter them in the classroom, and without realizing it, I was building a repertoire of concert music literature in my memory that would allow me to study these works years later in music school, and to teach them years after that, with a fluency and confidence similar to musicians who have visual access to the printed music scores.

Earlier in the fall, though just beginning the sixth grade, I wrote a letter to the headmaster of the Cambridge School of Weston, for I knew that I would be starting the seventh grade there in the fall of 1960.

October 15, 1959

You suggested that I should take typing, so this summer, my sister and I took typing down at the Belmont High. You also asked me to send any little poem or composition to you. This little poem down below is about what happened to Mother, who is a victim of ragweed hay fever. This poem is a parody of Robert Browning's *Home-Thoughts from Abroad*.

Oh, to be in England, now September's there,

Without any ragweed pollen in the air.

And to our great surprise, no stuffy nose and itchy eyes.

The Kleenex box was simply gone

Much to the joy of everyone.

And nobody was ever seen

Taking antihistamine.

Hay fever gone, anyhow,

And one can sleep in England now.

Last summer I read many fairy tales. All my reading of fairy tales inspired me to write one of my own. I have enclosed *The Leaf Princess* with this letter.

Most sincerely, Janne Irvine

The Leaf Princess, less than two pages long, was a thinly disguised Cinderella story. Its one claim to being different was in the choice of the ball gown. The heroine, Lise, is wandering in the woods and pondering that even if she could go to the ball, she has no pretty dress to wear.

Lise heard a rustling sound about her which sounded like the leaves. She looked up and saw that it was the leaves. Those were magic leaves and they spoke to her much to Lise's amazement and said "Little girl, why aren't you at the King's Feast?"

"I can't go because I do not have any pretty dress to

wear," Lise answered shyly.

"Well," said the Leaves,

"The prettiest dress ever to be

Is clinging on every tree."

After Lise had made a beautiful ball gown out of yellow and red maple leaves, the story ends this way:

And so Lise, a country girl, became a princess. Royal robes were offered her time and time again, but Lisa, the Leaf Princess would not touch them. She only wore her beautiful leaf dress.

The following spring, I wrote a play, *The Courtship of Miles Standish*, based on the poem of that name by Longfellow. This was not a school project. I just wanted to do it because I was so enthralled by the poem and the story and the romance of John and Priscilla Alden. I had already formed the Amateur Dramatic Society with my two girlfriends Linda and Mary. This consisted of spending nights at each other's houses, making up little plays out of fairy tales, presenting them to our parents, and keeping a cigar box with a few pennies in it as our treasury. Now, however, we had a purpose, for our sixth-grade teacher had offered us the auditorium and an afternoon to present the play to our class. I directed the play and took the part of Miles Standish; Linda was John Alden; and Mary was Priscilla.

Just see how my armor gleams! That is because I polished it myself and did not leave it for others to do. And, as I've always said, "If you want a thing well done, you must do it yourself, you must not leave it to others." And see here! My great Sword of Damascus! This sword has saved my life many a time and I am at home on the battlefield—but when it comes to talking to a woman, I am very timid and do not know how to act. John, I would like to ask a favor of you. Will you please go to the house of Priscilla and tell her that I love her dearly and wish to marry her?

To suit the part, I had my long hair cut to shoulder length. I wore the dark blue jacket I had worn two years ago when I was Henry VIII in our London living room. For the character of the pilgrim soldier, Mother made some starched cuffs and a large pilgrim collar, which she stitched onto the jacket. After all, I still had those wax candle figurines and knew just how the pilgrims had dressed. Linda wore a yellow sweater and gray wool slacks with red three-quarter knee socks; and Mary, as Priscilla, had a perfect little pilgrim costume that looked exactly like my wax figurine. The dress was gray, and the apron and cuffs were a pristine white. Priscilla had to sit at her spinning wheel and spin just before John entered with his friend's proposal on his lips and sublimating his own proposal in his heart. The best spinning wheel I could find was my bright pink-and-white Hula-Hoop—after all, didn't 1960 usher in the era of the Hula-Hoop? As the director, I had Priscilla sing a song while spinning. The budding and totally unrecognized musicologist in me knew that I had to use a composition appropriate to that era. Fortunately, in our singing class at school, we had learned the Tallis Canon, which was perfect. Though my play was short, it covered the major points of the story. Priscilla's rejection of Standish's proxy proposal, her acceptance of John's personal proposal, and Standish's jealousy of John were all represented. The play closed with the ultimate realization that if you want a thing well done, you must do it yourself.

As I look back on my years at the Winn Brook School, and they were good years, the only thing that could have been improved was the use of recess time. I couldn't participate in any of the games that involved throwing a ball, since I couldn't see the ball to catch it or dodge in time to avoid being struck by it. So I stood around outside with some of the other students who, for one reason or another, couldn't participate in the games. Then my friend Susan had an idea. She said that at the far end of the playground, there was a brook, and that was why the school was called Winn Brook. I knew that my brook was part of the Winn Brook system, and so of course I wanted to see the brook at school. At the very beginning of the recess period, we ran clear across that playground. I didn't know how big it was until we ran across it. Out of breath, we arrived at the chain-link fence, and there was the brook. It wasn't babbling and sparkling like my brook; at my house, there was a thirty-foot drop across the front of our property. At this point in the brook's journey, it was slow-moving and placid, but it was a brook. We just had time to run back to the school and return to our classroom as the school bell was ringing. How I wished

I could have spent all of my recesses walking and running across that playground. It was over forty years later that I began training to walk half marathons, and I wish I had had the chance to cultivate walking as an exercise over those intervening decades.

One afternoon, while walking across the playground to the school bus, I saw something shiny on the ground. There were a couple of coins there, but to my dismay I realized that I couldn't see what they were. Was one coin a half dollar? Was the other a quarter or a nickel? I squinted at them and realized after a while that I had a quarter and a nickel. I took them home and later to the school office; since they weren't claimed, they were returned to me. Today, I'd call this a reality check. I believed my vision was growing worse.

In those days, every morning began with a Pledge of Allegiance to the flag followed by a patriotic song. Miss Smarsh, my sixth-grade teacher, would select a student to lead the pledge, choose the song, and read out loud to the class some story of his or her choice. One day she chose me, and I was delighted. I believe the song I selected was "God Bless America," and I know the story I read was "The Beginning of the Armadillos" from *Just So Stories* by Rudyard Kipling. I had made this selection for several reasons. Of course I liked it, for I had grown up hearing Daddy read the works of Kipling aloud in his soft Missouri accent, and furthermore, the book from which this story came had large print. I thought back two years to that afternoon we visited that bookstore in Salisbury, when I had found that book with its dark red cover and oversized pages of dark ivory paper. I learned that Kipling had been ridiculed in school because of his poor eyesight, yet he, probably with little more sight than I had, went on to become England's poet laureate. Furthermore, he had illustrated his stories with imaginative pen-and-ink drawings. So I stood before my sixth-grade class and began to read. Those years of reading out loud to Mother served me well. I spoke clearly and slowly, and probably I added a touch of an English accent to this or that character for dramatic effect. The story was long, so I was asked to finish the second half the following day. When I finished it, I knew that something important had happened. My classmates enjoyed it, and I heard no murmuring about my holding the book so unusually close to my face. What an accolade of acceptance. Maybe that was because I did not feel the least bit self-conscious, and I was totally comfortable in what I was doing.

During the summer of 1960, we took a car trip across the country so that, along with visiting our family, we could go to several of the national parks. I remember spending restful green twilights in Missouri listening to my grandfather tell family stories. I enjoyed sleeping in the corner bedroom that had been my aunt's room, with a blue bedspread and gray-blue floorboards. Waking up to a new day was always filled with peaceful, pleasant things to do, which included swimming in the warm water of the community swimming pool and taking a trip to the Ozarks. I remember the intense blue of the Osage River, and the blues and milky greens of some of the great springs for which that part of the state is known. We took a side trip to Mansfield, Missouri, so I could see the house in which Laura Ingalls Wilder and her husband, Almanzo, spent their later years. The woman who gave us the tour actually had known Laura and remembered her as an active, bustling little woman, full of energy as she went up and down the narrow stairs up which we were climbing. On the second floor we saw calling cards and autograph albums that had been popular when the Ingalls girls were young. We saw quilts that Laura and Mary had pieced and sewn, and downstairs we saw Mary's organ as well as the desk at which Laura had penned her books. Since I knew the Laura stories so well, I enjoyed seeing everything I could in that house. Today, I still read the Little House books once every couple of years, and now I have the luxury of reading them recorded onto CDs. This trip predated cassettes and CDs, so we had to make our own entertainment as we crossed the plains from Missouri to Colorado. Kit and I would sing the old family songs in two-part harmony, or sometimes we would whistle them. We'd play chess on a small plastic traveling set we had been given, but that pastime ended when the plastic set melted. Once in Colorado, we visited Mesa Verde, climbed into some caves with ancient adobe buildings, and stood near another cave's entrance as thousands of bats flew out into the evening to catch their dinners of insects. We traveled to the Four Corners area and saw Monument Valley and the Mitten Buttes, which really did look like right and left mittens. I could see the expanse of turquoise-colored sky against which the red rock was the color of freshly cut rosewood or rare roast beef. I learned about the tablelands called mesas, since I could see those large land formations set in the middle of emptiness. We revisited Santa Fe; there I picked up a Navajo-style full-skirted dress and a velvet shirt, both of which were turquoise in color and trimmed with shiny silver braid.

Visiting my California grandparents included becoming reacquainted with their abundant garden, eating lush, fresh fruit salads, and enjoying the dry, hot smell of the eucalyptus-scented air. Traveling north, we went to a redwood forest, and again I enjoyed the scent of the trees all the more, since it was difficult for me to gauge their height.

Yellowstone Park offered smells and sounds along with sights. As we wound our way along specially constructed walkways, we heard the burbling of the "mud pots" and smelled the sulfur stench that hung in the air all around us. There was beauty in this volcanic landscape, and I enjoyed seeing the very blue color of the spring morning glories. I did get close enough to the Old Faithful geyser to see its waters blast off into the air, and as we drove through the woods, I saw the blurred shapes of large bears when they were pointed out to me.

By the end of the trip, we were tired and anxious to reach home. Mother did ask that we take a brief detour to see Niagara Falls. I remember feeling the pounding waters shake the wooden decks on which we stood, and from hearing the roaring cascade of the waters, I had a sense of the immense power of these falls. I have been told that now when one visits these National Parks, there is bumper-to-bumper traffic, and that one must make a reservation a year in advance. That was not the case in 1960. We came and went as we wished, and we enjoyed what we saw from the comfort of our car without being caught up in traffic.

It felt good to reach home, for we had been gone for over a month. There were so many memories to sort out and new things to think about, but there was not too much time to do that, for not only was I entering the seventh grade, I was attending a school that was new to me.

10

The Decision

By the end of that summer, I was beset by tears for which I had no explanation. Why was I crying? Often it happened in the evenings, and when it did, my parents would talk to me and try to find the source of my distress. Eventually, the three of us realized that I was reacting in the same way I had when, as little more than a toddler, I had cried from fear of going outside of the house into the backyard, where there would be unknown things I might trip over or bump into. There was always the fear that I might become lost, and in retrospect, vestiges of that fear were still present. I had found out through my parents' patient questioning that I was anxious about attending a new school and fearful of being confronted with new surroundings. I was relieved to be told that this was a not an uncommon reaction even from twelve-year-old students who could see clearly. It was Daddy who had the idea that we should go to the campus of my new school, walk around it, enjoy the beauty of the trees, and see the various buildings, and then, on returning home, I would try to make a map. We did just that, and during a subsequent visit to the school, I met some of my teachers, who were friendly and assured me that they would help me with anything I needed.

Within a short time, I learned the campus very well. The assembly hall/gymnasium flanked one side of the quadrangle, the

157

administration building was on another side, and the dining hall, below which the seventh- and eighth-grade classrooms were, was on the third side. A road ran along the fourth side, across from which was a building where I had science classes, and in another part of the campus, I learned my way to the art building.

That street that ran through the campus, on which the traffic was certainly not very heavy during the day, served as an important teaching tool for a subject I had started very late and at which I have never excelled. Amongst my school records was a comment that, although I was advanced for my grade level in vocabulary compre-hension and creative writing, in other areas I had the experience of a six-year-old child, for I had not crossed a street on my own until two weeks before entering seventh grade. Once, a couple of years before, I had been directed to cross the street in front of my house en route to a music lesson, but the street was not clear of traffic, for a car was cresting the hill and coming fast—far too fast to stop. I knew to keep running, and even now, I have not forgotten that spark of gut-fear of what almost happened, coupled with that inner drive to survive. It was my mother who had told me that the street was clear, and it was no wonder we never discussed what had happened, for she was as traumatized as I was by that incident. The campus street, however, was not threatening at all, and during my three years of study at the Cambridge School of Weston, I crossed it time and time again without any fear at all.

For the first time, as a seventh-grader, I had different teachers for my subjects, and I enjoyed all of my studies. For history and English, we read *The Old Colony of New Plymouth*, which was followed by a field trip to the historical attraction of the reconstructed Plymouth colony about one hundred miles away. For science, the subject for the entire year was the weather, and I'm sure my interest stemming from that time is why I am an avid watcher of the Weather Channel. I was so interested that my father offered to order weather maps for me, though we decided not to do so, since I knew I would not be able to see them well enough to take advantage of them. Instead, he installed an outdoor/indoor thermometer that I enjoyed using to track the temperatures as the seasons changed, as well as to follow the swing of annual temperatures from the occasional few degrees below zero to the occasional few degrees above 100.

During recess, I began to go next door to the eighth-grade homeroom, where there was a piano. Sometimes people would play it, and sometimes two eighth-grade boys would entertain their class-mates by singing such songs as "They Call the Wind Mariah" to the accompaniment of their guitars. I enjoyed singing in the weekly chorus rehearsals of the glee club. Joseph Schaff, the club's director, taught us English songs of the sea as well as "The Ash Grove," a touching Welsh air, to which I felt compelled to append a descant harmony. For the first time, I heard and sang "I Have Lost My Eurydice" by Gluck, a song I continue to enjoy through recordings of the great Italian singers Luciano Pavarotti and Cecilia Bartoli.

To my surprise, I was elected class president, and I felt most dig-nified standing in front of the class in my green plaid skirt, yellow sweater, and gray blazer from Harrod's, which Kit had worn in England and into which I had grown.

At home, music from England entered our record collection as more and more Gilbert and Sullivan operettas were acquired. Two discs of English country dances played on recorders, harpsichord, and strings captured my fancy, and soon I was playing many of those dance tunes on my soprano recorder. Kit would join me with her alto so we could play the lively melodies and compelling rhythms of "All in a Garden Green," "Nonesuch," and "A Trip to Paris." We still entertain ourselves by playing these tunes during Kit's yearly visits to Tucson.

The school year ended well, and the following summer of 1961 found us crossing the country again, this time by train. Daddy had teaching commitments at MIT and so had to stay near work for the summer. Mother had to tend to her ailing parents, so she, Kit, and I prepared for another trip. Mother found the perfect pastime for me while on the train. She read *Gone with the Wind* aloud to me, and from the first sentence, I was totally captivated. I was caught up in the world of Scarlett and Rhett, of voluminous ball gowns and battle-fields, and in a story that combined history and romance in such a compelling manner that even now, I read that book once a year. At my grandparents' house, I found a copy of the book that my grand-mother probably had bought the year it was printed. The print was a little larger than that of the paperback we had brought with us, so I spent the next several weeks reading that book three times. I never grew tired of it. I remember those lazy, sun-filled afternoons I spent sprawled on my stomach with my chin resting on the knuckles of my flattened hands. Occasionally I'd look out the window and see the blue California sky and a darker blur that was the range of the San Gabriel Mountains. I realize now that the movie probably came to the theaters that summer to mark the twenty-fifth anniversary of the publishing of the book. Whatever the reason, I insisted that we go to the movie more than once, and I knew that if I sat near the front of the theater, if not in the front row itself, I could see the bright Tech-nicolor greens of Scarlett's iconic gowns. I knew this was a movie I could appreciate as much as anyone, because by then I pretty much knew the book by heart. By the end of that summer, I could recite much of the dialogue, as I still can to this day.

When I began eighth grade, I was in familiar surroundings, since my homeroom was the classroom with the piano that I had visited during the past year's recesses. Soon I made friends with a trio of girls—sisters, in fact—and that piano was played more often than not during the morning and afternoon recesses, since my new friends were all accomplished musicians. My classmate Cora, the middle of the three girls, often played a concerto by Haydn. I listened and admired her dexterity and clear tone. Sometimes her younger sister Brooke, dashed in from the seventh-grade room and dazzled her audience by playing the dramatic Mendelssohn G minor concerto. Their oldest sister, Alexandra, always performed in a polished and competent manner, and my memory of her is that of her performance of the well-known Mozart Sonata in C major. The following year (or it could have been the one after that, for then I was attending as many concerts as I could), I was to hear these girls give a joint recital that qualified them as college-level musicians not only in piano, but in string instruments and voice as well.

After hearing my friends play, I would head for the piano and try to imitate their pieces. My fingers were clumsy and untrained, but my ear was growing sharper as I improved my ability to pick out themes from well-known piano pieces. When Cora played the first movement of Beethoven's Moonlight Sonata, I knew I wanted to play that piece, and within a short while I was able to play the first few measures of this hauntingly beautiful work.

Other subjects besides music demanded my attention. Our textbook for English consisted of a series of stories, some of them biographical. The one I read most often was the story of Paderewski, the pianist-politician from Poland. The science class exposed us to any number of geological formations, several of which I had seen two summers ago during our cross-country trip by car. I frequented the art studio, where I enjoyed ceramics classes. I found out how difficult it was to center a ball of clay on the potter's wheel, for if it was not centered, the slippery, wet clay would develop a mind of its own and flop off of the wheel unless it were held in check. I found it a challenge to build a pot with coils, for keeping the coils even and on top of each other was difficult for the beginning student I was. Working with clay did help to strengthen my hands, and in retrospect, I realize that it was fortunate for me to build muscles in my fingers. I learned about glazes and was always surprised when the chalky-textured, light-colored liquids, when applied to ceramics, would turn into bold, glistening colors under intense heat.

As the season changed from summer to fall, I was able to break away from homework to wander in the woods, pick a yellow maple leaf or two, and lie down in the summer-baked grasses of the sumac patch and sniff the beginnings of the autumn-chilled air. When the leaves fell, as autumn moved inexorably toward winter, it was too cold to spend as much time outside. I would look out the window in front of my desk and note how the predominant color was now gray. The leaves carpeting the ground were a warm brownish gray, the tree trunks a dark charcoal gray, and the overcast sky, not yet laden with snow clouds, was nevertheless a silver gray.

One day in mid-November of 1961, I came home from school and began to read my homework assignment. I was reading about oil wells in Ohio, and since the print was small for me, I had to stop every so often to rub my eyes. I looked up into the gray trees, enjoying the blurred airiness of their branches. I looked down to resume reading and saw a gray blur where, just seconds before, there had been a white page filled with black words. I rubbed my eyes again, but that made no difference, for the print was still illegible.

I stayed out of school for several days and was in bed to ease and possibly reverse whatever strain had affected my eyes, or to be specific, my left eye. My ophthalmologist and two of his colleagues, the top men in Boston, concurred that though they could see no change in the fabric of my left eye, the changes, slight enough to be undetectable to them, would naturally make a great difference to me. It was surmised that internal bands, maybe scar tissue, had altered the already delicate structure of the retina and that such changes could have been brought about by the natural process of maturity, for I was thirteen years old. I had noticed no warning signs that my vision would slip to this extent. It just happened. One minute I could read, and the next minute I couldn't. I was surprised to find that there had been warning signs of which I had been oblivious. My English teacher and ceramics teacher had both noticed that I was having more difficulty in seeing. The latter must have seen me squint for longer and longer times as I tried to read the names of pottery glazes that were printed in small letters on glaze-daubed labels affixed to the glass jars that, to make things more difficult, were stored on shelves in a dark corner of the ceramics studio. I was told that there was no reason to stay in bed, and though I saw strange, shifting colors, especially yellows and greens that finally dissipated without any further ill effect, I returned to school.

My mother had kept me current with my homework assignments by reading my books out loud to me. We read from the science book and studied the pertinent questions at the end of the chapter; we read history and English assignments, and Daddy helped me with my math homework. I found that I could respond to the questions in class without any problem, for I knew the answers and was confident in that knowledge. Sometimes, especially during science class, while the other students were reading to themselves, the teacher asked me to choose a friend, usually Cora, who would read to me as we sat in the hallway outside of the classroom.

Daddy bought me a mint-green typewriter. It was the smallest he could find and about the size of a medium-sized three-ring notebook. Today, with streamlined laptop computers and notepads, svelte and available in a dozen or more colors, my little green typewriter does not seem like anything special, but it was special to me. Some of my free periods were spent practicing my typing, for I was of an age to be writing term papers, and I had to improve my skills of thinking at the keyboard.

There was one period that was difficult to fill with a useful activity, and that was study hall. Of course I couldn't type in the study hall itself, so at times I would sit quietly in the dining hall where my classmates were reading, writing, and doing their homework. I could and did organize my thoughts on this or that project, but that did not seem the best use for my time for several hours a week. Then Mother had an idea.

She asked me if I wanted to take piano lessons. She had seen me hovering around the piano at home, and she knew I was picking out pieces that I had heard Cora and her sisters play. This time, I was interested—so interested that I could not wait to begin. Mother spoke with Mr. Schaff, the choral teacher, who said that, though not trained as a pianist, he could start me with lessons and give me whatever ear-training skills I needed. So the next day, I sat at the old upright piano in my eighth-grade room, awaiting the choral teacher under whom I had sung for the past year and a half.

I played for him what I could of the first movement of the Moonlight Sonata. Measure by measure and theme by theme, my teacher played, and I imitated. After three months, I was playing this somber, brooding, and beautiful piece accurately, with confidence and expression. The next piece I chose, since I had heard Cora's older sister play it, was the famous *Sonata in C Major* by Mozart. This was easy to pick up by ear, for the themes and notes made so much sense. Those two years of listening to the family stereo were standing me in good stead, for I understood, without knowing that I knew, the lucid and flowing eighteenth-century classical style. Once more, I found that I could imitate the notes I was hearing without much trouble.

Since I was not working from a printed score, mere imitation was not sufficient, for in order to learn this music, I was told I had to understand how it was put together. This unusual way of approaching the learning process opened my mind in so many ways, since I became attuned to compositional structure and the science of the interaction of chords, or music theory, all at the same time. I was avid to learn everything I could. After seven months of lessons at least three times a week, I was playing all three movements of that sonata by Mozart. In retrospect, I did not play them very well, but I could get through them, and that was thought to be unusual, considering the short period of time I had been playing the piano. Those right-hand scales running up and down the keyboard simply did not glitter. It wasn't until fifteen years later, in graduate school, that I felt truly comfortable playing that piece. After all, the music was by Mozart, and his music does need special handling!

What I could do when I first learned that sonata was a special skill that has stood me in good stead many times. Part lecture, part parlor trick, and partly as a way to sharpen my knowledge of musical structure, I would play the entire sonata while reciting a detailed and accurate verbal commentary on its harmonic analysis: "This piece is in the key of C major. The left hand is playing an accompaniment in broken chords that lay down the harmonic structure of the piece. Now the right hand has scales that conform to the left hand's harmonic presentation," and so on.

Music became the focus of my life, so much so that I never lamented the loss of my reading vision. I had too many wonderful things to think about, too much new knowledge to acquire, and too little time to practice at home, for there was my homework to be done.

Every afternoon, the school bus would drop me off at Belmont Center, which was just a couple of blocks down the hill from our house. Mother would pick me up and drive me the short distance home, or at times some of my classmates would walk me across the three busy streets and to the bottom of the hill, from where I would walk home without any problem.

Mother and I would begin reading, and we would usually start with English. Hadn't we always read books together? Only five years ago, it had been Laura Ingalls Wilder and tales of Robin Hood and King Arthur. Now we read textbooks on English grammar and whatever book was being assigned for a class. And if we weren't sure what book to pick up and read together, there was always Jane Austen, for now it had become customary to read at least two of her novels each year.

Before starting my next activity, I might take a fifteen-minute break to go outside and say hello to the woods. If it was winter, I'd breathe in enough crisp, cold air to give me energy for my next task and tramp around the house, making boot prints in new, fluffy snow, or in older, crunchy snow as the season advanced. Later, as winter began to think about retiring, I would pick the long, slender forsythia branches to bring inside to warm water and sunshine until the buds along their length would burst into a hymn of tiny yellow flowers whose message was that spring was not far away.

Once inside, it was time to concentrate on more homework. If I had to type a term paper, I would do what I could on my own, and then, since my typing was not yet accurate enough for final copies, Mother would retype the paper strictly in accordance with what I had written. While she prepared dinner, I would go downstairs to where the piano had been moved and practice my Mozart and Beethoven pieces.

After dinner, while Mother did the dishes, I would work with Daddy on my math. He would lie on the living room couch with his cigar in hand while I sat in a chair and concentrated on what he was explaining. Math was not easy for me, but at least by the following year, when I was taking algebra, I was able to do quadratic equations in my head, which did impress him. The one area of math at which I did excel was that of the "new math," so succinctly explained by Tom Lehrer, the talented mathematician, comedian, and a musician, whose catalogue of songs I knew by heart. His terse comment that "Base eight is just like base ten, really—if you're missing two fingers" got the point across, but to a budding pianist, it was not a wonderful analogy. I preferred explaining that to me, the different bases were akin to transposing a theme from the key of C major to that of G major.

After completing my math homework, there was still a block of time for more studying. Mother and I would do a little more work, reading an assigned book. It must be remembered that reading out loud takes a great deal more time than reading silently. Most people do not realize this, so in order to cover the assigned materials, every minute of my time had to be used wisely. Finally, by ten o'clock, it would be time to go to bed, knowing that the entire intensive schedule would repeat itself the following day.

One afternoon, after practicing my piano pieces by Mozart and Beethoven, I wanted to play something else. I couldn't pick up a piece of music and sight-read it. What could I play that was different? I began to think of a tune that was just a fragment, five notes long. I played it again with the right hand and found some simple chords so that the left hand could play in harmony. Phrase by phrase, my first little tune came into being, and when I played it for my teacher, he encouraged me to keep working with the vocabulary of notes and themes and chords. Within a few days, I had an idea for a second piece. This one was a little more advanced—first, my right hand played a melody with its supporting voice for eight measures, and this was followed by the left hand playing the same material in a lower part of the piano. A tiny middle section kept the piece going, and the end was a shortened form of the beginning, with both hands playing at the same time. I still play this piece, my little "Opus Two," which was in the key of A minor, my favorite key or tonality to this day. Now I was actively studying composition along with music theory, and by now I was having a few piano lessons from the school's resident pianist. He taught me a short piece by Beethoven called "Adieu to the Piano." For me, it might as well have been called "Hello to the Piano," for I was learning as much as I could.

Not all of the music I picked up was by Mozart or Beethoven. Some of the records in our collection were of humorous songs, such as the satirical and clever parodies of Tom Lehrer, who made everyone who heard "We'll All Go Together When We Go" quake with fear as well as with mirth when hearing about nuclear annihilation. Then there was the "Irish Ballad" to beat all ballads, which preached that murders of all kinds were an acceptable part of life, though lying was a sin! One of my favorite English music hall songs, learned from the recording by the incomparable actor/singer Stanley Holloway, that I still belt out in a chest voice while thumping out the chords on the piano, has to do with the ghost of Anne Boleyn, who carries her head 'neath her arm. Music was becoming a part of my life that brought pleasurable entertainment as well as serious study. There is no doubt that my immersion in so many aspects of music kept me from dwelling on my vision, which continued to deteriorate.

When it was clear that I was not going to recover my reading vision, my mother made an appointment to visit the school for the blind. She wanted to see what was available as an alternative method of education, and as a teacher she was interested in finding out what I would learn as an eighth-grader with other blind and low-vision students. I remember some of the conversations we had after she had visited the school for the blind. She said that if I went there, I would certainly be at the top of the class, since I was working at a more advanced academic level than were the children my age, and she knew, since it was she who was reading my study assignments to me. She knew that at times I must feel different from my peers, though I don't remember complaining about that. She said that if I went to the school for the blind, I could be of help to others by sharing what little I saw with children who hadn't ever had that opportunity, and I could in turn learn skills from my future classmates that I had not had the chance to develop. Furthermore, I would learn to read Braille, which would give me a great deal of independence.

It was that which caused me to panic. I had obtained a card with the Braille alphabet, so I knew a few of the symbols based on the combinations of raised dots. To the neophyte I was, the system was intricate and complex and, furthermore, it was a type of shorthand in which single letters stood for entire words, and combinations of dots stood for groups of letters and parts of words. I was concerned that I would fall behind in my studies in order to make the transition to what was tantamount to learning a foreign language.

At the age of five, when the same question arose as to whether or not I should embark on my education at the school for the blind or at the public school, the decision was made for me to start my education with my sighted peers. Now at the age of thirteen I was very much involved in making this all-important decision. I wanted to stay where I was. I had my friends. I knew I was doing well in my school subjects, and I didn't want to interrupt my instruction in several areas of music. Furthermore, though younger than the students in grades ten through twelve, I was to participate in the upper school's spring production of Gilbert and Sullivan's *Patience*. I was to sing in the chorus, and have two costumes, and learn everybody's solos just by listening to them.

I was not totally blind. This was as true as it had been eight years before. I could still see that the sky was blue or gray or black. I could see the tender green leaves of spring and the red and yellow leaves of autumn. All of my points of reference related to the sighted world, which is why I have always been able to take full advantage of verbal descriptions, even of things I have never seen. Of course, neither was I totally sighted. My vision could not be corrected, and I could no longer see to read, so where did I belong?

I knew where I wanted to be.

The definitive opinion was that of my ophthalmologist. He had seen me on a yearly basis from the time I was a few months old. He knew my parents well, both personally and professionally, and he respected the manner in which they had raised me. Unlike so many of the blind children he had examined, I had been taught to try to look toward people when I spoke to them, by directing my face toward their voices. I had been taught to smile, and I remember that it did not come naturally at first. My speaking voice was a flexible and expressive instrument and not the uninflected monotone adopted by so many. I had not developed the mannerism of rocking back and forth prevalent amongst those who had not been given sensory stimulation at an early age. My doctor was concerned that, unconsciously, I could revert to these mannerisms, which would gradually separate me from the world of the sighted in which I had functioned successfully for the first thirteen years of my life.

I had come to a crossroads. Two roads diverged in a yellow wood, and I could not travel both. Like Robert Frost, I took the road less traveled by, and that has made all the difference. It is the road in part chosen for me; and, in a larger part, it is the road I chose for myself. This is the road along which I have continued to travel with confidence and the knowledge that it was the right choice for me.

My doctor's advice, both medical and personal, was that I continue my education in the way to which I had become accustomed.

11

Song of the Crickets

During that spring of my eighth-grade year, I began to attend afternoon rehearsals for the production of *Patience*, an operetta till then unknown to me. I loved hearing the music and being a part of it. There were no grand solos for me in this performance as I had had years before in my beloved children's version of *The Mikado* and later in *The Pirates of Penzance*, for those were children's performances and this high school performance was to be a full-length production of the operetta. I learned the music as I always did: by listening to the strong singers and following them. Now I was hearing how the work was being put together. The choruses were rehearsed; the ensemble numbers that in some cases were for as many as five people were sung; the trios, duets, and solos were practiced day after day. Years later, I was to learn that Sullivan composed his scores in that way by writing first for the choruses, then for the smaller groups, and finally for the solos. The girls' chorus, a bevy of "Lovesick Maidens," presented the opening number. Our gowns were empire-waist dresses in pastel colors, and mine was pink. There were some excellent soloists among the upper school students; Patience had the high notes and flexibility that Sullivan demands for his heroines, and Lady Jane not only had the contralto needed for her role, but she really did play the cello (the original

172

called for a double bass) when such an instrument was needed as a prop during her solo. The men were splendid as the dashing Dragoon Guards, and the one chosen to be my Dragoon Guard was wonderful in helping me negotiate the stage during the complicated ensemble numbers that closed each act of the play.

Meanwhile, I still had my music lessons at least a couple of times a week. To my teacher's surprise, I began picking out all of the music I was learning from *Patience*. I could play the march of the dragoons and the tender quintet "I Hear the Soft Note," and I could accompany myself singing any of my favorite songs. Playing by ear means many different things to different people. For me, it was always a far more intellectual experience rather than an imitative one. My growing analytical ability was necessary in learning this operetta's music, since the music of Sir Arthur Sullivan, though seemingly simplistic, is in reality very subtle and complicated from the standpoint of music theory. The basic music theory I received during those early months of training helped to sharpen my ear, which made possible everything that followed.

I was reaching out and grabbing at any tune I could find, be it a piece for piano or a song from the operetta, and making it work for me, no matter whether I used the correct fingering or not! My teacher and I knew the time would come eventually when I would work under a piano teacher who would set me on the right road as far as proper keyboard technique was concerned. I wasn't quite ready for that yet, since those afternoon lessons, taking place for maybe a few minutes here and there during study halls, recess, or after lunch, were fulfilling my need to explore and learn everything I could. They were also making me realize, without a doubt, that music, in spite of my late start, was what I wanted to pursue as my life's work.

I brought my growing knowledge of music into my eighth-grade classroom when I gave an oral report on Scotland. Dressed in a plaid skirt and a velvet jacket that had been made for my mother when she was a child, I spoke about Scottish dancing. Just a few days before, my eighth-grade English teacher had taken me out of the classroom and into the hall to show me a couple of the steps and the high, uplifted, curved position of the arms that is used by Highland dancers executing the sword dance. I spoke about the butter-rich Scotch shortbread and brought in some cookies I had made. I spoke about the legacy of Scottish song and sang "Bonnie George Campbell," which tells the story of a man who goes to war: "But empty came his saddle and bloody to see. Home came his good horse, but never came he." I'm sure that one episode of presenting that particular project has stayed with me so clearly because now, clad in a long, black dress and wearing the Irvine tartan sash, striking with its blues and greens, I direct and perform with a small group of people who enjoy playing the music of Scotland and England.

Going from music to English, to history and science, and back to music made up the pattern of my days. The regimen of classes, term papers, and homework continued, but because it was spring, I had to take more study breaks to enjoy the emergence and flowering of that season. Lilacs. False blue, white, purple, color of lilac … May is lilac here in New England. April is forsythia, but May is lilac time. Amy Lowell's poem "Lilacs" is filled with as many images of lilacs as there are florets on the puffs of flowers. To reach the lilac hedge, I had to walk down the old king's highway, now a mere path to where at least three aged lilac bushes had intertwined their trunks and branches and had produced a bower of single lavender blossoms, double lavender, and double white flowers. The fragrance was as sweet as the May afternoon itself, and I would pick great bouquets of flower-laden branches and bring them inside to perfume the house. I learned to take a mallet to crush the ends of the stems so the flowers would last longer. Sometimes the flowers would be put into a large, square glass vase, but my preference was to use the silver pitcher. I still have that pitcher and the worn metal clippers I used for harvesting my crop of flowers, but now they are used for pruning oleanders or lemon branches rather than lilacs.

When school ended, Mother made an appointment for me. We traveled from Belmont into Cambridge to the Longy School of Music, where I had attempted to study piano five years before. This time, I was to meet Nicholas Van Slyck, the director of the school, a well-known, Harvard-trained pianist and composer, for whom I was to perform my eight small compositions.

The piano was a long concert grand with ivory keys and a tone much larger than I was used to hearing, since most pianos I had played were uprights or our square grand. I did the best I could as I played my piano pieces. Some were slow, others fast, and out of these pieces, all written within a six-month period, five of them were in the same key. This prompted the director to say, "Janne, the first thing you must do is to get out of A minor." The second thing he said was that I needed piano lessons, so he selected for me a teacher from whom I studied until I went away to college. I am still in touch with her.

As a teacher myself, I look back four decades ago to those beginning years of lessons and admire the way Trudi Salomon worked with me as a teenage beginner. There would be no more Mozart sonatas for me to play until I had gained sufficient technique. The first piece she gave me to play was by Mozart and was the well-known Minuet in F that Mozart had written at the age of six. Miss Salomon would play the piece at one piano while I listened, and then I would play it back to her on the piano at which I was seated.

As I recall my progress through miniature masterworks by the great composers, I remember studying several of the Short Preludes by Bach. Now I realize what good choices those pieces were, since inherent in most preludes is a repetitive pattern, which is such an aid to the beginning student. My first recital piece, played some six months after taking lessons, was "The Poor Orphan Child" from Robert Schumann's *Album for the Young*. This little piece was in my favorite key of A minor and was one of the first pieces for which I was taught to have a cello-like singing tone for the left hand. Trudi Salomon did more than to make that verbal image. She took me to the cello teacher one Saturday after my lesson, so I had the chance to hear another instrument, touch it, try to play it, and most of all hear a fine performer create that rich tone I was supposed to emulate at the piano. I learned early that part of playing the piano is a matter of imagination, for in a way, the piano is an orchestra. From the double bass to the high flute and piccolo, and from the warm, tawny sound of the clarinet to the soaring sound of the violin, the piano is capable of expressing the essence of these tones while never departing from its own identity.

Summer was the perfect time for beginning this new regimen of master piano lessons, since I had more time to practice. As always when I needed to take a break, I would wander in the woods, where one year I found some wild blackberries. Sometimes, to alleviate the tension brought about by constant studying and practicing, my parents and I felt the need of different surroundings, so we would take a short vacation. It may have been this summer that we visited our friends Wen and Fran, who spent several summers on a houseboat on Lake Winnipesaukee. I loved being on the water and the feeling of the movement of the boat. I didn't have to think of textbooks or assignments. It was summer, and I was reconnecting with being outside. I didn't have to worry about how much practice time I would have, since there was no piano on the houseboat. I couldn't stand being without music, so I did bring my soprano recorder, and after dinner I would pipe English country dance tunes and American folk songs across the waters.

Wen was clever at piloting his boat, and he took us on courses between mountains and through various inlets of the lake. One afternoon, he told me to take over. I grasped the wooden spokes of the captain's wheel. "Take the boat between those two mountains," he ordered.

"'I can't see where to go," I replied. It took my father saying that I really couldn't see the space between the mountains to convince Wen of my limitation. I got up from the wheel, but Wen wasn't through with me yet.

"Sit down," he commanded. He explained how I could turn the wheel to the left or the right a quarter, half, or whole turn. Thus, while sitting in front of me beyond the captain's wheel, he proceeded to steer us across the lake. "One quarter to the left," he would say, and I would react instantaneously. "One half to the right," was the next order. Faster and faster the directions came. "Put on more speed," he directed, and I could feel the boat surge forward. Wen was having fun, and so was I, although I knew I could not relax a muscle. I was on edge awaiting my next command, for I knew that Wen, scientist that he was, was calculating the nature of his orders in relation to the speed of my responses. He was piloting the boat by remote control, and I was enjoying the sensation of going fast. When had I ever had that opportunity to move quickly? I had never built up speed on my tricycle. I had never ridden a bicycle. Though I had had my feet strapped into child-sized skates and skis so few times as hardly to be worth the mention, I had never moved more than a few faltering steps on them. I had never soared. This was new. This was different, and I reveled in every moment. When I was asked to decelerate and finally to relinquish my seat, I knew that with Wen's help, we had created an experience that would always give me joy in the remembering of it.

Ninth grade found me continuing my piano lessons at the Longy school with Trudi Salomon, as well as continuing my studies in music theory and composition with my Cambridge School of Weston teacher who had introduced these subjects to me a year before. Other subjects that claimed my attention were my third year of earth science; for this year, it was the study of minerals. Of course I was interested in minerals after having studied what I could about the British crown jewels five years before. Along with science, I had a new subject called geopolitics, which was taught by the husband of the science teacher. This teacher, a man of culture and experience, spoke of things fascinating to me. With a German accent still coloring his speech, he told us about some of his travels, and when he showed slides to the class, he made sure that they were described to me. My seat was always at the end of the long table near the front of the room and near to where the teacher lectured, so he could make any comments to me if I needed any additional attention. Once, when showing a slide, he asked for an identification of a rounded conical structure. I heard someone say that it must be a beehive. When told it was not a beehive, my classmates didn't know what to think, but at that point I believed I knew the answer. Like any eager student wanting to give the right answer to the teacher, my hand was in the air, and when acknowledged, I said that if it was not a beehive, then it must be a beehive oven. I thought back seven years to that train trip across the country and to a clear blue New Mexico sky, the hot dry air, the reddish dust, and the reddish-tan adobe buildings. Before we even met the famous potter, Maria of San Ildefonso, I could remember my mother's voice in my ear saying, "This is a beehive oven. Look at it. See." She had put my hands on its rounded walls. "People would bake their bread in these outdoor ovens." The teacher was impressed and later told my parents as much. Furthermore, he said I knew how to concentrate, to listen, and to retain information. Because of this, I probably remembered 95 percent of what I was told, whereas others probably remembered 80 percent of what was presented, if that.

This gifted teacher told his class about Istanbul, and he spoke with so much feeling that it made a lasting impression on me. He spoke of that city as being the meeting of two great cultures, the meeting of the East and the West, and again, he told my parents that he wished I could experience just being there. Even without seeing it clearly, I would be able to feel the world go by and experience the different cultures present in that city. I have not traveled there, but whenever I hear of Constantinople or Istanbul, I think of this charismatic and cultured teacher with great appreciation for broadening my horizons.

My piano lessons were developing my skills of concentration, for I had graduated to a level of slightly more complicated pieces. I was introduced to a two-part invention by Bach, one of fifteen such pieces in which the two hands are virtually independent. This was Number 4 in D minor, a tonality I associate with several of Bach's massive works, such as the famous organ piece, *Toccata and Fugue in D Minor*, the *Chromatic Fantasy and Fugue*, and the *Art of the Fugue*.

To me, stemming from the days I played with that toy xylophone, keys continued to speak to me in color; D minor surrounds me still with the rich, silvery blue of a heavy silk brocade. It was not easy to control each hand as it played its own melody line. First, the right hand executed a difficult pattern of six notes going up in a row and one note leaping down, and then the left hand followed suit. Finally, the piece was learned and performed, and then it was followed by my learning a sonata by Haydn.

This piece had three movements: a fast one, a slow one, and a fast finale, rather like three books being sequels of each other. From the beginning, my teacher taught me in a most creative and analytical way. I was learning the piece theme by theme, but not just as a series of notes. I was learning it as a structure unto itself and studying it almost as though I were composing it. The sonata structure, the most common form used from the 1730s into the twentieth century and beyond, accounted for, at a guess, 75 to 80 percent of the music composed by the western composers. One of the most important aspects of this form is its reliance on repetition. Therefore, as I was learning a sonata, be it by Haydn, Mozart, or Beethoven, I was kept constantly in tune with the points of repetition that both accelerated the learning process and gave me an understanding of the form as seen from the composer's point of view.

I was learning and learning quickly. My ear was developing unusual skills as I studied these pieces by ear. During lessons, my teacher would play sonatas or preludes for me to imitate and learn, and sometimes at home my mother would play one hand at a time so I could pick up the melodies from her playing. I bought the appropriate volumes of sheet music, just as any fully sighted student would. These included the Bach inventions; Beethoven, Mozart, and Haydn sonatas; and later volumes of Schubert, Mendelssohn, and Scarlatti. Though I couldn't read the music, these scores became an integral part of my library, as they are still. When I had a question about a measure or a note or a chord, I could ask anyone who could read music to tell me what I needed to know. When my mother, with her own music lessons behind her, would play the phrase of a Haydn sonata so I could hear and repeat it, I knew she enjoyed working through my piano music with me, since this brought back memories when she herself had practiced for hours a day.

In the spring and especially the fall, I would take breaks from my studies to wander in my woods, observe what I could, and think about the changing seasons. Autumn, being nature's gift to the partially sighted, had allowed me a cornucopia of images, some of which are visual, some of fragrance and touch, and others that are more difficult to explain, because they are of thoughts rather than of actualities.

The change from summer to winter begins gradually. For me, autumn starts in late August, when maple and ash leaves are a tired green. Neither the tender green of spring nor the true deep green of July, these leaves seem to await their dramatic transformation, which is still six weeks away. Brilliant reds, oranges, and yellows are in abundance, but as yet, they are not seen in the trees, for they are in the garden bed in which I have planted nasturtiums, whose crayon-box colors speak of fall, though they are summer flowers. Their sweet, spicy fragrance and the sharp, spicy flavor of their leaves are a reminder that the almost clove scent of chrysanthemums and nutmeg fragrance of leaves drying under an October sun is not far off.

Summer's end or fall's beginning is the caress of a cooling wind. Two days later, a cold front could drop the temperature ten degrees in as many minutes. Then one night there's frost, and the garden's lost, and the lily-pad nasturtium leaves turn in to black slime, while a few tattered red velvet flowers sink onto a tangled mass of limp stems. Then the goldenrod and lavender lace woodland asters replace summer's abundant bouquets with shy and modest offerings for the little hand-blown glass vases that decorate the kitchen windowsill.

When the air is touched with a new coolness, and the woods appear restless in the presence of imminent change, the golden-leafed Solomon seals bend with the weight of scarlet berries, and the sumac branches splash arching rows of red leaves against woodland grasses dried by the September sun. Now, one by one, an early leaf, and then another, tired of being green, will drift to the ground, with pale suede underbellies reflecting and absorbing the color of sunshine, a sunshine that seems weaker than it was just days before. Waiting. Waiting. The woods are waiting. I am waiting.

Which is that special October day to be cherished and remembered until next year's memories supersede this year's images? Is it October 10, when maple leaves are gold against a crisp blue sky and the idea that leaves were ever green seems a fabrication? Is it the piles of orange pumpkins at roadside stands, so bright an orange I could revel in their color and know them by their name even before I sniffed their cool, smooth skins to catch a whiff of the pumpkin pie or candlelit jack-o-lantern concealed within? Maybe that special fall day to be treasured occurs a week later, when the sky is the color of leaf-smoke, and reds and yellows are muted by a misty sadness in the air, as sad as the memory of burning leaves. Another glimpse into the mystery of autumn happens when gray skies are laden with rain clouds, and the autumn rain falls on the leaves that remain, and the rain-spangled butter-yellow leaves glow in contrast to the India-ink wet-bark blackness of tree trunks, branches, and twigs. I can't select only one memory to cherish, so I keep all of them and add the concluding image of a gray November day when the orange, yellow, and red leaves have subsided into a quiet, tawny gray softness signaling the end of the leaf cycle, as the leaves subside and become one with the soil.

It was on a November day, one year after I had begun music lessons, when the English teacher informed my ninth-grade class that our class play was to be *The Insect World* by Josef and Karel Čapek. This play, a political satire in four acts, exposes the flaws of human nature and of society as observed in the world of insects. As the roles were assigned to my classmates, several girls became beautiful Butterflies, and one girl became a sweet little pregnant Cricket. One of the boys was her Cricket husband, and another became the Leader of the Ants. The English teacher found a role for me that would not demand my moving around on the stage. I was to be the Chrysalis with fragile, beautiful wings and a soft, glittery costume. All throughout the play, I was to announce that I was being born, and as the play drew to a close, I was to emerge, only to fall down dead.

I also had another role, for I was asked to write the incidental music for the play, and there could have been no happier composer of one year's experience to take on this project. I wrote a short piece of music to precede each act, and the job of each piece was to set the mood. The Butterflies, eventually all costumed with marvelous wings and antennae, flitted and flirted and were ridiculed for being fickle. I created a delicate little piece in the sunny key of F major, filled with gentle swoops and flourishes and a tender melody that floated into a minor tonality before returning to the delicate flirtations of the opening.

The Crickets were happy little homemakers whose lives were shattered. Since crickets are the only insects amongst those featured in the play that make a noise that can be imitated by a musical instrument, I had to figure out how to play their song. They make a high chirping sound—chee-yerp chee-yerp chee-yerp, if you will. Once I had decided that, I had to find the particular musical pitches to recreate their call. It was, alas, November, and no crickets were chirping at that time of year. I knew the music pitches in question were a G and an F sharp, which, on the piano, are two keys right next to each other, but I didn't remember whether the chirp should go up or down. I tried chirping both ways and chose going from the G to the F sharp. These notes certainly told me that I was to write this piece in the dark, rich key of C minor. The left hand opens with an energetic burst of notes, over which the right hand chirps the cricket call. The left hand repeats its statement, over which the right hand now presents a melody that contains the cricket chirp. Another short melody enters, and then the first two statements return in reverse order, so that the end is stark like the beginning and the final voice of the cricket is heard, altered, in the left hand. Needless to say, when I listened for the crickets' call the following spring, they were chirping in the key I had chosen for them, and their chirp, as I had guessed, was a descending rather than an ascending one.

The Ants were a militaristic society who thought they could save time by doing away with the number three. After a grand opening with left-hand octaves and a stirring and exotic chord, both hands play an ascending four-note pattern to which one can't help but count, "One. Two. Three. Four. One. Two. Three. Four." The notes are evenly spaced to give the feeling of the ants marching. Then the tempo increases, and the notes change their pattern to *short-short-*

long! short-short-long! in an ascending three-note motif. Here again, the automatic response is to count, "One. Two. FOUR. One. Two. FOUR," as dictated by the story.

The Epilogue, an introspective, haunting piece in E minor, is a reflection on life and death. It is delicate and short, and its steady rhythm of *long-short-short-long-long* gives it the aura of a processional. The final chord is stark and almost medieval in mood.

When our family friend the scientist Ivan visited—he is the one who had quizzed me on the kings and queens of England and on Thomas Jefferson—he asked if I had written any more short stories lately, for he knew about the story set at Stonehenge. I told him that, temporarily, I had switched from writing to composing, and on hearing my pieces, he was quite interested. He was also a little amused to hear a fourteen-year-old writing about life and death. It turned out that along with his numerous interests and talents, Ivan was an excellent pianist in his own right, so whenever our paths would cross, he had many lively tales to share with me about his love of music and of Mozart in particular.

I spent quite a bit of time in the Music Building as I finished my *Insect Suite*. Finally, I played the four pieces into a tape recorder, so on the night of the performance each piece was played in advance of the act that it represented. That was a night to remember and an amazing opportunity for me, considering I had been studying music for only one year.

Of course, I was still involved with writing, and throughout that year, I was assigned to write a series of term papers on gemstones, a subject of great interest to me. While my classmates were peering through microscopes and looking at rocks and crystals, Mother and I were reading from some of Daddy's scientific books about the histories of rubies, sapphires, diamonds, and emeralds. The most detailed paper was "Colorful Corundum: Natural and Synthetic," which opens as follows:

> The mineral corundum is 9 on Moh's Scale of Hardness. Although it is second in hardness to the diamond, the actual difference in hardness between corundum and diamond is greater than that which is between corundum and the softest minerals, such as talc.

I have always found that placement of corundum between the hardest and softest of minerals most interesting. Talc is so soft that you can scratch it with your fingernail, and the ruby is second only to the diamond in hardness. I wrote of the chemical composition of corundum being aluminum oxide, that sapphires are colored blue from trace amounts of titanium oxide, and that rubies are red from chromium oxide. I learned that Burma produced pigeon's blood rubies and that sapphires came from Siam, Ceylon, and Montana.

I wrote of imitation stones that have been around since antiquity. Though glass gems were found in ancient Rome and elsewhere, it wasn't until the dawn of the twentieth century that sapphires and rubies were synthesized with a chemical composition, hardness, and color indistinguishable from natural stones. It became necessary to develop specialized equipment to distinguish the man-made gems from natural stones.

I read of gems carved into idols and of historic gems such as the Black Prince's Ruby, first made reference to in 1367. Since so many famous gemstones were identifiable by size, color, shape, and history, it was only natural that I would want to write a story about such stones. "The Ruby," a thirteen-page short story written for my English class and handed in on January 7, 1963, was the result.

Since the kind of people I knew were academics and musicians, two of my main characters were London-based Geoffrey, a curator of historical gems, and Lynn, his concert pianist sister. The third character was an heirloom ruby ring missing for generations. Geoffrey is commissioned by Lord Wynthorpe, owner of the gem collection, to search for the missing stone. Geoffrey knows its history from the Crusades to the 1600s, and he follows a lead that takes him to Boston, where Lynn is giving a concert. Conveniently, her next concert and his next lead take them to San Francisco, where they discover that the ring had found its way back to Boston. Of course, they find the ring in the hands of the remaining descendent of the old English family, who, after meeting the brother and sister and attending Lynn's second Boston concert, wills the ring to the original gem collection.

Several areas of interest revealed themselves in this story. My newly acquired knowledge of the history of gemstones, my love of English history and bowing acquaintance with the era of the Crusades, and my trips to California along with my mother's stories of the Gold Rush and the San Francisco earthquake all came into play, as did my love of historic Boston and Beacon Hill. The piano works that my musician character played were all works I had heard within the past year, so I really was writing about what I knew. My English teacher's comments were favorable:

> Your story is fascinating and very well told. Actually the Ruby becomes a kind of character, doesn't it? Your young people are clearly drawn, and the atmosphere of your story is very convincing. I enjoyed it.

I was anticipating going into the tenth grade as an upper school student and was looking forward to new challenges, old friends, and a continuation of more music studies. Within a few weeks before the end of that year, I was told that other plans had been made and that I would be attending a different school. What had I done wrong? I thought about that year, and I didn't think I could be faulted for anything. I was earning high grades in spite of not being able to read my homework. I was continuing to cultivate my creativity in both music and in writing. I knew the campus very well by now and had to ask for very little help from anyone concerning anything I had to read or anywhere I had to go.

Yet it had been suggested that I might find the upper school too difficult unless my parents engaged the paid services of an aide, who would accompany me everywhere I was to go and to tell me anything I needed to be told. My parents believed implicitly in my ability to continue to flourish under the difficult circumstances inherent in my being a student with a serious visual handicap, especially since I had proven myself capable again and again over the past three years.

So my father made an appointment with a headmaster at another school, who was most interested in me and enthusiastic about accepting me exactly as I was. This headmaster, Charles Merrill, scholar, philosopher, linguist, author, poet, and gifted teacher, told my father, "I'll take any Irvine I can." He knew our family well, since my sister, after completing three very successful years, was graduating from his school.

So I left the campus in the country and prepared to go to the campus in the city, where I was welcomed on several occasions in advance of my matriculation. There, over the next three years, I was to accept challenges, develop skills, and cultivate interests, without which the thirteen years of post–high school academic pursuits, eventually culminating in earning a bachelor's degree, a master's degree, and doctorate would not have been possible.

12

❦

No Time to Spare

In April 1963, when the rain-blackened trunks and branches of the trees in my woods were tipped with the most delicate hint of spring green, I was invited to join my future classmates for a four-day weekend at the New Hampshire home of the headmaster of the Commonwealth School. I would be entering the tenth grade in a few months, and this weekend would give me the chance to become acquainted with future friends and fellow students. Once in the spring and once in the fall, the entire student body, as well as the faculty, would spend four days of country living that included daily classes, walks in the woods, and home-cooked meals. In addition, there were evenings of entertainment that ranged from scenes from Shakespeare and recitation of original poetry to singing folk songs to the accompaniment of any guitars that had found their way on the buses that transported us from the school to the country.

I enjoyed every minute of that weekend, along with the six others I experienced during the following three years. We'd have an English class while sitting under a large tree. The history teacher, a skilled naturalist, would take us on walks of exploration across fields and along woodland trails. When it rained, we'd sit on the floor of the living room of the headmaster's large, old New England house and sing French folk songs or play sophisticated games of Twenty Questions.

The students prepared the meals, and from the beginning my job was to help to core and cut green bell peppers that found their ways into hot stews for dinner served down the hill in the barn. The barn was also the setting for the dramatic or musical entertainments. By the end of that first New Hampshire weekend, I knew I would recognize any number of the people whom I would see the following September in English or history or first-year German classes.

This was to be my first exposure to the formal study of a foreign language, apart from the few French classes I had taken during my year in London. German was chosen for two reasons. It is completely phonetic, so once I learned how to pronounce the words, I would be able to write them; and furthermore, it was an appropriate language to study when preparing for advanced study in music.

I had the occasion to learn a few words in German, for that summer I spent studying *Kinderszenen* by Robert Schumann. My piano teacher, with whom I had been studying for a year by this time, made such fine choices for me, and that summer as I explored Schumann's *Scenes from Childhood.* I knew I had an affinity for these pieces; for ever since that November day a year and a half before, when my method of learning had changed from that of reading to that of listening, I had, for all practical purposes, left childhood; therefore, I was able to tune in to the element of nostalgia evoked by these pieces.

I learned all thirteen pieces in this set. Some covered a single page, and others were two pages long. I learned the titles in German, since my teacher, Trudi Salomon, knew that language, and I knew that just those few words would give me some vocabulary words with which to start German classes in the fall. The first piece in the set, known as "About Strange Lands and People," is still one of my favorite pieces to play; its tender and wistful mood always takes me back to that summer of learning. The sixth piece, "Important Event," is a bold piece in the style of a march, with solid octaves in the left hand and chords in the right hand, and a subtle, tricky rhythm to give the piece character.

It is the following piece, the seventh, that is probably the most famous. My mother knew "Träumerai," or "Reverie," from her early years of piano study at a time when that piece was played in almost every parlor. This short, perfect piece is used most touchingly at the beginning and end of the 1947 movie *Song of Love*, in which Katharine Hepburn plays the part of Clara Schumann, wife of the composer, Robert.

That summer found us hunting for a grand piano, since the square grand on which I had begun my lessons could not produce the range of expression I needed for my constantly advancing studies. We found a parlor grand, forty years old at that time, and this is the piano that now graces my studio and on which I have studied and taught for over forty-five years.

Another item I needed for my studies was a tape recorder. At this time, cassette recorders were new and somewhat unreliable, so Daddy brought home an enormous reel-to-reel machine that took great seven-inch reels of tape and occupied a good portion of my desk. Kit, then a freshman at Harvard, recorded my textbook for medieval history that summer, so for the first time, I had access to a textbook that I could study solely on my own time.

There were several MIT families living in Belmont who had children going to the Commonwealth School. Sometimes Daddy would drive us to school, and at other times one of the other fathers would do so. Fortunately the MIT campus was just across the Charles River from Boston, so arranging transportation was not difficult. The

Commonwealth School, located on the corner of Commonwealth and Dartmouth Street, was housed in a building that had originally been two massive brownstone-style mansions of an earlier era. Remodeled on the inside, but still with massive staircases and wonderful, heavy old-fashioned banisters, there were five floors and a basement that I had to learn as quickly as possible.

I remember that first day of classes as I attended English, medieval history, biology, and first-year German, among others. The incredible amount of work, and the level of intensity I needed to exert to listen, comprehend, and retain what I heard, was more than anything I had ever experienced. When my father picked me up at the end of the day, I remember feeling overwhelmed by the amount of material I had to cover. In his quiet and matter-of-fact way, he said that this was what advanced education was all about, and that in time things would sort themselves out.

In German class, I remember repeating, "Good morning. Good afternoon. Good day. How are you? Fine, thank you, and how are you?" While my classmates were reading the responses, I had to imitate by listening, and so I learned to copy the different sounds that another language gives to vowels. I know my exposure to hearing German spoken in Germany six years before helped me to develop a proper accent and intonation. Furthermore, my parents found a young German woman, an MIT faculty wife, who was hired to tutor me in her language. That tape recorder was put to good use as she, and later her successor, read the chapters and vocabulary lists from my textbook so I could study them. It was certainly helpful for my parents to have one of my subjects taught by others, and my continued use of the tape recorder also eased their schedule.

If *Romeo and Juliet* was not our initial assignment for English, it was certainly one of our first projects. I have always loved that play, and I reveled in the in-depth study of the plot and character analysis inherent in this level of education. "I think Janne knows *Romeo and Juliet* by heart," the English teacher wrote in November 1963. "She has entered intelligently and enthusiastically into class discussion and was the best actress in the Shakespeare scene we did."

I was Juliette's nurse, and in our scene, I exhorted Juliet to forget Romeo and marry instead with the County Paris. I assumed a slightly Cockney accent to show the common origins of the nurse, and I inflected my voice ever so intriguingly to emphasize any sexual innuendos. I had a wonderful time playing that part.

Medieval history seemed like an old friend, since much of it was a continuation of the English history I had picked up when in London. I read about the kings and queens I recognized, such as England's Henry II and Richard I, as well as those from other countries, such as Charlemagne and his father, Charles Martel, who were then unknown to me. When castles and cathedrals were mentioned or described, I had a warm feeling of recognition, for I still remembered seeing dungeons, austere stone walls, ramparts, and the great, heavy gates with pointed spikes known as portcullises.

I had few points of reference when it came to the study of biology. Even though I couldn't see the diagrams or use a microscope, I listened to the lectures, my mother and I read the textbook, and I had the chance to work with some of the animals under study, since I too had my jar of creatures pickled in formaldehyde. I handled the frog and the little fetal pig, even though I did not cut them apart. My major research project toward the end of the year was on the orchid family. After all, I had grown up with a greenhouse at hand whenever I wanted to walk into it, smell the moist air, touch a thick green leaf or a delicate fern, and above all, catch the whiff of a sweetly scented flower.

This project involved the study of the unusual nature of orchid propagation seen in nature and in the laboratory, as well as a discussion of placing specific plants in their proper genus and species. Two important aspects of this project were the dissection and mounting of some blossoms for the benefit of the class, along with a discussion of the genetic characteristics of two parent plants and their offspring. It happened that my father had crossed two plants and they, along with the offspring plant that he registered, were all in bloom at the same time. The flowers had easily recognizable characteristics in size and color that related them to the parent plants. I brought these three plants to my class and spoke about the characteristics in the shapes of blossoms and leaves that the offspring plant had inherited from its parent plants. I also prepared handouts for my classmates. I picked four large lavender flowers, so big and firm of texture that I could feel, identify, and manipulate the separate parts of the flowers. I separated the petals and sepals by hand and glued them onto pieces of black construction paper, so they could be passed around to my fellow students as I discussed the anatomy of the flowers.

The other major project for biology was a paper called "Bring Out Your Dead: Two Great Pandemics: The Black Plague and the Spanish Influenza." Mother and I read several books dealing with the Black Death, and any number of juicy details, such as the abandonment of dying people and even cannibalism, made it into my paper. I learned that several seasons of too much rain, beginning in 1306, led in time to famine, so when the plague came along the trade routes from China, so much of Europe was defenseless. I learned that the plague was not relegated to antiquity or the Middle Ages, since modern outbreaks have occurred. Here in Arizona, as well as else-where in the Southwest, it is endemic. I'm glad to say I have not heard of any outbreaks in a long time, and if occasional cases do appear and receive medical attention in time, this illness can be cured by antibiotics.

The Spanish influenza of 1918 is a study of how rapidly a disease can spread. My mother and her mother had the Spanish influenza in 1918, though they lived isolated on a farm at that time. My great-uncle, who was in the army, had it as well, knowing that this particular influenza caused more fatalities than did World War I. That gave me a personal reference to that particular era and event, especially since my great-uncle was one of twenty survivors out of a group of one hundred infected soldiers.

There were lighter subjects. I enjoyed taking modern dance, which served as physical education for me. According to the teacher's comments, I learned to move with more assurance and confidence, showing that this activity is excellent for acquainting someone with failing vision with moving through open space in comfort.

There was a piano on which I could practice during times assigned for study hall. It was an old upright piano in a small room on the fourth floor, and it was on that piano that I practiced sonatas by Mozart, Beethoven, and Haydn. It was to this room I went for solace when, during November of my tenth-grade year, the news of a president's assassination rocked the school; I played softly to myself whatever I could think of that was both mournful and comforting, such as the opening movement of the Beethoven *Moonlight Sonata*. It was certainly helpful for me to be able to practice at school, since that allowed me to spend more time at home to study for my classes.

There was also music in the form of a madrigal group. There were not enough people for a massive chorus, since during my years at Commonwealth there were only ninety students attending, so those of us who wanted to sing made a group of about twenty singers. Oliver Chamberlain, our teacher, was a musicologist and double bass player with whom I was later to study music history, theory, and composition. We sang songs of the great Elizabethan masters, and we sang songs in German, French, and Italian as well. As always, my way of learning choral music was to sit next to a strong singer and match whatever she sang. Whenever I hear these songs in recordings—and recordings of music of the sixteenth century do abound—I am transported back in time to our rehearsals and performances. I can't help but hum along with the recordings, and I do so when I present these songs to my music history classes!

It seems as though I was being led into the splendor of medieval and Renaissance music through several channels that fall and winter. A family friend, a dean at MIT, had a colleague that he thought I should meet; thus I was introduced to Dr. Jacquelyn Mattfeld, a Yale-trained musicologist and dean of women at MIT. I remember the first time she came to our house for dinner; later, as we visited around the piano, I had the feeling of entering a new world. Jackie was most interested in my being a teenage beginner pianist, and she understood the battle I waged constantly between my ability to express myself musically and the struggle I had from the standpoint of my late-developing piano technique. She saw through my fingers' hesitations and recognized my potential as a pianist, and she always gave me encouragement. When she heard my compositions, especially *The Insect Suite*, composed a little more than one year before, her immediate thought was to liken these little pieces to the suites of character pieces and atmospherically descriptive miniatures from the glittering harpsichord school of the French baroque composers. She mentioned names with which I was not familiar, such as Jean-Philippe Rameau. As always, whenever I wanted or needed a recording to further my studies, my father would buy whatever LP I needed to augment my education. I still have that disc of pieces by Rameau and Scarlatti, and over the years I have learned to play several of them. I did have a feeling of recognition when I heard such pieces as "The Roll-Call of the Birds," "The Cuckoo," and "The Hen." I was in good company. After all, hadn't I written "The Crickets"?

Jackie also introduced me to the lute, for she knew I enjoyed playing the recorder and singing Renaissance madrigals. At that time, the early music revival was strong in Boston, which abounded in studios and workshops where the finest harpsichords, recorders, and lutes were being handcrafted for intellectual audiences of performers and concertgoers alike. She found me a lute and a lute teacher, and by January 1964, I was having weekly lessons. The lute is a beautiful instrument that, due to its artistic appearance, graces many canvases contemporary to its era. Shaped like a half pear and the size of a guitar, it has a very wide neck and fingerboard that, unlike the guitar, bends at a sharp angle toward the shoulder of the performer. Like a guitar, the neck has frets that aid in the placement of the left-hand fingers. Like a twelve-string guitar, many of the strings are doubled. On a guitar, the sound hole is open, whereas on the lute, it is covered with intricate carving and is called the rose or rosette.

My teacher, Joel Cohen, a Harvard-trained composer as well as a master lutenist, became very well known in the years after I knew him, as a recording artist and the director of the Boston Camerata, a group that showcased fresh and enthusiastic performances of medieval and Renaissance music. I enjoyed those lessons most sincerely, though my progress on that instrument was slow and labored. It turned out not to be the right instrument for me, for I always found it awkward, and in a year and a half, I learned no more than a half-dozen pieces.

What I did learn, as it related to early music, has lasted me a lifetime. During our lessons, we spoke of composition and music theory as it pertained to this early repertoire. Not too many fifteen-year-old musicians can converse with comfort about the Romanesca, a popular centuries-old chord progression that appears in Mozart's *The Magic Flute* as well as in many much earlier pieces. Furthermore, I took every lute piece I could play, which included a French dance, an English tune, and, of course, "Greensleeves," and proceeded to play them, not on the lute, but on the piano, complete with the appropriate musical ornamentation. Years later, I was to learn several of the difficult lute works from the recordings by the British lutenist Julian Bream, whom I also heard many times live in concert. I added to my repertoire of lute pieces, thanks to a close friend and college classmate who is now a lutenist based in Boston. From hearing her practice, I learned such pieces as John Dowland's "Queen Elizabeth Her Galliard" and "Fantasia No. 10" by the Spanish composer Mudarra. To this day, I play them on the piano, on a harpsichord if I can find one, or if I can't find one, I turn to the harpsichord setting on my electronic keyboard.

I learned so much from these lessons that now, as a teacher, I can be most encouraging to students, especially my adult beginners, even when their progress is slow and labored. I know from my own experience with the lute that a world of invaluable knowledge can be acquired from musically rich lessons, even when the tangible progress, gauged by a level of technical proficiency of the student on the given instrument, is minimal.

In retrospect, part of the problem I had with the lute was lack of time, for I had so little to spare. Just as I was beginning the lute, I had my first major piano performance. It was on January 17, 1964, at the Longy School of Music. I was one among several student performers, and my presentation was Schumann's *Scenes from Childhood*. I could have played a selection from the thirteen pieces, but since I had learned all of them, it was deemed that I present the entire set lasting twenty minutes. I was nervous. Of course I was nervous, since that went with being a late beginner. As always, I felt insecure being in the presence of people my age and younger who were more technically proficient than I was, but that couldn't be helped. I had to present this work as well as I could. I began the opening piece and let its mood of wistfulness soothe me. The second piece was bold and rhythmic, and the third a little technical workout. One by one, each piece spoke to me and to the audience. Number four ended with a whimsical musical question that was answered in number five. Then came the march, "Important Event," followed by "Träumerai." "Knight of the Rocking Horse," always one of my favorites, thundered its way to the finish, and it was followed by the last four pieces, ending with the enigmatic "The Poet Speaks." At last I had finished. I had a slight memory slip at the end, but I kept going till the final notes were played and faded into silence. What I did not realize, and did not find out until a recent phone call with Trudi Salomon, now Trudi Van Slyck, was that the music faculty and all of the professional musicians, including her husband, who had auditioned me, were impressed by my level of pianistic expression and musical maturity after only a year and a half of lessons. That January evening, we were remembering and reminiscing about a performance that had taken place forty-six years before.

Jackie Mattfeld knew of a music camp that she thought I would enjoy. This wasn't just any music camp. It was a camp for junior composers that had been founded and was being run by a woman who was a well-known teacher from the Peabody Conservatory in Baltimore. The Peabody Junior Conservatory had been in existence for many years before I heard of it, and thanks to Jackie's recommendation, I was accepted.

Late in June, my parents drove me on that two-and-a-half hour trip out of Massachusetts and north into New Hampshire, where we drove by the iconic Old Man of the Mountain. Finally we drove into Vermont past a little town called Lyndon Center that was only fifty miles south of the Canadian border. There were no tears of anxiety as I embarked on this new adventure. Not only could I manage this new situation and new location; I was looking forward to this new experience. I was eager and excited, especially when we drove out of a wooded Vermont country lane into the open countryside of fields and hills, toward what was tantamount to a castle. It was there I was to live and study for the next seven weeks, and castles had always held a fascination for me.

13

The Thunderstorm

The house that crowned the hill was a monument to a railroad magnate's financial success, and though obviously not medieval, it was a castle of sorts that had seen better days. There were round towers with pointed roofs, a grand lobby two stories high, and on the second floor was a wide balcony where, I found out later, students would gather to hear the weekly concerts and recitals. There were enough corridors to please any heroine of Gothic romance, only the rooms, instead of being filled with mysterious locked cupboards, had one, and sometimes two, new upright pianos that had been shipped in for the use of the conservatory.

Mrs. Grace Cushman, dynamic, organized, and affectionate, welcomed me and showed me to my tower bedroom, which was directly above her office bedroom. I saw where the practice rooms and the dining hall were, and though I was confused for the first couple of days, I learned my way around very quickly. My parents left, knowing I was in good hands and ready to embrace a new experience.

"Today I had my first day of classes," I wrote in my letter home on June 29, 1964. "Annie is teaching the musicianship class I and II. This class covers the first two years of theory and harmony in the course of one summer. The hour before lunch is a practice period. Besides exercises, I worked hard on the first and second parts of my

Sonatina, as well as refining 'The Cricket' and 'Butterflies.' Today, I have to see Mrs. Cushman to find out what I will play tonight."

I would have written this on a Monday, since it was on Monday evenings that we had a weekly forum. This was a concert of our student compositions performed for the entire camp as well as for a moderator, a composer of some note who usually came up from New York City to participate and critique the students' works.

"Well, tonight I will be playing one of my pieces, and I am so anxious to hear the others play," I wrote. There never was a time when I was not learning something. "I have been having so much fun making friends," I continued. "There is plenty of time to meet new people and talk. In the lobby, we talk, and usually someone sits down at the piano and plays a little.

"The food is very good here," I continued. "I guess that is because the group is small. Last night for dinner we had chicken with water-melon for dessert. Even the hamburgers were quite good." When does one ever have the chance to praise institutional food? "A funny thing happened during lunch today. The meal was a ham and cheese casserole, and the group was asked to give suitable names to this new dish. While we sat eating, one table at a time would bang the milk pitcher for silence, and then they would give their name for the dish. I gave out the first name, Hamlet, and 'The Tragedy of Hamlet' is what the cook decided to call the dish."

Our morning classes were rigorous and taught in a direct, hands-on way. With two pianos, half a dozen kids, and one teacher in the room, there was demonstrating, playing, and commenting all going on at the same time. That first summer, I gained a thorough knowledge of the so-called white-key modes, or diatonic scales, or the medieval modes. Most people recognize the C major scale and can play it by going from one C to the next C on all of the white keys in between those two notes. Different scales occur when one begins on a D or an E or any of the other four white keys.

Some of these scales are brilliant and aggressive in mood, and others are introspective. The seven scales thus derived reveal their Mediterranean origins by their names—Dorian, Phrygian, Lydian, Locrian, and Ionian, for example. These modes appear in the body of Gregorian chant, in medieval and Renaissance music, and in a fragmentary manner in the later historical eras of music as well. They also appear in folk songs and are what give that music so much of its individuality.

"We have to make up a piece in Dorian in the style of a plain-song," I explained to my parents, reminding them that "plainsong" referred to medieval church music. "We are just expected to write a melody, but I have just made a little song. I took Robert Frost's 'Nature's First Green Is Gold' and made it into a one-line melody song in the plainsong style. I am also having fun improvising in the Dorian mode."

I was to study all seven of these white-key modes, and throughout that first summer, I wrote a series of short piano pieces exemplifying each one. Whenever I could, I used alliterative titles, so "Dignified Dorian," "Dorian Delight," "Phrygian Fantasy," "Lively Lydian," "Merry Mix-olydian," "Aeolian Air," "Locrian Lullaby," and "Ionian Imp" made their way onto the weekly programs of student compositions.

After working hard all week with taking classes, studying our com-position, and practicing the piano, the weekend brought a welcome change to our schedule. Every Saturday, we would take a trip up into the mountains and hike, have a picnic, and return, tired and happy, in the afternoon.

"Yesterday," I wrote, "I had a wonderful time on our all-day hike. We had a lovely drive to Jay Peak, the mountain we climbed. We had a sunny day for the trip, and drove by clear blue lakes surrounded by mountains and little rocky streams. Mrs. Cushman and I climbed for around an hour. We had to get back in time to fix the cookout hot-dog lunch in a little picnic area near the foot of the mountain. Apparently, Jay Peak is only two or three miles from the Canadian border. After climbing nearly halfway up the mountain and down again, we fixed lunch. I buttered hot-dog buns while Mrs. Cushman cooked the hot dogs over a little open stone fireplace. The mountain climb was beautiful. The trail we followed went through woods. It was quite steep and rocky in a couple of places. Once we walked up a nearly dry stream bed."

After Saturday night dinner, we had an event that practically rivaled the weekly Monday Night Forum in importance. I wrote, "Last night, we had another wonderful square dance. These dances are so much fun, and I find I can manage quite easily. I had the best time in the Virginia Reel. The resident concert organist played the music for us on the piano in the auditorium where we dance. We had the best music to dance to. Most of the pieces were Bach, but one was the Handel F major gigue I play on the alto recorder!"

We couldn't stay up too late on Saturday night, because on Sunday mornings, we provided the choir for the local church. After lunch we would attend a faculty concert, given by our excellent faculty resident musicians, all in their twenties and thirties, and filled with enthusiasm and talent.

"Today I sang in the choir again," I wrote to my parents. "Our Sunday afternoon faculty concert starts in around an hour from now. I will tell about it later on. It was just perfect! First, a Couperin cantata, then the Mozart cantata with the 'Alleluia' that I already knew; a Liszt organ piece was played, a Bartok piano sonata was played, and the last piece was the Beethoven string quartet Op. 18, No. 3. These concerts are always so exciting. I have to rush to dinner now."

It was such an important part of our education to hear these concerts every week. Mozart wrote the "Alleluia" when he was seventeen years old—that was the age of the older students at the camp! The camp's organist, himself a graduate of the Junior Conservatory's preparatory program, later was in residence at one of the large Lutheran churches in New York City. Years after my camp experience, as a college student attending many concerts in the city, I had the chance to hear him play.

What made these concerts special was that we knew the performers, since each headed a table in the dining hall. What better way was there to have casual conversation with young professionals who were between seven and fifteen years older than were we ourselves. They were the best role models for us, since many of us hoped to become professional musicians too.

After the concert, we had a free evening, so letters home could be written. Then the week would start again, beginning with Monday Night Composers' Forum. Not all of the details I sent home pertained to music. Of course, in my letters home, I described my tower bedroom to my family. The tower was four stories tall, and my room was on the second floor. The room was a semicircle, since the walls were rounded to conform to the tower structure. Against one part of the wall was a pair of bunk beds, next to which was a door leading to the fire escape. My bed was the next one over, and another double-decker bed was beyond mine. There were dressers enough to go around, and there was plenty of space in the extremely roomy closets. Off the bedroom was a long bathroom that merited additional description in a letter:

> P.S. I want to give a description of the house; it is like a big old castle with towers, many staircases, 126 rooms, and several large closets. The bathrooms seem as old as the house! Apparently, a few summers ago, the girls named the toilet off of our suite "Vesuvius," as it gurgles and snorts and has the reputation of periodically overflowing!

Week after week, we added to our knowledge of music theory. We learned a shorthand by which chords can be written down as Roman numerals. I found out I could take down dictation by listening to a piece of music and by writing the chords on the blackboard. After all, since I had grown up with a blackboard in my bedroom, I was in some ways more comfortable using it than I was in using a piece of paper. The hand movements were larger, and the arm movements were engaged in a different way, just as they were when I wrote in the sand all those years ago when vacationing on Cape Cod. Furthermore, since I am ambidextrous, I developed the skill—yes, part showmanship and part practicality—of taking a piece of chalk in each hand and writing in a hand-over-hand manner. I was able to keep my place on the blackboard in this way, and I built up enough speed to compete in this skill with my classmates.

Sometimes we took newly learned chord progressions or scales and incorporated them into our newly composed "masterworks." Other times, we'd discover these same progressions or scales in the masterworks of the great composers, for we were always playing our favorite piano pieces for each other. Maybe my roommate would play a sonata by Haydn that sounded like a piece I might want to learn. Sometimes before dinner, one of the boys would sit at the grand piano in the lobby and play the first movement of the Mozart piano concerto in D minor, a piece I knew well from listening to recordings of it at home. Another boy might play a cadenza he had written for the Beethoven piano concerto in C minor, and I was always an eager listener, listening and learning. For the first time I was enjoying the company of boys; at school, I never had the chance to do so, since my schedule for finishing my homework precluded time for developing an active social life. Here, with music as our common language, we could communicate, and laugh, and compare notes on our favorite pieces. Now, not only could I recognize the boys by their voices, I knew that it was Peter who played the Mozart concerto and Charles who favored the Beethoven.

Halfway through my sojourn at camp, my parents came to visit. I played my new compositions for them and bubbled over with excitement and enthusiasm concerning what I had learned. I introduced them to my teachers and friends, and it was in the way I did it that revealed my process of growing up. This gave them even more satisfaction than did their recognition of my advancing musical skills.

"Hello there," I would call out to a group of friends I recognized by their voices. "I can't see who you are, but I'd love to have you come over to meet my parents."

Sometimes, Mother and Daddy would stay for the Monday Night Forum, so they had a chance to hear one of the most important aspects of my learning experience. My contributions were either newly composed pieces with their clever alliterative modal titles, or they were movements I had composed for a new sonatina. I wrote three such pieces during those high school years, and each sonatina, or little sonata, had three movements. Mine were filled with familiar tonalities, since that was the idiom best known to me. Others of my fellow students wrote in a tonal manner but were a little more adventurous than I was. One of the most gifted composers wrote several pieces of Greek liturgical music that became so popular on first hearing that by the end of that summer, most of the camp members could sing those hauntingly beautiful compositions. Another student, who may have graduated the following summer, wrote a full-fledged sonata in the most unusual tonality, for the scale he used had eight and not seven tones in it. This octatonic scale delighted me, and in subsequent years, I was to work within its boundaries and explore its unusual harmonies.

Then there was the composer who was so fluent with the avant-garde movement that his weekly works were memorable at that time for their shock value. There was no recognizable melody, only notes such as blips, bleeps, plucked strings, and a high note on the piano, a growl in the bass, and a squawk on the clarinet. In retrospect, I realize that young composer was both daring and innovative, and for me, instructive. Actually, I am indebted to this fellow student, since it was through him that I had my first exposure ever to the type of music I was to study throughout my college and graduate work, during which time I took a major in piano and a minor in composition. I, with my pseudo-eighteenth-century harmonies, and the avant-garde composer, with his totally modern creations, represented styles that were as opposite as any two styles could possibly be. Interestingly enough, for the three summers I attended this camp, both of us presented compositions at each and every forum.

To keep our curriculum in balance, our intensive study of music was our morning activity. We looked forward to modern dance and swimming for our afternoon engagements. During this first summer, swimming took place in a man-made pond quite close to the castle/house. My main memory of that pond was that it was known to have leeches, though I never became attached to one.

On July 22, I wrote, "Our resident composer is away, so the moderator last night was Dr. Vincent Persechetti, a well-known composer and teacher of composition at the Juilliard School. The forum, which lasted for three hours, was one of the most exciting and interesting evenings I have had. Dr. Persechetti took an interest in all the pieces, and he spent a long time discussing each one. Every comment he made was useful. All the pieces on the program had been either finished or completely composed during the previous week, and I finished the first movement of my sonatina on Monday morning. Everyone liked my piece, and even though it was in the early baroque style, they thought it was very original. This experience of playing for people has helped me a great deal in getting over stage fright. So far, I have not been bothered by it."

For the first time, I was in a situation in which music surrounded me. From morning to evening, pianos spoke to us from every practice room, or a singer or violinist could be heard warming up with scales.

Music was the essence of our class work. Whether we were learning new chord progressions or studying scales from musical antiquity, we were adding to our basic knowledge of the subject.

Music was the substance of our creative endeavors. Most, though not all of us, were junior composers. Those who didn't create their own music helped in creating performances of their friends' works.

Music was the accompaniment to our entertainment. Of course we sang songs while we traveled on the old yellow school bus through the Vermont countryside, on the days we climbed mountains. Some of these songs were those that we had learned from scouting camps or church camps, or from other places where people gather and sing. Sometimes while we waited for an evening event, someone would start up a round, and the rest of us would follow, coming in with the second, third, and fourth voices. Everyone knew "Frère Jacques" and "Three Blind Mice," since early childhood was not that far distant from some of the younger campers. Sometimes one of the young faculty members or older students would start singing a round in French or German that, within five minutes, would be joined by the rest of us. Even after seven weeks, as the time for learning and sharing came to a close, we had songs of farewell, which also served as songs of reunion to be sung the following summer for those of us who were planning to return.

Above and beyond the study of music, I learned many things about myself. I could make friends easily. I could laugh and make jokes, and be "one of the crowd," and enjoy the company of boys as well as girls. I was Janne. I was not the girl with low vision or the girl who did some things differently. I had become formidable in my own right, and people looked up to me for my fluency and facility with my newly acquired musical skills. My ear was open to learning anything and everything, and I could undertake all of my assignments without asking help from others. This was truly the gift of independence. My ability to learn by ear had kept me totally competitive with my classmates who learned by both eye and ear. Also, this was the first time ever that I was able to devote all of my time totally to the study of music. After all, I had begun my music lessons just two and a half years before, and during that brief period of time, my extensive homework assignments always needed to be completed before I could play the piano or compose.

That first summer, an incident perfect in its drama, timing, and orchestration occurred outside the confines of a concert setting. It was late at night, and my four roommates and I had been entertaining each other with scary stories. Finally I got to sleep, but I was awakened by the rumbling of thunder. The storm came quickly, the thunder grew increasingly louder, and the lightning flashed relentlessly. So much for our stories of maidens stranded in the tower of an old burning castle! We were in a very old building atop a hill, and we knew we were vulnerable. How could the lightning not strike us? Yes, there was a fire escape, but it was rickety and made of metal, and we had not set foot on it before. Would it be safe if we had to flee the decaying castle of a building? All of us were awake, but we didn't talk, since we were enclosed in our own little bubbles of terror. That storm seemed to go on forever. Finally, and it seemed a long time later, the cracks of thunder came at widening intervals, and the lightning flashes came from farther away. Then, after a distant rumble of thunder, I heard the notes of the first bird as it welcomed the dawn. As the silences between the mutters of thunder grew longer, one bird and then another joined the first bird. Finally, the thunder ceased altogether as a chorus of birds sang to the sunrise.

My immediate thoughts were of gratitude for being able to welcome a new day. All five of us frightened fifteen-year-old girls had survived the fabrications of our overactive imaginations as well as that thunderstorm. I don't think the others heard that avian hymn to the dawn that had affected me so profoundly, since the other girls did not discuss it that following morning.

Somewhere, somehow, I knew I had experienced that same situation before. As I thought back over the storm, I could hear the thunder rumble, but I also heard the frightened shriek of piccolos and flutes. I heard the low, throbbing notes that only double basses can make, and I reexperienced the fear-laden instability of shifting chords and dissonant harmonies. Eventually, as the thunder in the low strings grew softer and less intense, I heard the tentative notes of the clarinet followed by the stronger answer of the horns. The orchestral harmonies had already told me that the danger had passed, since everything was coming to a full and safe resolution, or harmonic conclusion. Then came a theme played in the strings that was so perfect and so much a tender celebration of life that, as I realized what it was, I was overwhelmed and humbled to have heard what I considered nature's reenactment of Beethoven's sixth symphony, the Pastoral Symphony! Beethoven had captured the spirit of a thunderstorm from the awareness of its approach, through the onslaught, and finally to its peaceful conclusion. That night's adventure had blended the past and the present into a shimmering recollection, and I knew that it would become a profound memory that would stay with me always.

14

❦

Making Friends with Other Trees and Flowers

After my summer of total immersion in music, I was ready to tackle the academic challenges of the eleventh grade. Ancient history was of interest. I learned about Doric and Ionic columns, so I linked those terms immediately to the Dorian and Ionian modes I had studied the previous summer. I looked for every reference to music in second-year German, and I had no problem adding *das Klavier* to my vocabulary, for that was the word for piano. English was always a favorite subject, and it may have been in eleventh-grade English that I handed in a book report or a term paper on Jane Austen's *Emma*. In spite of our heavy reading load, Mother and I read through the six Jane Austen novels on a regular basis, especially during vacations, when other assignments weren't pending.

First-year Spanish was an addition to my curriculum, and Mother enjoyed working with me on that subject as much as I did. Thirty years before, she had taught in the California school system, and decades before Spanish was accepted as a second language, she was allowing her little pupils to teach her their songs in their own language. She took classes in conversational Spanish throughout her entire life, and she had a love of the language, which I share.

My music classes in composition continued under the direction of Mr. Chamberlain. Since I was now comfortable in writing within the three-movement sonata allegro form, my project was to write such a piece, but not for piano. It was to be for a woodwind quintet. Writing the piece down for others to play was not easy, since I could never see well enough to write music. Today, I can do so in a very limited and simplistic manner because I figured out how to create raised, lined, oversized music paper, and even with the tactile lines, lining up notes on top of each other is something best relegated to others. My teacher copied the piece down as though it were a piano piece, and then, theme by theme, we talked about how it should be orchestrated for flute, oboe, clarinet, French horn, and bassoon. I learned that every instrument was to have a chance at playing the melody, and as we discussed the instrumentation, I began assigning specific instruments to the themes as I composed them at the piano. The andante, the slow movement, began with a melody in the left hand, with a fragile wisp of a secondary melody in the right hand. It was obvious that the left-hand melody would be played on the bassoon, and the flute was to be its accompaniment. Working with these instruments and associating their tones with the melodies I composed at the piano marked a new development in my training in composition.

My piano lessons that year took me well into the intermediate level of piano studies. I learned all four movements of Beethoven's first piano sonata, followed by an impromptu by Schubert. That piece, redolent with water imagery and wistful melodies, is one I play to this day. I was introduced to a new form when given the Third French Suite of Bach to learn. Since the baroque suite is based on the structure of court dances popular many decades before Bach lived, I became familiar with such words as allemande, courant, sarabande, and gigue.

A true breakthrough in the learning process came when my piano teacher recorded this piece on my large reel-to-reel tape recorder. The result was phenomenal, and I came to my next lesson with several of the movements learned. I had the luxury of learning these pieces on my own time, without having to ask anyone about this or that note. Since I have what is called perfect pitch, I can recognize the name of any note that is played and know whether it is a B or an A, I could listen to the tape, repeat, and play. What made this recording different from a professional LP record was that the two hands were played separately, so I could focus first on the right hand and then on the left. From then on and through college, I was to learn my music by having such pieces recorded for me, either by my teachers or by advanced fellow students.

As commencement approached, I was given an unusual honor, although I was only a junior. My woodwind quintet was played in its entirety by my fellow students as part of the graduation ceremony program. In a letter to my parents dated June 16, 1965, my head-master, Mr. Merrill, wrote, "I can imagine how proud you were to hear Janne's quintet played at commencement, not only for what she has done, but for the way it was received by her schoolmates. For the amateur there is a magical quality to musical composition that no other art form really enjoys, and I was pleased to see what she had received from her work with Mr. Chamberlain."

This letter continued with the discussion of a different matter. For some time, I had wanted to take off a year between high school and college to spend exclusively on the study of music. Because of my late start, I felt sure that such a year for catching up would be necessary before I could enter college as a freshman. At first Mr. Merrill agreed with this plan, since he, of all people, knew that the time

I had spent to achieve the high standard of work in my academic subjects had shortchanged my time allotted to music, especially to piano. When he consulted with Mr. Chamberlain, he was told that I already knew much more about all forms of music than the average good musician in the first year or two of college. Mr. Merrill advised that I plan on entering college at the same time as my classmates. We just had to find the right college.

On the same day that Mr. Merrill wrote to my parents, a letter was being written to him by Grace Cushman, the director of my summer music camp. It reads, in part, as follows:

All year I have been planning to write to you about a Commonwealth student, Janne Irvine, who spent last summer at our camp and who is now to return for her second summer with us.

Because we had expected her visual handicap to be a deterrent to progress, her rising to advanced heights of productivity was such an amazing accomplishment that I think you should know that she was one of two students who produced new compositions for each weekly forum—the "ultimate" at our camp!

That she has facility to use at the keyboard the material which was presented in our classes, is, of course, due to a remarkable piano teacher. So few piano teachers are capable of explaining structure as they teach notes—which is, of course, the way this girl learns—that again, it is a tribute to parents and school that Janne should have such excellent instruction.

To my amazement also, she was able to work at the blackboard (again one of the fastest we have ever had) and prepared

217

a notebook record of her own "gleanings" of the Musicianship course. She seems to find her own way out of her problems!

Perhaps the greatest contribution we had for Janne was the social adjustment and the freedom of discovering for herself some of the limits of her capacities. In the dormitory she was valuable as a "mixer," completely unselfish in her reaching out to help others with an initiative that is—I'm sure you understand—gratifying to administration! She made a place for herself inconspicuously in the entire camp program (including square dancing), even to climbing mountains. After a strenuous climb on Mt. Mansfield, she decided for herself, I think, that she had gone as far as she wanted to with that kind of experience. She didn't give up; she just decided not to try any of the Mt. Washington climbs.

I am continually amazed at the home and the school that could produce such success with a handicap. As I see Janne's problem for total fulfillment as time goes on, I believe it is one of helping her to find a means for her own independent direct contact with knowledge when she has gone beyond the reach of a wonderful home and a wonderful school as "middleman." If you have any suggestions for us for this summer, I should be very glad to hear from you.

During that second summer at camp, I wrote another three-movement sonatina, and more importantly, I learned the circle of fifths, which presents a pattern of all major and minor chords. Usually this circle appears as a chart in college-level music theory books, and though it is discussed, it is rarely, if ever, played. I had the good fortune to learn to play it, to derive countless pianistic exercises from it, to learn my music theory thoroughly because of it, and to use it as the core of teaching piano technique, especially to adult beginners, throughout my years of teaching piano.

I still remember the morning sun pouring into our classroom. It shone on the warm brown of the wood floor and on the brown wood of the two upright pianos, once again imported for the summer of study. The sun also shone on a most beautiful fuchsia silk that covered the walls, for we were in a different location for that summer of 1965. If last year's location was a castle, this one was a grand manor house that also topped a hill. Several of the ground floor rooms had silk brocade on the walls, and I remember touching that fragile fabric with my fingers, which were rough enough to catch on the threads of the cloth. My fingers also discovered the wool or cotton batting that was coming out from around the edges of the silk, for this great old home was a little shabby as well, though in better repair than was last year's residence.

A gentle, grassy hill went from the house down to the barn that had been converted into a concert venue and square dance hall. Again, the best of classical music was played for our Saturday night Virginia Reel, always the closing dance, and that sent us outside smiling as we walked back to the main house. One such night, my fellow students were looking up at the stars. We were so far out into the country that the stars could be seen. There were times in the past when I had seen the faintest flicker of stars, but with growing up among so many trees, stars were never easy to find. I looked up into the black Vermont sky to see what my friends were admiring. There were no stars at all, as far as I was concerned. The sky was completely dark. I couldn't help but ask, "Are there many stars up there?" and I was told that the sky was filled with them. Fortunately, nobody challenged my question or commented on my asking it. I was glad to let the subject drop. So rarely was I confronted with the fact that I was missing out on something that it was a shock. Yet that reaction shows, in its own right, that such an experience, with its negative overtones, was the exception rather than the rule. I was making my own rules, by which I would not succumb to any obvious limitations.

That summer, once again I presented a composition at every forum. My woodwind quintet was arranged for strings, so that gave me a different sound picture as far as orchestration was concerned. I did prefer it played on the winds, but it was still interesting to hear it played on instruments other than the piano at which it had been composed.

As I entered my senior year at Commonwealth, there was a hint of sadness as I took part in various activities for what I knew was to be the last time, and that included the New Hampshire weekend that took place in the fall. I remember walking down a country road, and since I was alone, I didn't go very far. I would examine one small red swamp maple tree whose leaves glowed like carnelians, garnets, and rubies in the rain-spangled air. After picking a couple of leaves, I would find a tree filled with amber and citrine and topaz leaves and pick some of them to add to my collection. As always, I could not decide whether the autumn leaves were lovelier on sunny days or on rainy ones. I still have those miniature maple leaves harvested in New Hampshire, since I dried them between heavy books and then mounted them between two sheets of Lucite. These three displays, each about the size of a long-playing record, decorate my kitchen wall, and behind the clear plastic, the little leaves are still bravely rust or tawny in color, though they are over forty years old by now.

It was Jacquelyn Mattfeld who suggested that I visit Sarah Lawrence College during the fall of my senior year. She had become dean there, and she invited me to visit the campus and meet members of the music faculty. Monday, October 12, 1965, was filled with sunshine and gold and red maple leaves as I began that journey that took me from my home outside of Boston to begin my adventure at the college that was to nurture me for five wonder-filled years. My visit was skillfully and affectionately orchestrated by Dean Mattfeld, who saw to it that I met the right people at the right time.

I visited with music students, Professor Kenneth Wentworth of the piano department, and composer Meyer Kupferman. I also met with teachers of Italian and of German, as well as with the dean of admissions. My appointments with them seemed more like social visits rather than interviews, but indeed they were interviews to see if the college and I would be right for each other.

I fell in love with the music building as soon as I saw it. I wanted to live in that wonderful house that was filled with music from its basement to its attic, and I wanted to become a Sarah Lawrence girl and study music there. On that October day, I did not know that I would have the opportunity to fulfill both wishes. Mr. Kupferman invited me into his sunshine-filled studio, which was dominated by a Steinway grand. We sat on the sofa opposite the piano, where he proceeded to ask me a number of questions. I don't remember the exact questions, but he would have learned about my two summers spent at the Peabody Junior Conservatory, where I had received excellent training in theory and composition. I also told him of the past seven years in which I had been listening to and absorbing many pieces of music from my father's collection of LP records, including the Bach Brandenburg concerti, Mozart piano concerti, Beethoven symphonies and sonatas, bagpipe bands of the Scots guards, English country dancing recorder music, and recordings of English music hall ballads.

Mr. Kupferman seemed pleased with my remarks. Knowing he was a clarinetist, I made a point of commenting on the Mozart Clarinet Concerto as well as Schubert's "Shepherd on the Rocks," an ethereal work for soprano, clarinet, and piano that I had heard in concert at my music camp. Finally, a question came for which I did not have a good answer. He asked me if I knew much about opera, and I replied that I knew very little about it. He rephrased his question.

"You have not listened to much opera?" He sounded shocked.

"I have not listened to much," I stated quietly.

"Then how do you expect to be any kind of a musician, if you don't know anything about opera?" he shouted at me.

Somehow I knew his thundering voice held a note of playfulness, so I told him, oh so seriously, that I would hope to learn about such things if I were accepted at Sarah Lawrence College.

When I left the campus that October afternoon, I felt as though I were a Sarah Lawrence girl, but I would not find out whether I would be accepted for another five months. Furthermore, I had to fill out what was known to be one of the most demanding college application forms, consisting of twelve questions, the last of which was a page-long autobiography.

If a writing sample wasn't an official part of the application form, it was a part of the application packet; after all, the college was extremely well known for its writing department. I sent "One Golden Day," an essay about the changing of the seasons. Over the years, I had observed that six weeks before the official change of each season, one special day heralds its approach. For example, in February, though there may be snow on the ground, that one day may have a sky of a lighter blue, almost a spring blue, and the air will be touched with special warmth belied by the snow on the ground.

I was asked, "Who was your favorite teacher?" I wrote about Seymour Alden, my medieval history teacher at Commonwealth. Quiet and scholarly, he was equally informative discussing the French kings Charles the Simple and Charles the Pius as he was in New Hampshire, taking his history class of students through a forest where he pointed out the cellar hole of a house long since burned, and showed us trees that were leaning in a certain direction from being buffeted by the famous hurricane of 1938. The year after my application was written, when I heard that Mr. Alden had died of cancer at age forty-one, he was one of the first people for whom I grieved.

Another question was, "What is your favorite book, and why?" Of course, I had to select one of Jane Austen's books, and I chose *Emma*. Though forty years later I was to explore Emma's character in detail, since I was portraying her in my two-hour play, *If Emma Had Practiced*, even at the age of seventeen, I could appreciate the metamorphosis of Emma's character from being willful and manipulative to becoming contrite and humble.

Another question, "Tell of your experience of employment and earning," was given an answer equally terse. Because of my visual problem and my being somewhat overprotected, I informed the committee that I had not searched for a job, especially since my summers were used for furthering my education in music. Within my first year at Sarah Lawrence, I was given the job of being a dormitory hall adviser, and by the time I had graduated from college, I was earning a goodly amount from being a teaching assistant, teaching a fellow college student for credit, and teaching both recorder and piano to any number of local children and teenage students.

Returning to my senior year in high school, I had a full program, including third-year German and second-year Spanish. Following my year each of medieval and ancient history, my senior class was American history. The text for the latter course was a two-volume work by Morison and Commager, *The Growth of the American Republic*. Finally I had the chance to study about Thomas Jefferson, so if quizzed about his role in history, as I had been at the age of ten, I would no longer have to plead ignorance!

Since I had missed the chance to study more modern European history beginning with the Napoleonic Era, one summer, Mother and I read *Vanity Fair* and *Les Miserables*; the next summer, we read *War and Peace*. The following summer must have been that of 1970, since that was when we read an extensive biography of Beethoven that came out on the two hundredth anniversary of the composer's birth. Because my mother and I had read my high school materials together, we were able to discuss these books in their historical context as well as enjoy them as great literary works. Because reading aloud is so time-consuming, we took advantage of its slower pace to discover and discuss details of both content and style. This constant verbalization has helped me to keep these books within my memory, and I'm sure that this way of learning has allowed me to retain much of this information to the present day.

During the four and a half years that my mother read out loud to me on an intensive and daily basis, I never once heard her complain. Because I can read voices to an extent, picking up on unspoken emotions by focusing on the tone and inflection, I'm sure I would have noticed any hint of complaint, but I never was aware of such. Mother would say to her friends that she was receiving what was tantamount to another college education. She always enjoyed learning, and books remained an important part of her life throughout her productive years. At times she became tired. At times I became tired, but in spite of that, we completed what we had to do. On a level that was totally unspoken, I knew that the best way to express my thanks was to excel in my studies, though the main reason I achieved good grades was that I wanted to learn what was presented to me. Doing well academically was almost a by-product of the way I learned. By listening to materials being read aloud, I developed a long concentration span, and by knowing that there was little or no time to review before final exams, I had to commit to memory whatever information I would need to know.

Besides studying together, my mother and I would go into Boston several times a year to visit one of the great art museums or attend a concert. After seeing a most unusual exhibit of gold at the Boston Museum of Fine Arts, Mother knew that I would enjoy this chance to see the most beautifully crafted objects in gold that she had ever seen. This treasure was from the time of Alexander the Great, and I was looking forward to seeing what would have been in existence during the times that had become real to us during our year's study of ancient history. I remember a vast room filled with people who were murmuring and exclaiming in awe. We stepped into line and finally came within view of the shadow boxes, for there were specially constructed showcases to hold this treasure. They were lit from within, and I remember seeing the gorgeous colors of silk—turquoise, royal purple, fuchsia, and that clear, bright green that is so wonderful in silk. I loved seeing those bright colors, but that was virtually all that I saw of the exhibit, for once again, as with the crown jewels, I was too far away from the treasure to see it. My mother, with fine powers of description, told me of the most marvelous pendant earrings as well as earrings wrought in the forms of tiny chariots. There were plenty of pins and necklaces for ladies to wear, and I enjoyed the description of the golden net crafted to cover one's coil of hair. The one piece that was large, so large that I could see it, was a larger-than life-sized sheaf of wheat made of pure, gleaming gold. Seeing that exhibit did make an impression, even though most of what I had experienced was through description. I was as upset as anybody when I heard that en route to another location, several crates of this irreplaceable gold had been conveniently "lost."

Shortly after seeing the exhibit of ancient gold, Mother had seen an art show that she discussed in such glowing terms that I was anxious to see it. She spoke of colors, of the most magnificent use of color, but when I went to see the pictures, the colors were to me no more than shades of brown. Where were the glorious colors about which Mother had been so enthusiastic? The wines and blues she had described were not there for me, but as before, I relied on her descriptions, which gave me a positive impression of having seen the works of Andrew Wyeth. It startled me, but did not bother me to any great extent, that parts of the color spectrum were now outside my ken. Being a realist, I accepted this gradual loss of the perception of subtle colors without being disturbed or panicked. By now Mother and I had a comfortable understanding of such things. No longer did we have battles over what I could and could not see. She knew that I always wanted to enlarge my experience of many things that some people might consider being out of reach. She was valiant in taking me places and describing things that she knew I would store in my increasingly well-trained memory.

It was during my senior year that I went on a school outing to the Boston Museum of Fine Arts. This was indeed my kind of outing! We had the chance to visit the display of musical instruments. Oh, how I loved seeing those lutes and recorders and harpsichords, early pianos, violins, and horns, and I had the chance to play some of those instruments.

At the Isabella Stewart Gardner Museum, which I had visited about twice a year for as long as I could remember, there was plenty to entertain both the eye and the ear. That museum was intimate enough that, as we wandered through what had been a Venetian palace brought over from Italy stone by stone, Mother and I were able to get close enough to things that I could see. We saw stone carvings and statues, and some of the pictures were painted in bright enough colors that I could appreciate them. Others, such as *El Jaleo*, John Singer Sergeant's mural of the Spanish dancer, though muted in color, were large enough for me to enjoy. To this day I have a copy of it in my music studio. My favorite display happened once a year. In April, I could see brilliant orange nasturtiums cascading down four stories from the top floor to the ground floor in the atrium. Sometimes this show happened when Mother and I attended concerts there; it is one of the finest venues for chamber music and recital performances. In fact, more than once, I heard my marvelous piano teacher, Trudi Salmon Van Slyck, perform there.

We also attended the solo piano recitals presented in Boston's Symphony Hall by the greatest pianists of that time. After studying a Beethoven sonata by listening to a recording by Rudolf Serkin, I had the chance to hear Serkin in person, performing the splendid works by Beethoven, Schubert, and Mozart for which he is so well known. I still have the concert program dated April 8, 1962, during which Serkin played the *Moonlight Sonata* by Beethoven. It was his recording of that very work that helped launch my study of the piano just four years before. I also heard the great Arthur Rubinstein play the *Twenty-Four Preludes* as well as the *C-Sharp Minor Scherzo* by Chopin. Sometimes if a concert was sold out, people could buy tickets to sit on folding chairs on the stage itself. Once I must have been seated ten feet behind the maestro, and I was not close enough to see his hands, but I did see a blur of white: his shock of white hair. I remember hearing him play the *C-Sharp Minor Scherzo*, and at that close range, I could pick out many nuances in dynamics that might not have made it farther out into the hall. The cascading broken chord fragments sounded like sparkling, gentle, brief showers of rain, and it was a never-to-be-forgotten privilege to hear a twentieth-century pianist most closely associated with the music of Chopin play the music of that composer. Not all of the pianists whose concerts I attended were of an earlier generation. I heard Van Cliburn near the beginning of his career as he played the very Russian work *Pictures at an Exhibition*, preceded by a solemn, dignified, and powerful performance of "The Star-Spangled Banner."

The major piano pieces I learned during my senior year were the enigmatic and beautiful *Arabeske* by Schumann, which combined the wistfulness of the *Scenes from Childhood* I had learned two years before with the development of a more mature technique. The other work was a sonata by Haydn, a three-movement piece that displayed a multitude of personal aspects of the composer. The second movement favored a melody in the middle to lower register of the piano where a cello might sing, and the cello was an instrument favored by Haydn. The third movement of this sonata has a hint of Gypsy-inspired music in it, and it must be remembered that Haydn grew up on the border of what is now Austria and Hungary, where he would have heard such music. This movement also contains a hidden set of variations, but to explain that calls upon me as the musicologist and theorist I am today, rather than the eager piano student I was at the age of seventeen.

How many people have the chance to study music history while in high school? I was one of the lucky ones. There were only two of us students who listened with interest and amusement as Mr. Chamberlain took us through the opera *Don Giovanni* and explained how Mozart's extraordinary talent in setting his music to operatic libretti set him apart in that field. I still remember our analysis of the "Catalogue Aria," in which Mozart itemized the Don's many conquests. When a large lady was being described, the music portrayed her with a rich orchestration and long, strong notes held by the singer. When a small and delicate woman was mentioned, the music, using lacy, melodic fragments and high-toned instruments, evoked her image.

When our studies changed from the operatic to the symphonic, we explored the Fifth Symphony of Beethoven and learned that the iconic rhythmic motif that opens the first movement, *short-short-short-LONG*, was not relegated to the initial statement of the opening theme. As we listened further into the first movement, at first we couldn't find that motif until our teacher, a former double-bass player, pointed out his instrument playing the bass line underneath the second theme. Beethoven wasn't through with us or with that *dit-dit-dit-da* theme either, for that which was imperative in the first movement was now ponderous in the second movement. In the third movement, that theme returned as delicately as though autumn leaves were dancing to it; in the fourth movement, that four-note motif became a song of triumph. No wonder teaching this symphony is special to me.

For a similar reason, I experience a special pleasure when I teach the Beethoven *Violin Concerto*; the final movement of that work was the first work I ever presented in front of a class. My class consisted of myself, one other student, and our teacher. They listened patiently as I described the thematic layout and traced that opening sparkling melody as it wound its way through the entire piece. I discussed orchestration. Though the violin was the solo instrument, Beethoven paid special attention to other instruments of the orchestra, especially when he gave a solo part to the bassoon while the violin solo danced in circles around it. Beethoven too could express humor in music, and I smile from the joy of hearing this piece whenever I teach it.

On a weekend that heralded the beginning of spring, I went for the final time to the headmaster's home in New Hampshire for our school retreat. This was the last time my classmates and I sat around the dining table singing Renaissance madrigals, and the last time we sat in the living room singing French folk songs. It was the last time we took our history classes while walking in the rain, or sat in the barn after dinner, enjoying scenes from Shakespeare. As I left this retreat for the last time, a quiet spring rain was falling, and the hedges of forsythia, rain-laden with yellow blossoms, seemed as tearful as I.

Yet as one experience was drawing to a close, another was opening for me. Once again, I visited Sarah Lawrence College, but this time I was a future freshman. My letter of acceptance marked the beginning of a new stage in my life. I visited with student friends I had met the previous October, and I attended student plays, for the college was well known for its department of drama. I heard student recitals held in the music building, and I knew that within a few months I too would be performing with my classmates in that same venue. I made more friends, and for the first time I saw what my dormitory room would look like.

I spent time with my future professors of piano and composition and showed them my current projects. I also discussed with them how I would study my materials outside of the classroom, for I would be on my own now and would rely on the help of tutors and fellow students to read to me. Mother would not be reading out loud to me. I discovered one of the many differences between the routines set by high school and college. My classes would not be every day; they would happen two or three times a week, so I would have more time for fulfilling homework assignments. For my one non-music class, I was to take first-year French, for which the resident teacher's aide from France would read my homework assignments onto a tape recorder. For my piano studies, my teacher, along with the occasional advanced student, would continue Trudi Van Slyck's practice of recording the repertoire I was to learn, one hand at a time. For my assignments in music composition, an advanced student or my teacher himself would write down from dictation what I had composed.

I was busy creating music while completing my senior project in composition at Commonwealth. I was writing *Three Pieces for Four Recorders*, and unlike the woodwind quintet of the previous year, I had firsthand knowledge of the instruments. No longer was I working within the eighteenth-century idiom; I had graduated to the twentieth century with a touch of the medieval, given the origin of the instruments. The first piece had flowing melodies that were not written in the traditional major or minor scales; instead they showed influence of the medieval modes along with some twentieth-century twists. The second movement, my favorite, was based on an unusual rhythmic pattern that sounded both old and modern; and the third piece bordered on being twelve-tone, yet it was a passacaglia influenced by the great *Organ Passacaglia* by Bach! This piece was being written not only as a homework assignment, for I was entering it in a competition to be held by the Boston chapter of the American Recorder Society. My composition won second prize and as such was given a public performance by some of the finest recorder players in Boston, in a concert presented on Sunday, May 1, 1966. Forty-five years later I had the occasion to contact Mr. Friedrich von Huene, who had been one of the expert performers at that concert. "Thank you very much for your kind and extensive letter regarding the 1966 Boston Recorder Society concert," he wrote me. "I certainly remember you very well as that young and eager recorder player and composer." Now I always think of this musician whenever I play my soprano recorder, for it was just a few months ago that I ordered my sweet-toned ebony soprano from his workshop, the Early Music Shop of New England in Brookline, Massachusetts.

Along with music composition, I was involved with composition of a different kind, for in English class, after reading some of Chaucer's *Canterbury Tales*, we had to write such a tale of our own. "The Root of Evil's Greed" was our theme, and we could hand in the finished product either in verse or in prose. This was one homework assignment I could accomplish at school, for it did not involve anything being read aloud to me.

For the past three years, I had been allowed to practice on the old upright piano in a small room on the fourth floor. Since there was a small hole in one of the glass panes in the window, for at least five months out of the year, the room was very cold, so I had to wear my green woolen cape when I went upstairs to practice. I wore that wool cape on a winter afternoon as I climbed the stairs to the fourth floor, and as I entered what had become my special room, I reached out my hand to say hello to the old piano and touch its chilly ivory keys. That afternoon, however, I had to practice on a different keyboard, for my mint-green typewriter was my companion for this particular assignment. Setting my small portable typewriter on the desk near the window, I inserted the paper and touched the cold green keys as I settled my pointer fingers on the F and the J.

Clenching my jaw so my teeth wouldn't chatter, I imagined myself back five hundred years. I was sitting in the tower of a medieval castle, which would have been just as cold as this, I thought. Cold and damp, and if there had been glazed windows, they would have had cracked panes, or maybe there would have been no panes at all. My castle bower in that fourth-floor tower wouldn't have had a piano, since lutes and recorders would have been used for music-making at the time of Geoffrey Chaucer, and besides, a fourteenth-century poet would have used an ink horn and quill rather than a mint-green typewriter.

I thought of those pilgrims journeying to Canterbury, for I had seen the Canterbury cathedral and had touched the intricately carved pillars of the cloisters. That had been nine years ago, I thought; just a little more than half my lifetime. But I had to write a story and not lose my way in memories. "The root of evil's greed," I wrote: the saying from which I was supposed to spin a Chaucerian tale. Lines from the *Canterbury Tales* were humming through my head, so I let my thought patterns fall into the rhythm of the iambic pentameter. "The root of evil's greed, I know it well. Here is another tale that I will tell." The thrust of the phrase took me into the next line. "To keep you from succumbing to that wrong. Now listen as I tell to you. A long time ago there lived a gallant knight ..."

From there on, there was no stopping. The rhyming words were like the cadences of the medieval music I loved. Two years before, in advance of studying medieval history, my mother and I had read two lengthy novels about the middle ages. From those hours of reading, I had learned a great deal about medieval life. I could see the castle in my mind, for hadn't I seen several medieval castles in England and France? I could picture the knights in their armor, and the ladies in their velvet gowns and jewels. I could imagine the rushes on the stone floors and the dogs snarling for food scraps under the banquet table. I could hear lutes and recorders and the singing of ballads. Even the cold room in which I was working and the folds of my wool cape were atmospheric.

I populated my castles with a knight and his ladies, since for my knight, Sir John, his sin of greed was that he had not one, but two wives. One was a beautiful blonde.

> She came from Cornwall, and her name was Kate
>
> For her husband there was no better mate.
>
> But of Sir John, remember what I said?
>
> Something was strange which I foreshadow-ed.
>
> With one wife he could not be satisfied
>
> Or happy. So he had another bride
>
> The other maiden's name was Edith, and she had
>
> long raven hair
>
> She always went to Church on every day
>
> And like her unknown rival she did pray
>
> To God that her dear husband would not waver
>
> And let another woman gain his favor.

I typed, and soon I had written four single-spaced pages of rhyming couplets.

As I placed the pages in my notebook, I stared at my work for that afternoon and saw an indistinct gray blur on a white page of typing paper. When I went home and showed my effort to Mother, she saw that very little had to be changed when she read that rough draft out loud to me. A few weeks later, when the little room on the fourth floor was no longer cold and when the green wool cape had been put away until the following winter, I handed in my paper to my English teacher. When the papers were handed back to the students of the senior English class, there was an A+ on the front of my paper, and at the end of it was the rejoinder "Shame on you, Janne!"—for the last lines were, "The moral of my Tale, I'm telling you: You cannot have your Kate and Edith too!"

My *Three Pieces for Four Recorders* received its second performance at my commencement on June 10, 1966, the sixth graduation to be held at the Commonwealth School. I played the soprano part, and my classmates who had played my woodwind quintet the year before performed the other parts on the alto, tenor, and bass recorders.

As I received my diploma from Mr. Merrill, I felt the deepest gratitude for all of those who had made this moment possible. This school had nurtured me and had given me advanced studies in music that would make my transition to working at the college level as smooth as any such transition could be. I thought of my parents, who believed in me so much that they had given me countless hours of their time and had done everything they could to give me the best in education. On a personal level, they had given me the strength and feeling of worth that would allow me to compete on an equal level with anyone. They knew that my continuing gradual loss of sight, though it would always present me with challenges, would, in the long run, not be a major defining factor establishing who I was or what I could accomplish.

That summer was a time of new beginnings. Kit married a fellow scholar, with whom she moved to an apartment near Harvard. During my last season at music camp, I composed not another sonatina, but a full-fledged three-movement piano sonata. I would not be returning the following summer, for by then I would be caught up in college classes, concerns, and commitments. What I took with me from that music camp was the pure joy associated with the fulfillment of learning skills in music that would last a lifetime. I also treasure a series of memories of three summers of Vermont sunshine, of enjoying the company of my musical peers, and of taking the first steps in learning how to become independent.

At last, it was time to prepare to leave for college. Daddy packed the car with everything a college freshman would need. I had three different tape recorders and a turntable and speakers, for then I could listen to music LPs in my dorm room as well as listen to whatever recorded books for the blind that I could borrow. I had my little green typewriter, which had been my companion since the eighth grade and which was to see me not only through college but through graduate school as well. Of course I had my soprano recorder, which by now had been joined by an alto and a tenor. I had a hot-water pot and a teapot and cups so I could serve tea to my friends. I had clothes that ranged from hot-weather cottons to winter wools, accompanied by sandals as well as boots.

As we drove out of the driveway, I said goodbye to the redwood modern house where I had lived for the past fifteen years. This house and woods had been my home since I was a toddler taking those tentative steps into a world filled with sunshine and dandelions and things I couldn't see until I bumped into them. I said farewell to the stream and the footbridge, to the large hickory tree and the leaning ash tree. Red and orange flowers were still blooming in my nasturtium bed, and I knew that within a month, the sumac leaves would be scarlet, and within a few weeks after that, my favorite maple tree at the top of the driveway would turn red.

This was a final farewell, for I was never to live in that house again. I would be elsewhere, making friends with different trees and other flowers and accepting new challenges in my life. I was aware that meeting challenges was something for which, from the beginning of my existence, I had been carefully schooled, and I knew, unquestionably, that this was a task for which I had been unusually well prepared.

Postlude

March 15, 2010, 12:00 noon

That two-hour class—part story, part recital of poetry, and part performance on the recorder as well as on my beloved Steinway grand piano—ended with a smile as I finished reciting my Chaucerian tale. I was exhilarated by the telling of my story. I didn't expect to be, but I was. A powerful feeling of well-being flowed from me out into my audience, and it came back to me even stronger as I sensed my friends' reactions and knew that all had gone well. The present was wonderful, and for the first time in a long period of time, I sensed an inner satisfaction and a feeling of profound contentment. I also had the feeling that the future held opportunities for me, though at that time I was not yet tuned in to what would develop within the next three weeks, something that could have the power to enhance and redefine my career along literary as well as musical lines.

I could sense a rising level of energy from people's voices as they began talking to each other as soon as the class was over. So many people came up to me radiating excitement, enthusiasm, and interest as well as appreciation for being allowed to enter my inner world. For now, after sixty years, I was ready and willing to share.

"I am a nurse," one woman said, "and I wrote a paper on retrolental fibroplasia when I was in college in the 1950s!"

"It must have been after 1953," I interjected. "That is when doctors discovered the cause for so many cases of blindness among premature babies."

Another woman said, "I was a young teacher in the 1950s, and some of my first students came to me with your same eye condition." She continued, "The description of your mother's style of educating you during those early years was most interesting to me."

Then a man spoke not of the past but of the present, saying several of his grandsons were born premature, and though none had lost sight completely, several did have problems with their vision.

Others spoke not of disability but of experiences gained from traveling. "We were a young married couple living in Heidelberg in 1958, the year you were visiting Europe," the husband of a couple from Concord, Massachusetts, said.

"That must have been when you lived in a two-room apartment with no kitchen and a bathroom down the hall," I said with a smile, for his wife had told me that detail after I had described that when Johannes Brahms had moved to Vienna, his apartment had been equally austere.

Another person mentioned living in London at the very same time I had lived there. So many people said that my vivid memories of Europe had activated their memories of having visited the same places at the same time, and they enjoyed revitalizing their memories as I shared my experiences with them.

Then a man shared with me, "I loved your description of the Matterhorn. I was there the year you were. That was fifty years ago, which was the year that I climbed it."

As this flock of positive comments and compliments pulsed and swirled around me, I realized that something had happened to me of extreme personal importance. What I had done this morning freed me of inhibitions and misconceptions, for this presentation was not an admission of weakness but an acknowledgment of strength. Now

I realized that being different, rather than setting me apart, had made me one of many, for each person in that class, or anywhere else, travels within the bubble of his own world. My bubble was one amongst a multitude of bubbles that, I now realized, meant I did not stand out in a crowd by virtue of what made me different. What I had thought of as an unavoidably identifying disability was, in reality, just one of my many personal attributes like height, hair color, musical ability, or a facility with words that, from the beginning, has helped to define my being. I would not have known this if I hadn't abandoned my reticence and self-imposed uptightness and shared my story with my students, who were also my friends.

I was soon to share my story with others, and though they were strangers, they were drawn into my tale of opportunity and struggle, of creativity and education. The golden strand of music, the silver one of writing, and the velvet strand of blindness not only continue to intertwine the aspects of my means of expression, but they also draw in onlookers who want to know about details I have considered not out of the ordinary, but which I have found that, to others, are unusual.

I discovered that people wanted to know more about the tiny infant whose head at birth was small enough to fit into a teacup. Those who had heard my story wanted to sympathize with the fragile child who was fearful of stumbling over rough terrain and tripping over unknown things she couldn't see. I assured my listeners that the nine-year-old girl who stared at the crown jewels just out of reach and just out of sight is still within me, only she has found ready access to jewels of knowledge and gems of memory. The teenager, writing a poem one minute and playing a sonata the next, definitely is active within me, and the fifth-grader who said she wanted to become a teacher has done so, many times over. The protected child, described as "delicate," has become someone who walks half marathons at sixty, and who knows that tired feet and exhaustion are the intangible medals earned at the end of every race, just as feelings of well-being and contentment are the emotional rewards for sharing what hitherto was an untold story.

Today's class was different. I knew that as soon as I began speaking, and it was confirmed most positively after I had finished. Today's class was different, and now, most fortunately, so was I.

Postscript
Messages through Time

I. The Root of Evil's Greed (A Chaucerian Tale)

II. The Ballad of Sir Geoffrey

III. The Treasure

IV. My Father's Hands

V. A Note to Mary Jane

VI. A Note to Kit

VII. A Note to Jackie

VIII. English Rose

IX. Self-Portrait

The Pardoner's Second Tale

A Chaucerian Story (1966)

Radix malorum est cupiditas

The Root of Evil's greed, I know it well.

Here is another tale that I will tell

To keep you from succumbing to that wrong.

Now listen as I tell you. A long

Time ago there lived a gallant knight

Whose name was John. He always loved a fight,

A hunt, or any knightly deed. To save

A lovely maiden by a rescue brave

Would thrill him to the heart. Now this Sir John

Had something strange of which I'll tell anon.

He had one wife, noble, fair, and true

Who did all that a woman ought to do.

She was to him a gentle loyal wife

And swore that she'd be faithful all her life.

She bore his children willingly. She knew

How to be a mother, good and true.

She ruled her castle well, and like a queen,

The keys, the stores, the herbs were her domain.

She trained the maids in all the skills she could

That would help to advance their livelihood.

This girl was talented, and also fair,

She had blue eyes, long gleaming golden hair,

Pearl white skin, and graceful slenderness

And a gentle heart of tenderness.

She came from Cornwall, and her name was Kate,

For her husband there was no better mate.

But of Sir John, remember what I said?

Something was strange which I foreshadowed.

With one wife he could not be satisfied

Or happy. So he had another bride

Who also was to him gentle and true

And worshiped everything that he would do.

She knew exactly how to rule her home

And did so when her husband went to Rome

Or to Jerusalem. He knew that she

Could manage the estate as well as he.

Edith was the second maiden's name,

And it was from Northumberland she came.

And she was also beautiful and wise

She had long raven hair and flashing eyes

She always went to Church on every day

And like her unknown rival she did pray

To God that her dear husband would not waver

And let another woman gain his favor.

It was a trick to lead this double life.

He kept his wives in ignorance, for strife

He wanted to avoid at any cost.

If they found out all would indeed be lost.

He wisely kept his homes from one another

To keep one from discovering the other.

With Kate in Cornwall he was called Sir John

Richard was he when he was called upon

By Edith or by any other friend

Who knew him in the north. He had to spend

The rest of all his lives as people two

With two great houses, twice his revenue,

With all his riches doubled, two noble names,

Two eldest sons, for wives, two loyal dames

And all the other knights who were his peers

Who equaled him in courage, rank, and years

With half his wealth they must be satisfied,

They only had one house and one fair bride.

To keep his friends unknowing and apart

Was fun, and also showed his craft and art.

Now of our friend, Sir John, and of his double

This love of lives and wives gave him much trouble.

But first I'll tell what happiness he had

For many years before his luck turned bad.

For several months Edith would be his mate,

But then a dreadful longing for his Kate

Would quickly overcome him. He would leave

And tell his wife who always would believe

All that he said concerning shrines or Rome

Or other holy cities. He went home

As we all know to see his other wife

To live for several months a happy life,

And when he got the least bit tired of her

This episode would always reoccur.

And sometimes he would even keep his word

And was a pious pilgrim. He assured

Himself that he was a virtuous knight

And always did the thing he knew was right.

Perhaps we might condemn his greed and lust,

But he himself did think that he was just.

He had such haughty scorn and condescension

For mistresses and others, not to mention

All other kinds of women whom he knew

Distracted all his friends. But he had two

Lawfully wedded wives who loved him well.

He did not think this sin enough for Hell.

He was not concerned with interdiction.

He was married with the Church's benediction.

But Fate stepped in when he was not aware

And wrecked his happy life which was so fair.

He spent six months with Kate, then setting forth

He went to be with Edith in the north.

But when in London he fell very sick,

He got the priest and doctor to come quick.

He worsened, and deliriously did rave,

The priest was worried how his soul to save.

Oh Kate, my bride, I love you tenderly.

Oh Edith, my own wife, how dear to me

You are. They were amazed, to say the least,

The doctor and the flabbergasted priest.

If he recovers he must indeed repent

And undergo a dreadful punishment.

The priest then solemnly proclaimed the sentence

Which Sir John had to follow for repentance.

From now on you must be a celibate.

You cannot have your Edith or your Kate

Or any other woman. You must be blind

To happiness and love of any kind.

You've sinned against the Church. Twice you did marry

You must abide within a monastery

And eke your days out in a lonely cell

To try to gain a better place in Hell.

Oh, what a penance for our gallant knight

Who always loved a hunt or worthy fight.

He had to end his days among the sages

And every year he went on pilgrimages.

The moral of my tale I'm telling you

You cannot have your Kate and Edith too!

II. The Ballad of Sir Geoffrey (1976)

He was a Yorkshire lad by birth

And Geoffrey was his name.

I'll tell to you the story

How he gained honor and fame, m'lads

He gained honor and fame.

He first went west to Canada

To do postdoctoral work.

At the Atomic Energy Program

There is no time to shirk, m'lads,

There is no time to shirk.

The spirit of adventure

Possessed by every knight

Sent him forth to Berkeley

For him that move was right, m'lads,

For him that move was right.

For there he met fair Lise

Who was his Danish bride.

Now England and Denmark

Were ne'er so well allied, m'lads,

Were ne'er so well allied.

Once more he had to travel,

He came to MIT

From Nuclear he changed

To Inorganic Chemistry

To Inorganic Chemistry.

Harvard also knew him

But soon he had to go.

For England now had called him,

And he could not say no, m'lads,

And he could not say no.

Because for all those many years

He had gained so much knowledge

They gave to him a Chemistry Chair

At Imperial College, m'lads,

At Imperial College.

He wrote a book on chemistry,

A veritable tome.

He then acquired in Sussex

A gracious Tudor home, m'lads,

A gracious Tudor home.

One thing led to another.

He continued to rise.

Not long ago he gained great fame

When he won the Nobel Prize, m'lads,

When he won the Nobel Prize.

Now kneel before the Queen, m'lad,

Receive the accolade.

Once on the right, once on the left,

A Knight has now been made, m'lads,

A Knight has now been made.

III. The Treasure

Receiving and Sharing a Mother's Gift, 1999

You gave me life against all odds

and nurtured me with love

and taught me every day that life

is a gift. A privilege.

Something so special it should never

be taken for granted.

You taught me how to come alive with music.

Prenatally? We'll never know for sure,

though Mozart is that golden thread

whose music gives us serenity and joy

and can keep loneliness and fear at bay.

You taught me to rely on myself

and learn deep from within

that no matter what has gone wrong

there is no substitute for a good mind.

You gave me pride in my ability to surmount

problems and obstacles, blindness, and loneliness.

And so I learned never to give in to self-pity.

Now it is your turn to learn

through all that you gave to me.

How not to lash out in loneliness and fear.

How not to make self-pity your ruling concern.

It's time to find the ability to say

I'm glad I'm alive for another day.

For fifty years I have grown through your wisdom.

I have nurtured it. Cultivated it. Made your ideas mine.

Now, the greatest gift I can give you, along with my love,

is to give you back your own wisdom.

Your own love of life.

Your special ability to find beauty

in the Tucson blue sky,

in the exuberance of a small brown dog,

in the knowledge you are alive

for another day,

and that life is to be treasured

and not thrown away.

IV. My Father's Hands (1998)

Your careful hands

brushed against giant delicate ferns

touching fragrant faces

of lavender orchid blossoms.

Knowing fingers untangled long white roots

separating bulbs and leaves

to make two perfect plants

where there had been just one.

Your skillful hands

wired our house on Hickory Lane

and built the greenhouse for those orchid plants

where lavender and white cattleyas

and tiny yellow Dancing Ladies danced above a sea

of rich ferns.

Your chemist's hands

fashioned glass equipment

infusing ceramic lumps

with radioactivity.

You glazed them

to look like rocks

designing cork cradles

for a Geiger counter's trip

through minefields fifty years gone by

radioactive pebbles

hidden with buried mines

waited for discovery.

Your strong hands chopped down locust trees

and planted striped bark maples

making the perfect place

for me to grow up and enjoy

the grape juice-colored lilacs,

the woods, and dog-toothed violets,

the brook and wooden bridge,

the old stone wall, and aged hickory tree.

And all those memories were ours to treasure

that we took as the Woods was left behind

when hickory trees gave way to oleanders

and Arizona ash gave shade instead of maple trees.

Your dexterous hands

built a pancake griddle and record player

and then you collected the best there was to hear

the Pirates of Penzance on seventy-eights

and later you obtained on thirty-threes

a repertoire my world can't do without

from Mozart to Mussorgsky, Beethoven

and bagpipes.

Your competent hands

drove that dark gray Mercedes

through snow-lined Alpine passes

of Austria and Switzerland,

through Holland's tulip fields

and the Roman ruins of France.

You parked that car in a London mews

and drove it through England into Scotland

and into that west coast town in Ayrshire

which bears our name.

And then we drove across America

and waded in two oceans.

We ran along the beach at Cape Cod

and climbed down clumsy steps

to wade in sea-sand at La Jolla.

Your hands

gave me "hands-on" experience with

flame red flowers on steep Colorado mountain sides,

obsidian cliffs, and fragrant redwoods,

iron red rocks, and silver waterfalls

from Montreal to Mexico City.

Your sensitive hands

taught me to find the rich silk threads

within the weave of firmer, thicker wool

so I would know a Tekke Turkaman by its touch

and realize that a room without an Oriental rug

is hard to call a room at all.

Your capable hands

made the most delicious waffles

delicate and airy

with savory syrup.

Your chef's hands created

chicken and wild rice burritos

which were your own invention.

Oriental pot-stickers, pasta with pesto,

Missouri ham and fried apples,

roast chicken with the smoothest gravy

were creative delights

which now feed my memories.

Your tender hands

have petted little furry backs

and scratched behind the ears

of more than fifty years

of tiny sharp-nosed chihuahua dogs.

Your loving hands

held my hands

so I would not be afraid

of chemotherapy.

Your firm hands poured the wine

when it was time to celebrate

my Red Hibiscus Day

Symbol of recovery.

Then, two days ago you lay as though you slept

with one arm resting above your head.

I slipped my hand into your hand

and held your gentle, sensitive fingers

and found the most profound comfort there.

The vibrant warmth of fifty years of love

pulsed between our fingers,

and made me almost forget

the gentle, inexorable, and irrevocable

loss of heat.

My hands felt a quivering beat.

The pulse of life. The heat of awareness.

A tingle of hope.

Then came the devastating realization

that the heartbeat I felt

in my fingertips

was my own.

V. A Note to Mary Jane (2010)

You speak to me of color.

There's a bluebird and a red cardinal

right outside my kitchen window.

They show up well

against dark green leaves.

I pick up the phone

and you are there

in your Virginia woods

describing fuchsia azaleas.

Black-eyed Susans droop

from drought

but perk up again

after a rain.

Orange nasturtiums cascade

from that pot on your terrace

and awaken memories

of my garden patch.

My nose can smell their tart sweetness

and I taste the tang

of lily pad leaves.

It's the blue-purple and purple-blue

that sings to me

that speaks to you

for violets have ever

linked us two

and you won't let the lawn mower run

until the violet blooms have gone.

You tell me how you

match your yarns

to what you see

around you

I understand completely

for I know

clashing dissonance when two notes

themselves so close to colors

sound together

and don't agree.

You speak of colors in wintertime

but now the colors are on your loom

and I have seen your weaving room

laden with yarns

whose colors you recite to me

Teal. Aubergine. Avocado.

And I imagine what your next project

is going to be.

VI. A Note to Kit (2010)

Alternative reality.

I was confused.

Reality was reality

or so I thought.

I am here.

I am sitting on this chair

talking to you.

That is real.

How can it not be so?

Alternative reality?

The words seemed unrelated

Out of tune

You did not force the issue.

All you said was

The concept exists.

I thought about it

from time to time

and thought again

when the phrase brushed

against my brain.

Lack of understanding

bred rejection.

Two years later

I played a minor scale.

Chopin used this

I told my class.

I played a six-tone scale

so different

from the other.

Listen to the six-tone scale

An alternative tonality

is what I said.

An alternative

tonality?

and then I knew!

Reality? Tonality!

They were the same.

I knew they were the same.

Even Schoenberg's Twelve-Tone Row

had its own reality

far beyond Tonality

I've known that concept all my life.

How could I be so dense!

My world is my own reality.

It belongs to nobody else.

I thought about those summers

Going to Cape Cod.

You could see the red truck

and read its license plate.

I saw a smudge of red

then it was gone.

You could read a page with print.

I saw a grayish blur.

Then I began to redefine

my personal reality

specific to me

different from yours

hitherto defined by limitations

yet beautiful in its own way.

Now my own reality

Alternative alternative reality

attacks the flawed perception

with tools of ingenuity

imagination

memory

creating a new entity. A new reality

powerful and positive

still different from yours

defined with pride

not apology

for being different

for being

different

makes it

unequivocally

mine.

What took me so long?

VII. A Note to Jackie (2010)

We've been out of touch

for many years.

There is so much to share

for we are linked by ties

ties of music centuries old.

You listened to my Song of the Crickets

and heard beyond the hesitation of fingers

not yet skilled enough to play my own works

but you trusted in Time, and in time

that trust was rewarded.

You knew I needed to find new horizons

as well as independence

in the hilltops of Vermont

from Medieval Modes

to the extreme avant garde

I heard it all and gradually found

where I belonged.

I still play that Spanish cantiga,

the French basse-danse

and Greensleeves

not on the lute, but on the harpsichord

if I can find one

and on its electronic cousin

if I can't.

You informed my Muse

to direct me to Sarah Lawrence College

where I made Toll House Cookies

(both cooked and raw)

for your Christmas parties

at the Deanery.

I followed in your footsteps

to the New Haven Green

(for you, it should be New Haven Blue

for blue was your favorite color).

And after that Yale degree

I struck out across the country

to find Mozart in the Arizona Desert.

You visited me in Tucson

and found how I had worked with fragments

manipulating, transposing, and reconstructing

themes so I could play

a Sonata and Fantasy

Mostly Mozart.

But you don't know about

Janne on Jane.

Music in the Novels of

Jane Austen

For now, clad in a Regency-style gown

I become Emma Woodhouse

handsome, clever, and misguided

telling her story at the pianoforte

in a two-hour concert/play of my devising

for I know the keyboard sonatas

the Italian art songs

the songs by Robert Burns

and English country dance tunes

she would have played.

And I play them as though I were Emma

or Jane Fairfax or her other friends

for that hint of comedy lurks

within as it always has

just below the surface of scholarship.

Years ago you told my parents

Music was one of several forms of expression

that could be mine.

I could be a pianist or composer.

I could be a writer

or an artist within my limitations

and I believe

I have fulfilled your expectations

communicating through expression

in many different ways

any way I can.

It may have been the second time we met

I mentioned the name of a scholar.

"You sound just like a musicologist"

was your response

with a smile in your voice

to the fifteen-year-old I was then.

I wish you could hear me now

lecturing on music history

from the troubadours

who sang of love and dancing

to the modern composer/teachers

with whom I have studied,

for music history is your subject

as surely as

it is mine.

VIII. English Rose (1997)

We met as schoolchildren

in our woolen plaid skirts and blazers from Harrod's

and stood in the cheering crowds and watched

A distant brilliant sparkle in a coach

White fur and diamonds and a white-gloved hand

as the young Queen of England waved and smiled

as her coach passed by.

Years passed as we grew up a continent apart.

We shared our high school and college experiences

by letter and by phone.

You saw the wisteria in bloom and attended

my Senior Piano Recital

and I saw you receive your Masters

in International Relations.

We earned our doctoral degrees the same year

and found out English History for you

and Music for me

were not as relevant to college curricula

as they were to us, but we were creative

and managed to find students who would listen.

We loved to share what we had studied over the years.

You told me about your college students

and I had stories about my high school pupils.

Then three years ago you had a new adventure to relate

about surgery and how it felt to undergo chemotherapy.

Just this spring your mother told me about wigs,

the shorter, the blonder, the better

and four months later I had the occasion

to take her advice.

Now when I tell my music students about England

and talk of palaces and castles,

or when I take them through the genealogies

of nine hundred years of English royals,

I think back forty years to those two little girls

and I have a feeling, deep from within

I'm carrying on your life's work as well as mine.

And when I watched the funeral of a Princess

I traveled in my mind from the Palace to the Abbey

and heard the hymns of the British Isles

starkly beautiful and moving in that setting

of medieval stone

I heard, and was haunted by a modern song

powerful and poignant as it rang out

against the ancient abbey walls

And I knew without knowing that I knew

I was saying good-bye not to one English Rose

but to two.

IX. Self-Portrait (2010)

Little girl

of fifty years ago

brown braids down her back

and a hand extended

to catch butterflies

lives in her portrait

sepia on paper two centuries old

Young child

senses the seasons

dancing through New England woods

Picking dew-sweet violets

lavender lilacs

Eager girl

travels through time

medieval castles

London palaces

learning English history

a nine-year-old can absorb

Eighth-grade student

looks up from small print

to outlines of November gray trees

the book now

lying open on her desk

undecipherable

permanently

A finger's touch

cool ivory keys

pianist in the making

needing to be heard

late beginner

fighting against time

C sharp minor

dark as grape juice and chocolate

Beethoven's Moonlight

sound pictures

Sixteen-year-old

opens her being

to Vermont mountains

composer in training

music everywhere

even the thunderstorm speaks

of Beethoven's Pastoral Symphony!

High school years

listening out loud

books and textbooks

a mother's patient reading

a daughter's concentration

learning

memorizing

education for a lifetime

College student

music and poetry

deepening exploration

French short stories and

fresh apple cider

dormitory parties

singing spoofs of

well-known songs

Lilac Time senior piano recital

in a lavender gown

sadness at graduation

end of a half decade

beginning of new experiences

Yale student

lessons and concerts in neo-Gothic halls

professors renowned for skill and scholarship

playtime chess

cultivates concentration

Gilbert and Sullivan singing parties

white wine

clouds gather

sidewalks slick with black ice

glaucoma headaches cloud recollections

summer surgeries

March recital

June commencement

seeking sunshine.

Tucson woman

dry heat

eucalyptus-scented air

five more years of study

teaching while learning

learning to teach

The Completion of Fragmentary Keyboard Works

of W. A. Mozart

flowing doctoral robes

mortarboard with gold tassel.

academic hood velvet lined

pink for Music

Placid years pass

a decade and a half

teaching

performing

enjoying the company

of friends

Summer of 1997

the performance was halted

would the symphony be left

unfinished?

chemotherapy

realization

I am Janne

in a red wig or blonde

or no wig at all

Long hair again

I celebrate being alive

and share with others

that journey

through space and time

Now I walk in the

Race for the Cure

wearing the pink ribbon

and pink T-shirt

for survivors only

One by one

music lectures are presented

one by one

a poem is published

an article written

a program presented

Stately woman

reaches out her hand

new adventures are

within reach

The child in the portrait

still reaches out for butterflies

~The End~

About the Author

In her debut book and autobiography, *Making Friends With Other Trees and Flowers: A Story of Low Vision and High Expectation,* Janne E. Irvine brings a full and rich portrayal of the world of low vision, coupled with her story of hard-won academic and personal success. Optimism, energy, and an eagerness to learn about whatever is put in her way, whether she can see it or not, makes her story compelling and memorable.

Originally from Boston, Massachusetts, Janne Irvine has lived in Tucson, Arizona, since 1974 and has established herself as a pianist, piano teacher, musicologist, and writer. She holds a BA from Sarah Lawrence College, an MM from the Yale University School of Music, and a Doctor of Musical Arts from the University of Arizona. Her dissertation topic was The Completion of Fragmentary Keyboard Works of W. A. Mozart.

Her yearly series of lectures, Music: The Art of Listening, has gained popularity among music lovers from around the United States who winter in Tucson.

Janne Irvine is internationally recognized for her lectures on music in the novels of Jane Austen, and she has published articles on this subject. She is also a published poet.

Dr. Janne Irvine has designed and taught the following classes:

- The Evolution of the Keyboard Sonata from the Pre-Classical through the Present

- The Evolution of the Fantasy, Toccata, and Fugue from the Baroque through the Present
- The History of the Keyboard Concerto from the Baroque through the Present
- The History of the Instrumental Concerto from the Baroque through the Present
- From Concerto Grosso to Symphony – from the Baroque through the Present
- The Evolution of the Piano from Its Plucked and Hammered Predecessors
- Bach and Mozart – A Century of Genius
- Bach – His Life and Music
- Mozart – His Life and Music
- Beethoven – His Life and Music
- Genre and the Changing Style from the Classical Through the Present
- Nineteenth and Twentieth Century Nationalism in the Music of Germany, Spain, France, Russia, England, and The United States of America
- The Music Dictionary: 100 Facts, Terms, Dates, Composers and Compositions You Should Know
- Biographies of the Major Composers and the History of Their Times
- Music in Literature: Books Whose Plots Revolve Around Music and Musicians
- The Church Modes in the Folk Music of Scotland and England

- Gilbert and Sullivan – Satyrical and Sublime
- Birds, Beasts, Fish, and Insects Portrayed in Music
- The Musicology Behind Certain Film Scores
- A Composer A Day – an in depth look at composers from the Baroque through the Modern Eras focusing on biography, history, and carefully selected repertoire

CPSIA information can be obtained at www.ICGtesting.com
Printed in the USA
LVOW111826021111

253221LV00007B/23/P